Borde Hill Garden

In memory of Stephie, whose hard work, foresight and enthusiasm inspired generations of gardeners

Borde Hill Garden
A Plant Hunter's Paradise

Vanessa Berridge

PHOTOGRAPHY BY
John Glover

FOREWORD BY
Stephen Lacey

MERRELL

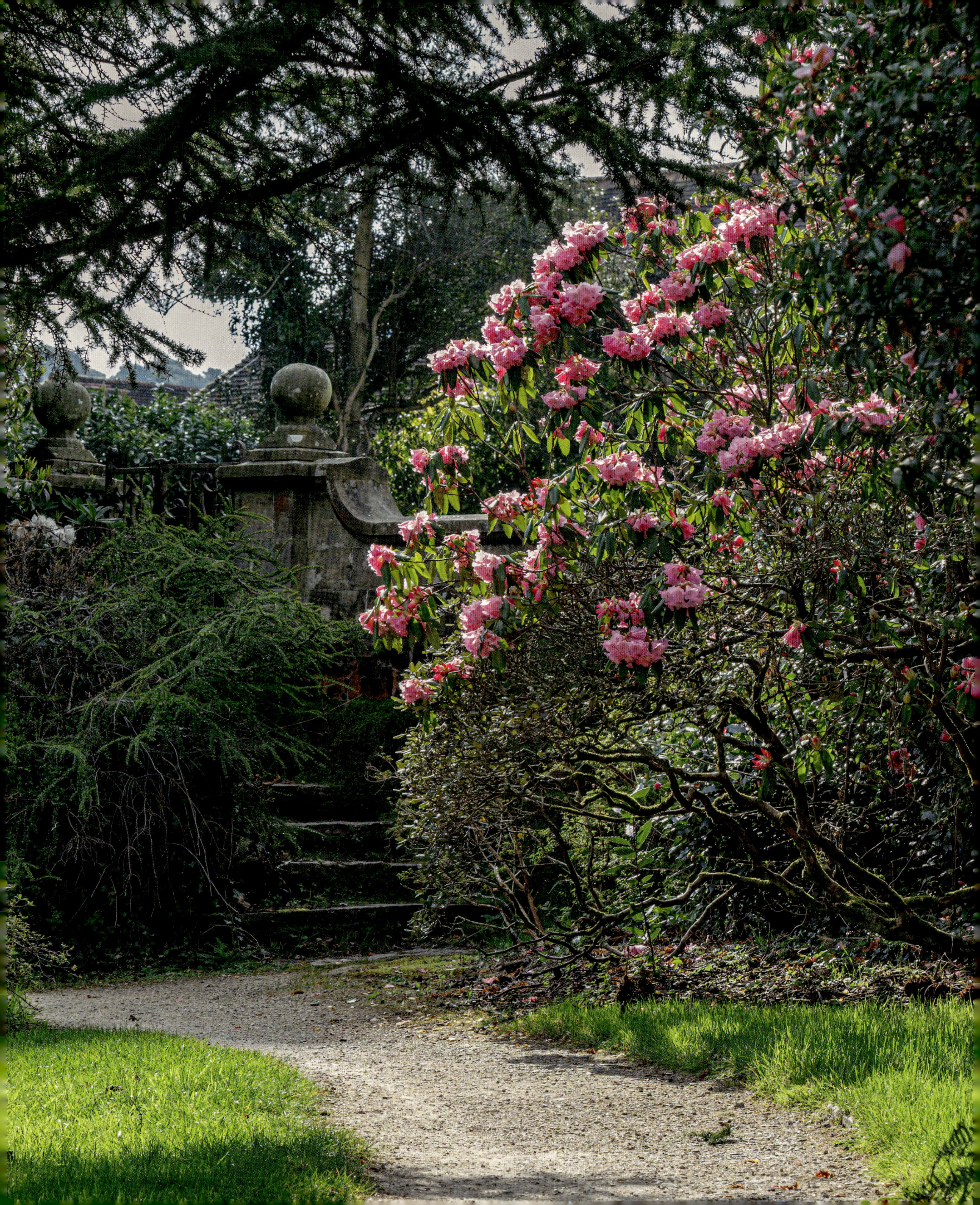

Contents

- 6   Map of the Garden
- 9   Foreword *by Stephen Lacey*
- 13   INTRODUCTION
  The World in One Garden

The History

- 19   Beginnings
- 29   COLONEL STEPHENSON ROBERT CLARKE
  The Great Project
- 37   COLONEL STEPHENSON ROBERT CLARKE
  The Colonel and the Collectors
- 49   SIR RALPH STEPHENSON CLARKE
  The Transitional Years
- 57   ROBERT NUNN STEPHENSON CLARKE
  Resilience and Rhododendrons
- 65   ANDREWJOHN STEPHENSON CLARKE
  Consolidation and Reinvention

The Garden

- 74   Introduction to the Garden
- 76   Old Rhododendron Garden
- 84   Jay Robin's Rose Garden
- 92   Mediterranean Garden and Victorian Greenhouses
- 98   White Garden
- 104   South Lawn and Mid-Summer Border
- 115   West Bank
- 120   Paradise Walk
- 128   Italian Garden
- 138   Round Dell
- 147   Old Potting Sheds
- 152   Long Dell
- 154   West Garden
- 157   Garden of Allah
- 166   Azalea Ring
- 174   Warren Wood

- 186   Historic Borde Hill Plants
- 190   RHS Awards of Merit for Plants Cultivated or Bred at Borde Hill
- 192   Borde Hill's Champion Trees
- 194   Timeline: History of Borde Hill and the Clarke Family
- 196   Clarke Family Tree
- 198   Select Bibliography
- 199   Acknowledgements and Picture Credits
- 200   Sponsors

Map of the Garden

1. Old Rhododendron Garden
2. Jay Robin's Rose Garden
3. Mediterranean Garden and Victorian Greenhouses
4. White Garden
5. South Lawn and Mid-Summer Border
6. West Bank
7. Paradise Walk
8. Italian Garden
9. Round Dell
10. Old Potting Sheds
11. Long Dell
12. West Garden
13. Garden of Allah
14. Azalea Ring
15. Warren Wood

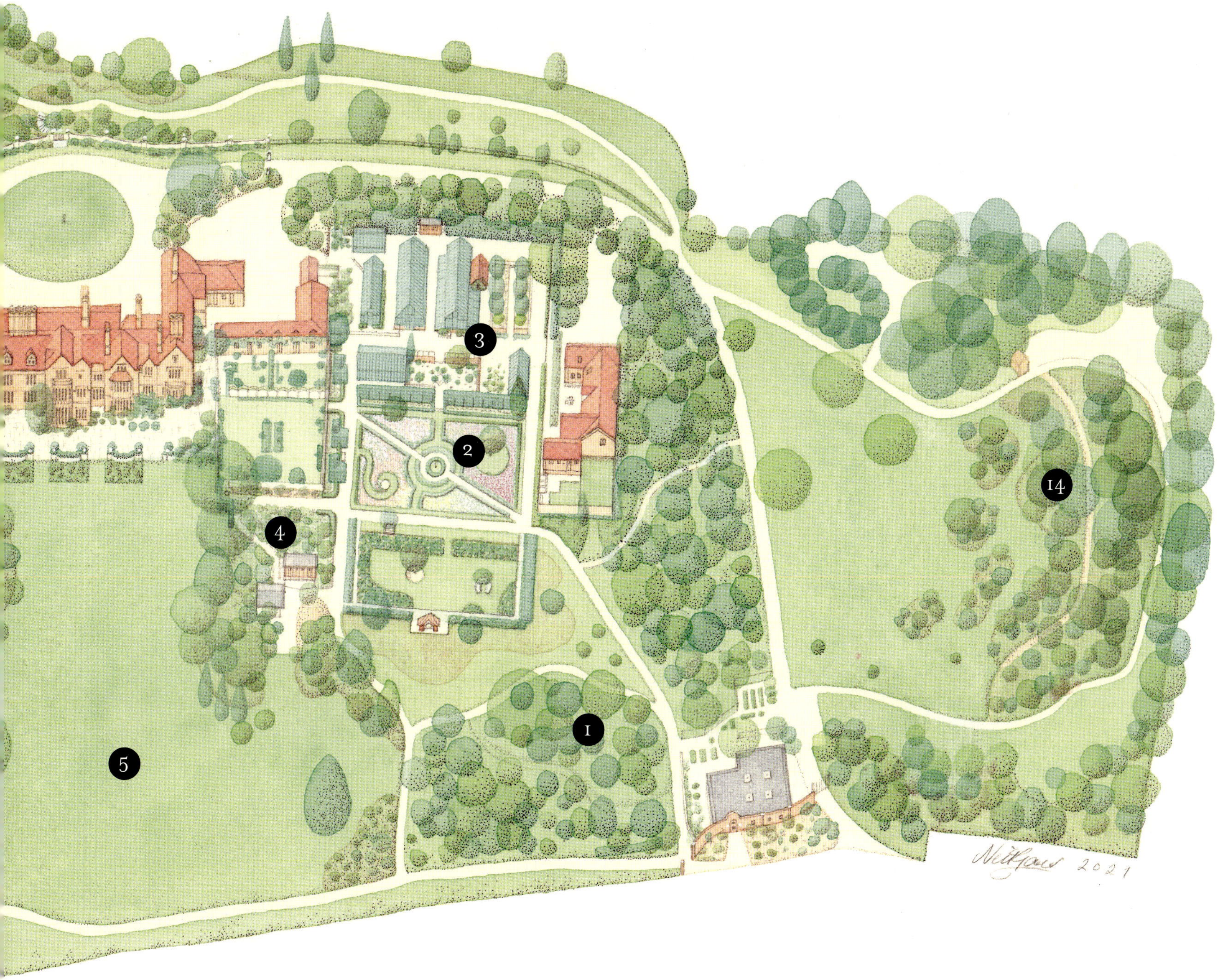

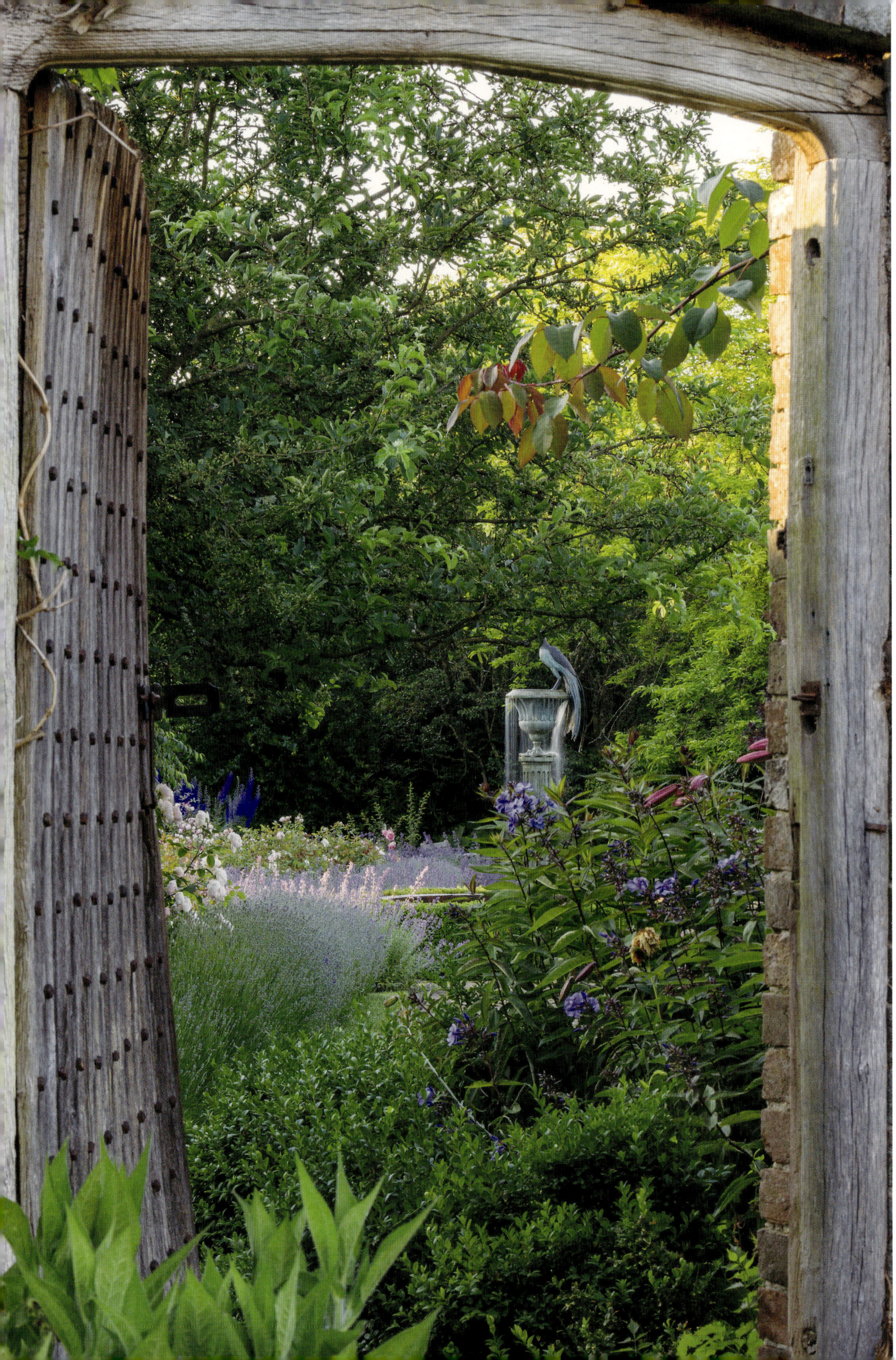

Foreword
Stephen Lacey

Plantsmen's and plant collectors' gardens are my favourite sorts of garden, and, boy, did those Edwardians know how to collect. Porcelain, paintings, stuffed birds – Borde Hill's creator, Colonel Stephenson Robert Clarke, collected them all. And out in his newly acquired landscape, he indulged his even greater passion for plants, filling acre upon acre of parkland and woods with trees, shrubs, bulbs and perennials.

It was some thirty years ago that I first encountered Colonel Clarke's wondrous legacy of sprawling magnolias and towering rhododendrons, explored the jungly dells and imagined myself catapulted to China and the Himalayas. Since then, I have returned to Borde Hill many times, and I still have that same frisson of excitement, not only from hunting down the veteran plants and catching them in bloom, but also from seeing the changes.

This is a garden that is never allowed to get stuffy. The changes are often subtle – planting gently refreshed – but sometimes they are bold, with artists invited to replant or reimagine areas of garden. In Edwardian style, Borde Hill's overall design, with its string of formal gardens linking to the woodland, is as eclectic as its plants, and the interventions of these artists – including biennial summer sculpture exhibitions – underscore its character.

But there is also a calmness and harmony at Borde Hill, and this comes from its setting. A strong feature of the garden is the way its introspective spaces are partnered by expansive views, so that as you walk the grounds, you are continually refocusing, from close-up planting to broad sweeps of parkland, from tiny flowers to ancient oaks, from exotic colours to the myriad greens of the Sussex Weald. Unspoilt countryside encircles the whole garden.

Remarkable, too, is the fact that, three generations on, the same family is gardening here – and with gusto. Andrewjohn and Eleni Stephenson Clarke are such enthusiastic and hands-on owners, forever floating new ideas, visiting other gardens, drawing in expertise and researching new plants. Tours with them are always lively.

A book about Borde Hill has been long overdue, and I am delighted it has found its champion in Vanessa Berridge. I have known Vanessa for a long time, too; indeed, as a magazine editor, she gave me one of my very first writing jobs. She has tackled her subject with characteristic thoroughness and panache, reading a mountain of historical documents – the colonel kept copious notes and records, and all his garden correspondence – and venturing fearlessly into grand-scale woodland gardening and the rarefied world of the rhododendron (with its hundreds of species, thousands of hybrids and minefield of identification challenges).

The result is a book to cherish, telling in engaging style the story of this beautiful place past and present, conveying the significance of Borde Hill as one of Britain's great heritage gardens, and explaining its botanical importance as a repository of invaluable genetic material and as a living link with the golden era of Edwardian plant hunting and horticultural derring-do.

A metal-studded door opens in a wall on to Jay Robin's Rose Garden, created in 1996.

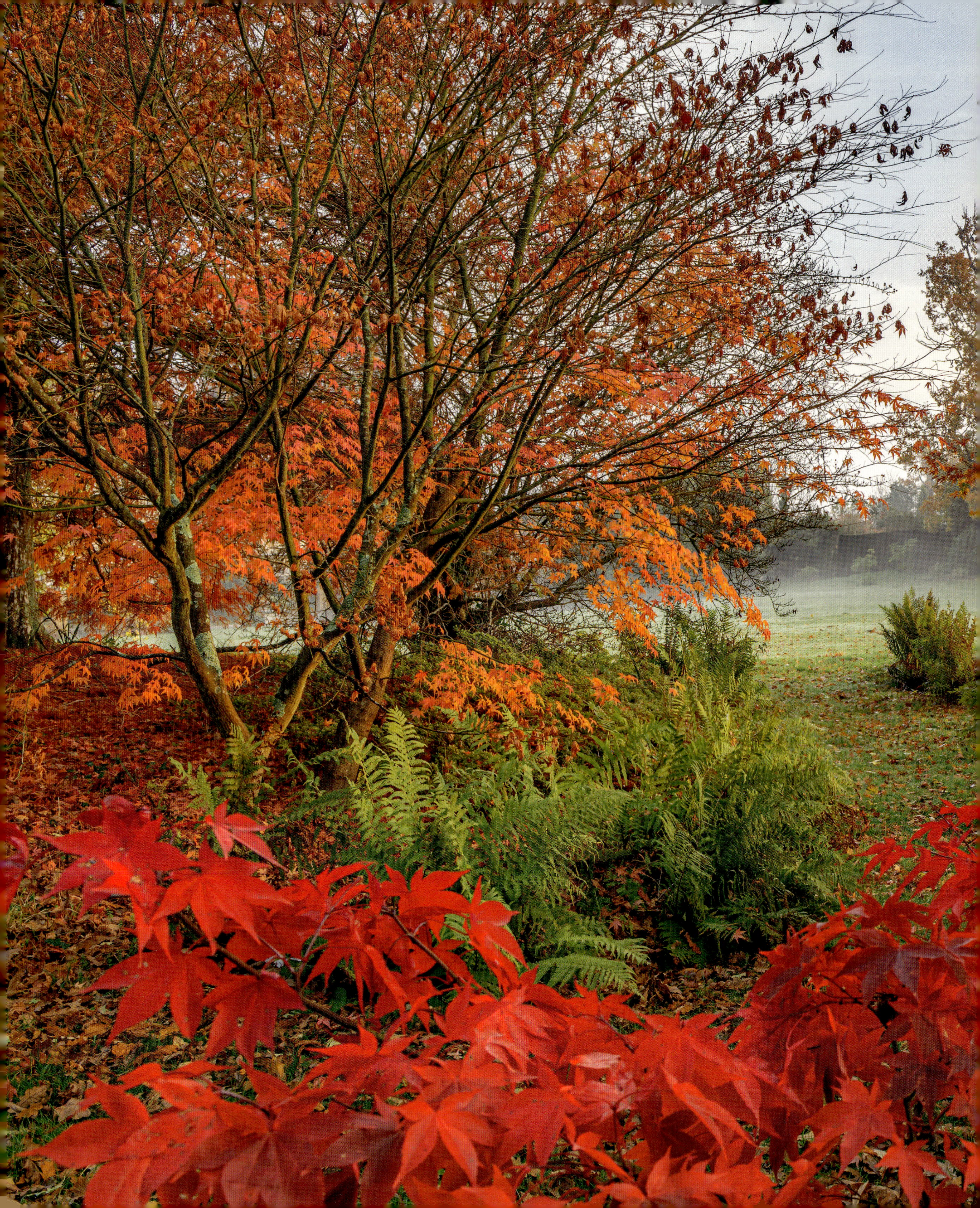

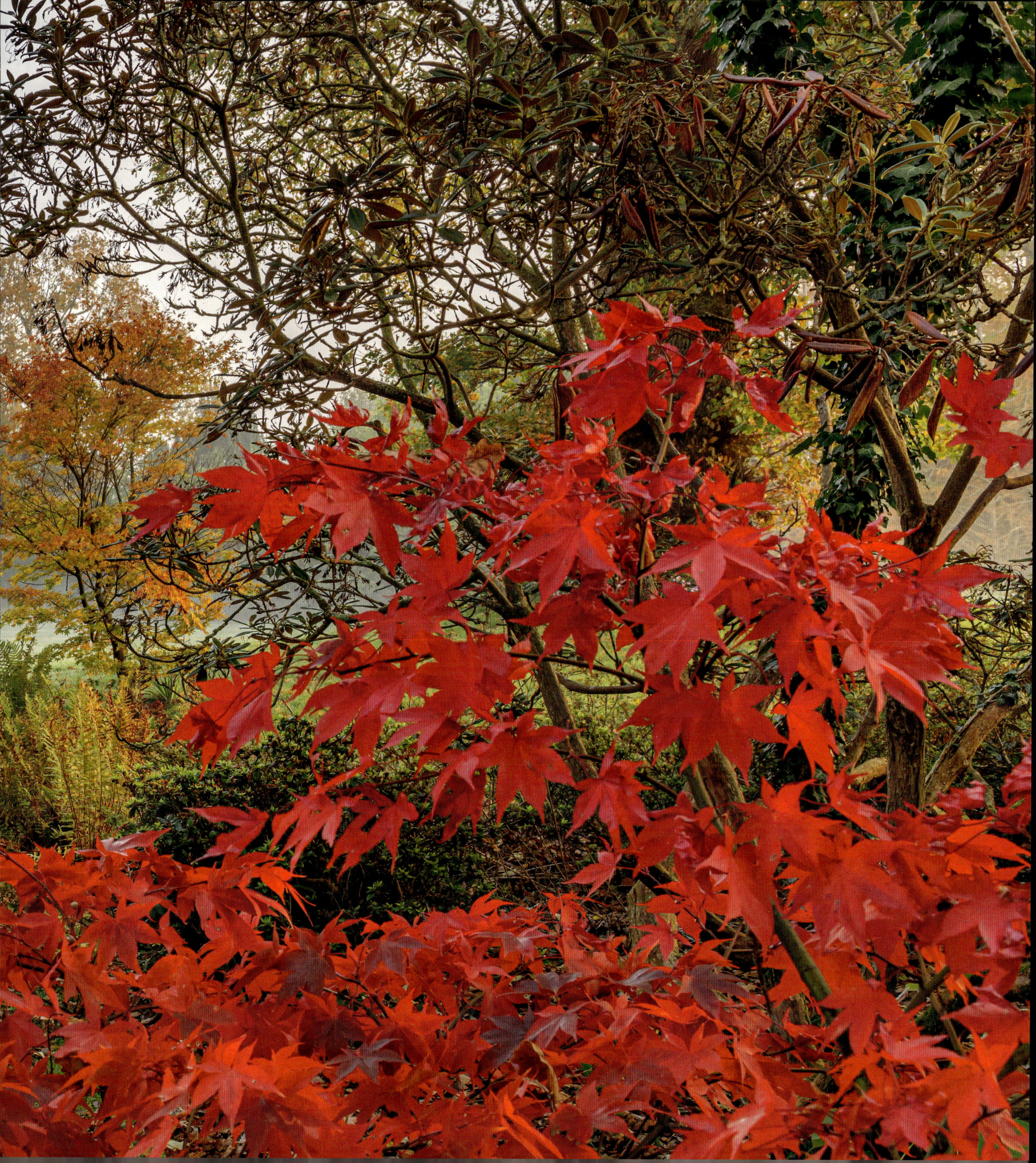

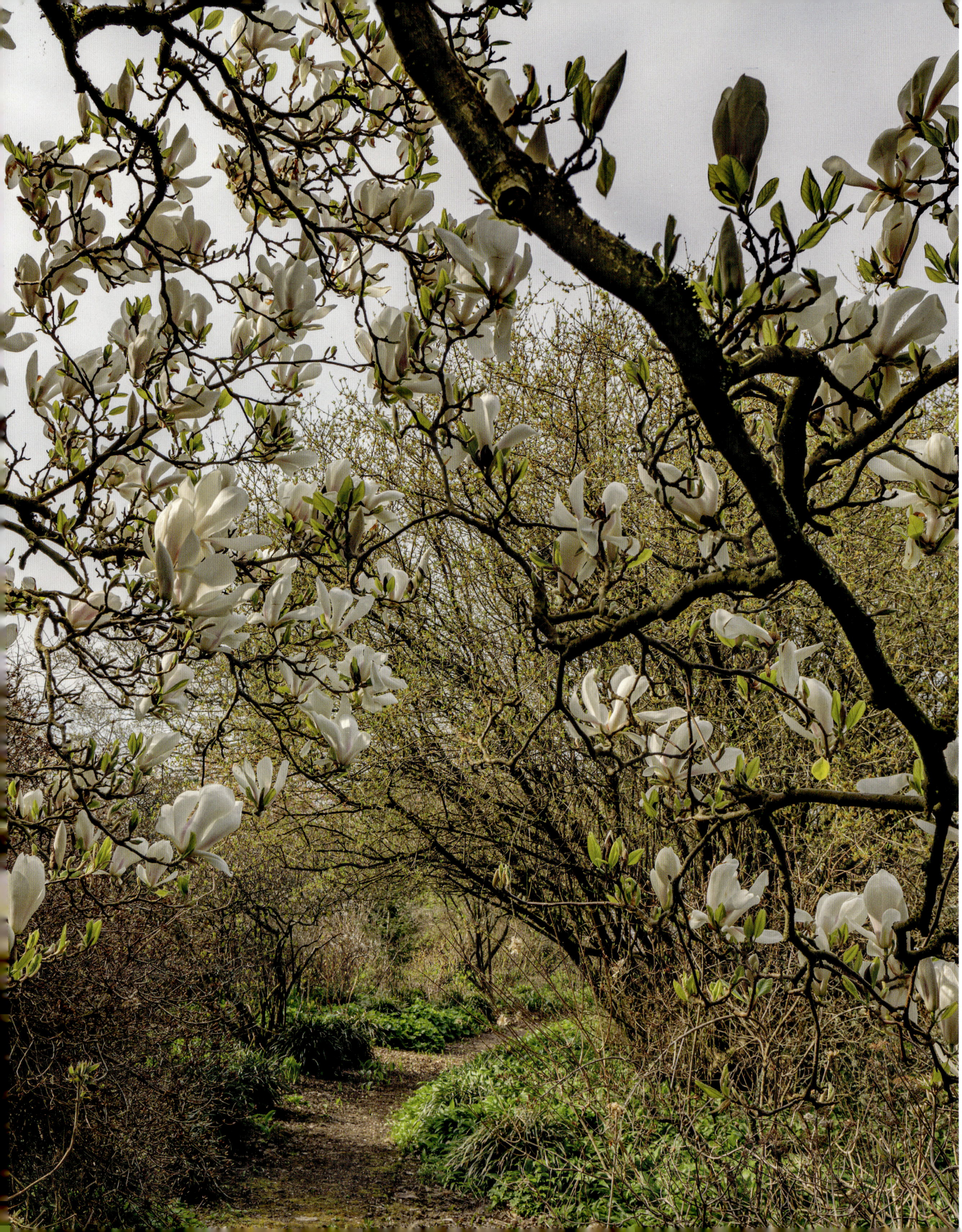

INTRODUCTION
The World in One Garden

Borde Hill in West Sussex is approached through softly undulating countryside. This is the High Weald, an Area of Outstanding Natural Beauty, and the perfect frame for Borde Hill's magnificent collection of trees and flowering shrubs. The Elizabethan mansion surrounded by 35 acres (14 ha) of formal gardens and woodland is at the heart of 380 acres (154 ha) of Grade II*-listed parkland. A very English scene, yet many of its rare plants were collected in remote areas of China, Burma and South America by death-defying botanists.

That fusion of the foreign and the indigenous has defined the British garden for centuries. Look at any great example – be it the Royal Botanic Gardens at Kew, Nymans, Stowe, Hidcote, Kiftsgate or Sissinghurst – and you will see how these gardens assimilated design influences and plants from overseas within a uniquely British aesthetic. Borde Hill, created from the 1890s onwards, embodies this rich mixture, and is a supreme example of the best in British gardening.

Gardens are among Britain's chief glories. Blessed with a temperate climate and a range of geological conditions, the British have adopted diverse gardening styles. Whether large or small, formal or informal, urban or rural, British gardens have embraced their surrounding landscapes, each with a profound sense of rootedness and scale: even the grandest garden will have its intimate corners.

From stately home to country cottage, British gardens feature an almost unmatched wealth of planting. For the British, not wanting to be confined to a small island, have been prodigious travellers, absorbing inspiration from France, Italy, Persia, India and beyond. The values and strategies of the British Empire are now questionable, but the reach of British trade and authority over the course of more than three centuries enabled gardeners to import plants from across the world that enriched our native stock to make gardens of variety and beauty.

So what defines a British garden? After all, fashions have come and gone: the formal was succeeded by the flowing lines of the eighteenth-century landscape movement. In the late nineteenth century William Robinson advocated choosing plants suited to a garden's soil and conditions, a reaction against the Victorian taste for extravagant bedding displays of tender exotics.

All these different styles share a focus on plants. 'Capability' Brown, the eminent eighteenth-century designer renowned for his naturalistic parkland, also planted roses, hollyhocks, honeysuckles, Persian jasmines and sumac in the garden at Petworth. A century later, Joseph Paxton, head gardener at Chatsworth, delighted in introductions from the Americas, and used the structure of the Amazonian water lily leaf as a template for his design of the Crystal Palace at the Great Exhibition of 1851.

Borde Hill illustrates many of these themes. Its wide lawns, flowing out over a ha-ha into the countryside, have the feel of an eighteenth-century landscape garden. The terraced Italian Garden displays influences from Italy and Persia, while the Old Potting Sheds are an intimate corner of shrub and perennial planting. Victorian greenhouses, once used for nerines and orchids and restored in 1997–99, recall Paxton's world. And with its variety of soils, Borde Hill has provided perfect conditions for trees and shrubs from several continents. To the visitor today, Borde Hill offers, quite simply, the world in one garden.

Borde Hill House has been occupied by the same family for almost 130 years. Its garden was the vision of Colonel Stephenson Robert Clarke (1862–1948), presiding genius for more than fifty years. Since his death, three generations of his descendants have successively reshaped and developed the estate. They have maintained the garden and enhanced one of the largest collections of privately owned rare trees in Britain.

After he bought the estate in 1893, Colonel Clarke laid out herbaceous borders around the house before focusing on collecting, and becoming a major player in a key period of

A path snakes through the back of the Azalea Ring beneath the white blooms of *Magnolia* ×

An aerial view reveals the complexity of the garden's layout, but also its splendid framework of parkland trees.

botanical gardens and other landowners, he subscribed for over three decades to plant-hunting expeditions that introduced species to Britain from across the world.

Colonel Stephenson Clarke's son Sir Ralph Stephenson Clarke (1892–1970) restored the garden and woodlands after their wartime decline, while his wife, Rebekah, devoted herself to raising nerines. In 1965 he set up the garden as a charity, managed by a council with members drawn from botanical gardens at RHS Wisley, Kew, Edinburgh and Cambridge.

Robert Nunn Stephenson Clarke (1925–1987), Sir Ralph's son, became a leading expert on rhododendrons. He raised the garden's profile by winning dozens of awards at Royal Horticultural Society (RHS) shows in the 1970s and '80s.

After Robert died prematurely in 1987, his younger son, Andrewjohn Stephenson Clarke (b. 1955), took up the reins. For more than thirty years, he and his wife, Eleni, have consolidated their predecessors' work by planning for the future while conserving the past. They have struck a balance between tending a collection of vital importance to botanists – Borde Hill features many plant species not found elsewhere in Britain – and providing year-round interest for the visiting public. They have reinstated the perennial planting of Colonel Clarke's Edwardian flower garden around the house, and have commissioned work from Chelsea medal-winning designers. Their achievement has been to safeguard the integrity of Borde Hill and its collection while ensuring its relevance for the future.

I have been fortunate in having been granted unrivalled access to Borde Hill's archive by Andrewjohn and Eleni. The correspondence between Stephenson Robert Clarke and nurserymen, directors of botanical gardens, other landowners and plant hunters gives unique insight into the horticultural world and social history between the wars. Letters reveal acts of courage by the plant hunters and the professional level of accomplishment of Colonel Clarke and his gardening friends. Also notable are Robert's painstakingly detailed handwritten lists of the rhododendron collection. It has been a joy to write this book, and I hope it will bring alive for readers the fascinating story behind the creation of Borde Hill and its continuation as one of the country's truly great gardens.

BORDE HILL GARDEN
14

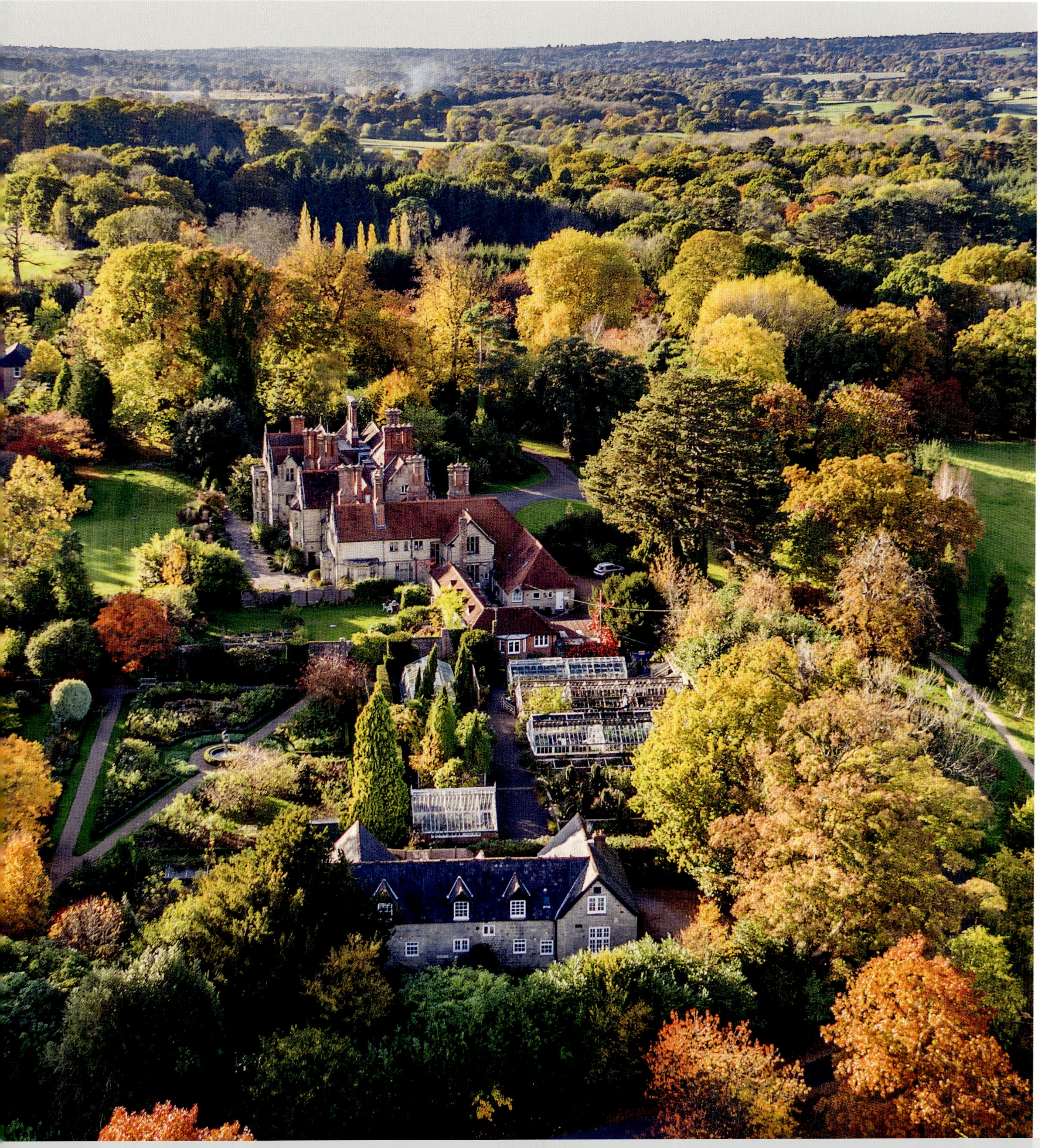

The History

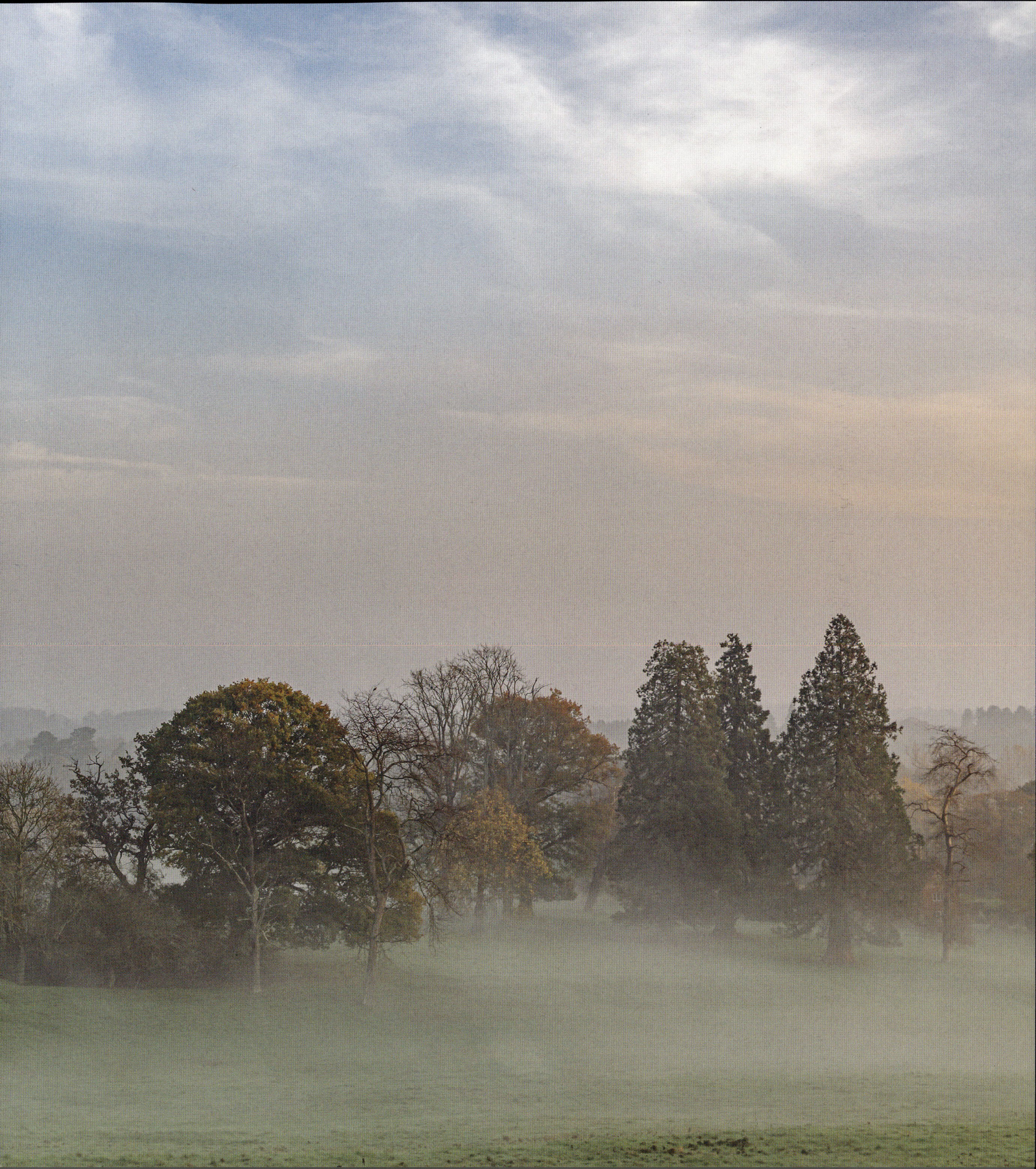

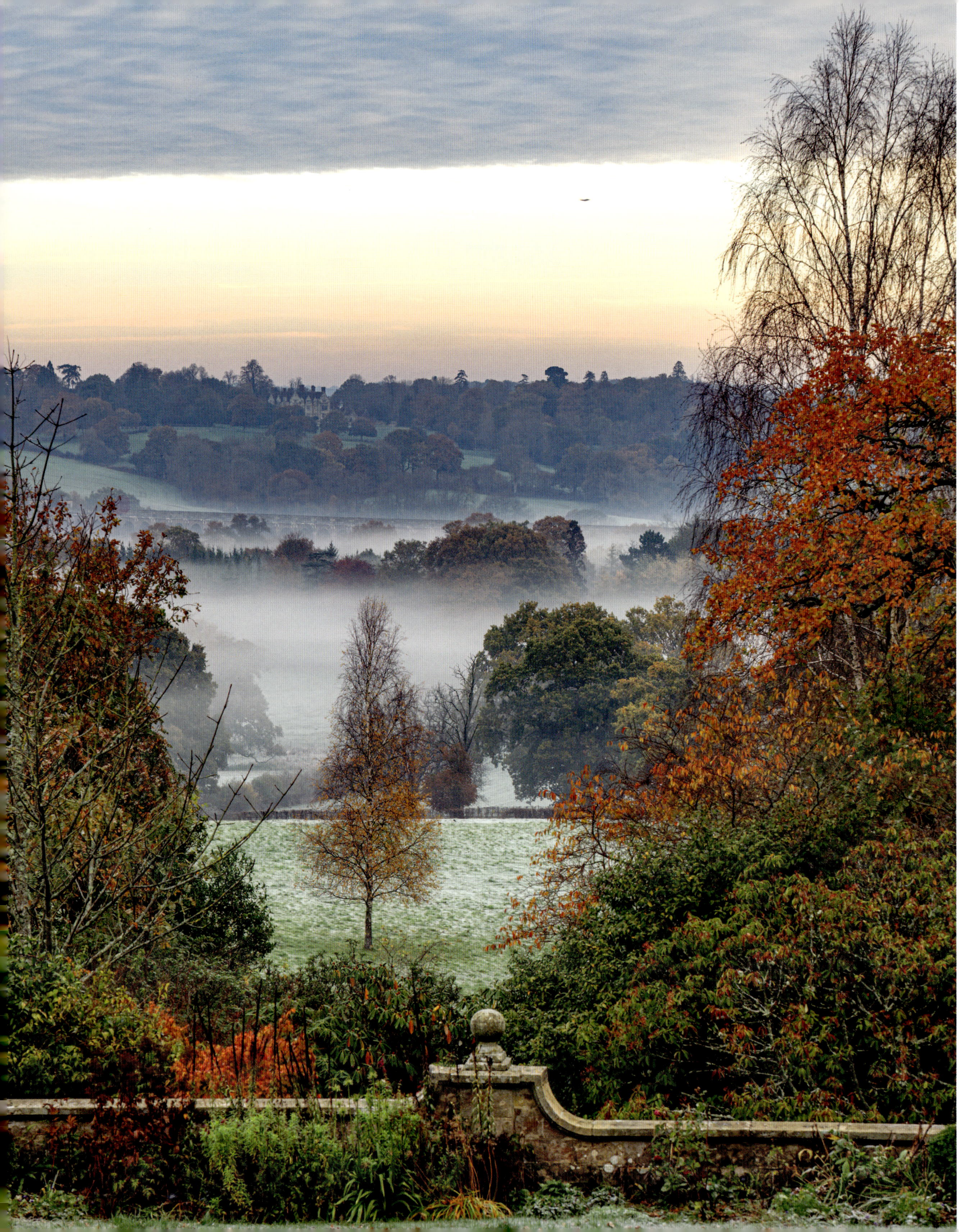

Beginnings

A railway viaduct sweeps majestically across the Ouse Valley, visible from the north front of Borde Hill House. Built in 1841, the viaduct still carries trains from London to Brighton over its soaring brick arches. It seems fitting that this imposing Victorian structure lies within sight of the Clarkes' home, for their family business, Stephenson Clarke and Company, once ran the biggest fleet of privately owned railway wagons in Great Britain, along with a fleet of ships. There is scarcely another building in sight, so it is hard to believe that a motorway and airport are less than a dozen miles away. In the early morning this seemingly timeless prospect is especially magical, with fields, trees and hills half-shrouded in mist. Were Stephen Borde, physician and builder of Borde Hill House in 1598, to stand here today, he would find much that is familiar. Certainly, it is clear to see why the Elizabethan courtier made his home in this English pastoral landscape.

Both the Bordes and the Clarkes rose from obscure origins to positions of wealth and influence. The Bordes, once Sussex serfs, were emancipated at the turn of the sixteenth century. In the early 1500s John Borde (or Boorde) sent his son Andrew (c. 1490–1549) to Oxford. Andrew was a Carthusian monk in Somerset for twenty years before informing his prior in 1528 that he was 'not able to byd the rugorositie of your relygyon' because of his fondness for wine and women. 'Merry Andrew' became an itinerant doctor and was recommended by the Duke of Norfolk 'to wayte on his prepotent Mageste' as Henry VIII's physician. He travelled between England and European universities, acquiring an extensive knowledge of plants and plant hunting that links him with Stephenson Robert Clarke, creator of Borde Hill's garden centuries later. Andrew spent time at the University of Montpellier, alma mater of Petrarch, where he would almost certainly have encountered Rabelais, who taught medicine there between 1534 and 1539.

Andrew wrote the first printed guidebook to in England. He worked as a medical practitioner in Winchester and London, but was convicted in Winchester of keeping three loose women in his house, and died in Fleet Prison in 1549.

By the late sixteenth century, the Borde family owned land from Somerset to Kent. Stephen Borde was knighted in July 1603 by King James I, possibly because, like his ancestor Andrew Borde, he was a court doctor. Stephen rebuilt his mansion in the Elizabethan style on its commanding site on the High Weald, surrounded by small fields and ancient woodlands. He planted orchards and herbaceous beds for medicinal plants. Rich inlaid wood and plasterwork, and a fine drop ceiling in the drawing room, were expertly installed, while over the fireplace in an upstairs bedroom are the initials 'S.B.' and the date 1601.

Stephen's initials can also be seen in the stonework of the west porch (the original front door), with 1598, the year of the house's construction. With his predecessor in mind, Stephenson Robert Clarke had his own initials carved into the north porch (now the house's main entrance), with the date of his extension, 1912.

There are other echoes across the centuries. In 1588, the year of the Spanish Armada, Stephen Borde subscribed £30 for the defence of England. Three hundred and fifty years later, in July 1940, Stephenson Robert Clarke

Opposite: The view towards the Ouse Valley Viaduct from the north front of Borde Hill House on a frosty

Below: The Ouse Valley Viaduct was built in 1841.

Right: Stephen Borde's initials were engraved above the west porch when he built Borde Hill House in 1598.

Below, right: Following suit, Stephenson Robert Clarke's initials were carved over the north-front door in 1912, the date that he added the east wing and extended the south-bay windows.

The view of Borde Hill House that featured in an 1870 sale catalogue shows the oak tree (on the right-hand side) that still remains on the South Lawn.

received a letter on behalf of the Chancellor of the Exchequer, Sir Kingsley Wood, thanking him for his 'generous action in lending to the country free of interest the sum of £2,000'.

Stephen's great-grandson William Borde moved further along the Ouse Valley to a larger family property, Paxhill Park, previously owned by a Ninian Borde. In 1705 William sold Borde Hill to a yeoman, Walter Gatland. William died without issue in 1720. Other parcels of land were taken over by the Burrells, the original owners of the land on which Borde Hill House had been built. In another stitch in the tapestry, the Burrells remain West Sussex landowners: Sir Charles Burrell, the 10th baronet, and his wife, Isabella Tree, have worked on the controversial and highly publicized rewilding of their estate at Knepp Castle, south of Horsham.

Over the years, Borde Hill House was sympathetically extended and altered by various owners. A watercolour illustration from the 1870 sale catalogue shows pleasure grounds around the house with gravel walks, and a formal parterre and croquet lawn in front of the house, on what is now the South Lawn.

In 1893 the Clarke family enter the Borde Hill story, when Stephenson Robert Clarke, a newly married man of thirty-one, bought both house and estate.

BORDE HILL GARDEN

Robert Clarke (1715–1786) played an important role in establishing the family business in the eighteenth century. Portraits of Robert and his wife, Dorothy Vanholt, are in the dining room at Borde Hill.

The Clarkes trace their origins to a John Clarke living in Northumberland in about 1530. Sir Ralph Stephenson Clarke, however, begins his family history of 1967 with another John, admitted in 1680 as tenant of a copyhold farm at Whitely in the Manor of Tynemouth. When he died in 1694, John's will described him as a 'Gentleman' with property across North Shields, including several houses and other copyhold property, and, most significantly for the family's future fortunes, a quay at Shields. Like later Clarkes, he was fecund: his estate was divided between thirteen children.

Intended, like Andrew Borde, for a religious vocation, Ralph, the second son of John's second marriage, went to St John's College, Cambridge, in 1693. In post-Reformation England that vocation meant the Anglican priesthood, and Ralph was inducted in 1703 to the living of Long Benton near North Shields. According to Sir Ralph's history, Ralph was a light-hearted man whose enjoyment of country life set the pattern for future generations of Clarkes. He perhaps lived above his means, as he left little property on his death in 1733. He did, however, leave two sons by his wife, Elizabeth Brown: Ralph and Robert, who both went to sea in the Merchant Service. While shipmasters, they bought shares in ships and a 300-ton sailing vessel, the *Cleveland*. Thus, they laid the foundations in the 1730s of the shipping and coal business that was eventually registered in 1850 as Stephenson Clarke and became one of the largest firms of collier owners and managers in the United Kingdom.

The younger brother, Robert, married Dorothy Vanholt, from a Dutch family resident in England, and the couple lived in Dockwray Square, overlooking the mouth of the Tyne, the base of North Shields shipowners. Both his and Dorothy's portraits are at Borde Hill, Robert shown with a globe and chart. Robert continued to live above the shop, so to speak, at the heart of the jostling waterside community of shipowners, shipmasters, sailmakers, ropemakers and ships' chandlers involved in the coal business. The coal was brought down the Tyne from the inland pits in lighters, known as keels, and trans-shipped at Shields. It was then taken by sea from Tynemouth to London, and sold there through agents to the Coal Factors' Society. Robert became unsure of these agents' trustworthiness, so in 1776 he dispatched his twenty-three-year-old son John to run the family's operations from London. John joined the Coal Factors' Society, and the Clarkes remained members until the twentieth century.

From then on, the business was primarily London-based, and John set up home there with his wife, Jane Stephenson, a woman with a fiery temper allegedly inherited from her ropemaker father.

Robert Clarke left over £12,000 on his death in 1786. His sons, John and Ralph, also prospered, increasing their share in the Coal Factors' Society. John took out a long lease on The Rookery at Tooting, a house with an 11-acre (4.5-ha) park, from which he rode to the Coal Exchange at Billingsgate on horseback or in his

BEGINNINGS

John Clarke (1753–1792) was painted by the royal portrait painter Johann Zoffany, an indication of Clarke's social position.

own carriage. John's social standing is illustrated by his portrait in the dining room at Borde Hill, painted by the royal artist Johann Zoffany. There are also miniatures of John and Jane.

When John died in 1792, Jane, unusually for a woman at that time, worked alongside her brother-in-law running the company until she married Captain James Strachan in 1796. The deeds of this marriage are still at Borde Hill, along with a small tortoiseshell box on which Strachan's initials are engraved. Despite Jane's remarriage, she remained important in the Clarkes' life, her maiden name adopted as a forename and used for the family business.

In 1805 Ralph set up in partnership as Clarke and Burgess, coal factors, shipping and insurance brokers, and the partners were joined in 1806 by John's son, Robert. Since 1790 Ralph had been a member of the Clothworkers, one of the 'Great Twelve' livery companies of the City of London. In 1828 he was master of the company, an office held by subsequent Clarkes; family membership continues to this day. Ralph retired in 1818 and died in 1843 aged eighty-one.

The life of John's son, Robert, born in 1781, is documented by letters, account books and Coal Factors' Society records. In 1815 he married Maria Elizabeth Nunn, and they had six sons and four daughters. Another fruitful and judicious marriage: Maria was the daughter of a banker, William Nunn, and the granddaughter, on her mother's side, of Henry White, a sugar merchant and chairman of the West India Dock Company. The Nunn family were also lacemakers; they had a factory on the Isle of Wight, where they made lace for a daughter of Queen Victoria (a letter of thanks from the queen is in the family archive).

Robert and Maria moved further out of London, buying Croydon Lodge, where their second son, Stephenson, father of Stephenson Robert Clarke, was born in September 1824. Robert hunted with the Old Surrey Hounds, shot, entertained, played cricket, and bought books and pictures. He was also a churchwarden and became a captain in the Loyal Tooting Volunteers, whose regimental drum from a Napoleonic war campaign is at Borde Hill.

Between 1812 and 1816, Clarke and Burgess was the principal house in the Coal Factors' Society, with more than a ninth of the society's total import business. Robert involved himself in every aspect: a letter of August 1818 records that one day he spent seven hours in the saddle visiting collieries in Northumberland. In 1825 he became chairman of the Coal Factors' Society, a post he held until his death in 1849.

But Robert, more concerned with detail than the bigger picture, failed to notice that the London coal trade was changing. Until the mid-nineteenth century, the coastal coal trade was carried on by little sailing brigs like those the Clarkes had managed for over a century,

Generations of Clarkes were military men. The Loyal Tooting Volunteers' regimental drum from the Napoleonic wars (right) and a drum from the Boer War (left) are both kept at Borde Hill.

BORDE HILL GARDEN

22

In the late eighteenth century John Clarke took out a long lease on The Rookery, a house with an 11-acre (4.5-ha) park at Tooting.

plying regularly between Newcastle and London. Steam appeared first in the collier trade in the 1840s, but Clarke and Burgess was slow to catch on. Robert did not appreciate that old-established customs and procedures within the exchange were being superseded by fiercer competition for business, nor did he spot the implications of new coalfields opening in the Midlands, and growing competition from railways in the transportation of coal.

Robert's shrewder son Stephenson had been in the business, but had also traded on his own account for some time before Robert's death. According to Sir Ralph, Stephenson inherited 'little but the name of an old-established family business, and from a financial point of view [he] had to start again almost from scratch'. In 1850 he amalgamated his father's business with his own, registering it as Stephenson Clarke and Company, at offices in St Dunstan's Alley in the City of London. With capital advanced by relations, he built up the fleet of colliers and moved into steamships; by 1876 the company had disposed of all its sailing vessels and owned a fleet of seven iron steamers. He also invested in railways, which, in 1886, were delivering almost twice as much coal to London as was arriving by sea. Stephenson ensured that, for more than a century, the distinctive black-and-white Stephenson Clarke livery would be seen on colliers sailing up and down the coast and on railway wagons speeding through the countryside. London's population increased rapidly, and with it the demand for coal. Stephenson Clarke, owning both ships and railway wagons, and by then collieries as well, responded quickly to trade fluctuations. As railways became overstretched by the demand for coal, the company began again to buy sailing ships as well as adding to its fleet of steam colliers.

London's expansion led to the growth of the gas industry, in which Stephenson also involved himself: he was a director of several British gas companies, and helped develop others around the Mediterranean and Asia Minor and in Denmark and Ceylon (now Sri Lanka).

In 1861, aged thirty-six, Stephenson married twenty-four-year-old Agnes Maria Bridger at a society wedding at St George's, Hanover Square. They probably met through their Sussex connections, for Agnes Maria's father, Charles, owned a Sussex estate near to Stephenson's country home, Brook Cottage, at Ardingly. Stephenson developed the medieval hunting lodge into a shooting box, where he spent weekends. He renamed it Brook House and bought further land to avoid encroachment on his shoots. The house was extended in the Arts and Crafts style, with half-timbered gables and stone mullioned windows inspired by Tudor architecture. An imposing mansion, it became the long-term home of many of Stephenson and Agnes Maria's ten sons and four daughters, all of whom lived to be at least twenty-four.

After the birth of each of his children, Stephenson took Agnes Maria abroad to recover (and presumably to conceive another).

BEGINNINGS

Marble busts of Agnes Maria and Stephenson Clarke, commissioned in about 1871 from the Milanese sculptor Antonio Tantardini. Their son Stephenson Robert Clarke (Stephie) would create the garden at Borde Hill.

Family legend has it that the nanny, left to name the children, selected forenames from the surnames of Clarke brides, including Strachan, Bridger and Vanholt. Family names run through the generations: Sir Ralph's elder son, Robert Nunn Stephenson Clarke, was given the maiden name of his great-great-grandmother.

Sir Ralph describes Stephenson, his grandfather, as 'a very small, neatly made man with good eyes, rather good-looking; a heavy cigar smoker, but moderate in what he drank … At shooting lunches he had a strange mixture of sherry and ginger beer, which his old keeper used to call "the Guvnor's lush".'

White marble busts by the Milanese sculptor Antonio Tantardini of Stephenson and Agnes Maria, which once stood on plinths in the Old Potting Sheds, are now in the main reception room in Borde Hill House. Sculpted in about 1871, Stephenson epitomizes the Victorian paterfamilias. He has a full head of hair and

Brook House was developed during the nineteenth century from a shooting lodge into an Arts and Crafts-style mansion by Stephenson Clarke (1824–1891). Members of the Clarke family continued to live there until it was finally sold in the late 1980s.

BORDE HILL GARDEN

mutton-chop whiskers that meet under his chin above a plain white shirt and loose bow tie, with a flourish of gardenias in his buttonhole. Agnes Maria, already the mother of eight children, looks perhaps older than her thirty-four years, her face, not surprisingly, slightly strained. Her dress has an unfussy buttoned blouse front with a cameo brooch at her neck, and her hair is braided at the top of her head.

Agnes Maria can also be seen in later life in one of the first English works by the Anglo-Hungarian artist Philip de László, portrait painter to royalty and aristocracy. Dressed in velvet and silk, Agnes Maria appears as she was described by Sir Ralph in his family history: 'Grannie was highly intelligent and possessed energy and character, and was extremely generous and kind.'

A true Victorian, Stephenson Clarke was both businessman and benefactor. He contributed to building Highbrook Church, where family members would be baptized, married and buried, and made gifts in his lifetime and his will to the Clothworkers' Company, St Bartholomew's Hospital, and Whitgift School in Croydon. On his death, a tribute in the school's magazine read, 'Mr Clarke's name is familiar to all generations of Whitgift boys, and there are few of them who have not in some way or other benefited by his munificence … Those of us who knew him personally were strongly attracted by his kindly geniality of manner.'

Stephenson Clarke died aged sixty-six on 3 April 1891, leaving a net estate valued at over £940,000. His coffin was borne to Highbrook Church by seven estate workers, dressed in new black suits. Agnes Maria survived him by more than thirty years, dying at Brook House in July 1921.

Ten months before Stephenson's death, his eldest son, Stephenson Robert Clarke, had married. Although he inherited Brook House, he decided to leave his mother's home and start afresh with his new wife, Edith, and young son, Ralph. In 1893 he bought Borde Hill and began writing a new chapter in the history of both house and family.

A Victorian bath chair used by Agnes Maria Clarke (1837–1921) is in the entrance hall of Borde Hill House.

Above: Agnes Maria was the first of three generations of Clarkes to be painted by the society portraitist Philip de László.

Overleaf: An aerial view of Robertsmere in the South Park.

BEGINNINGS
25

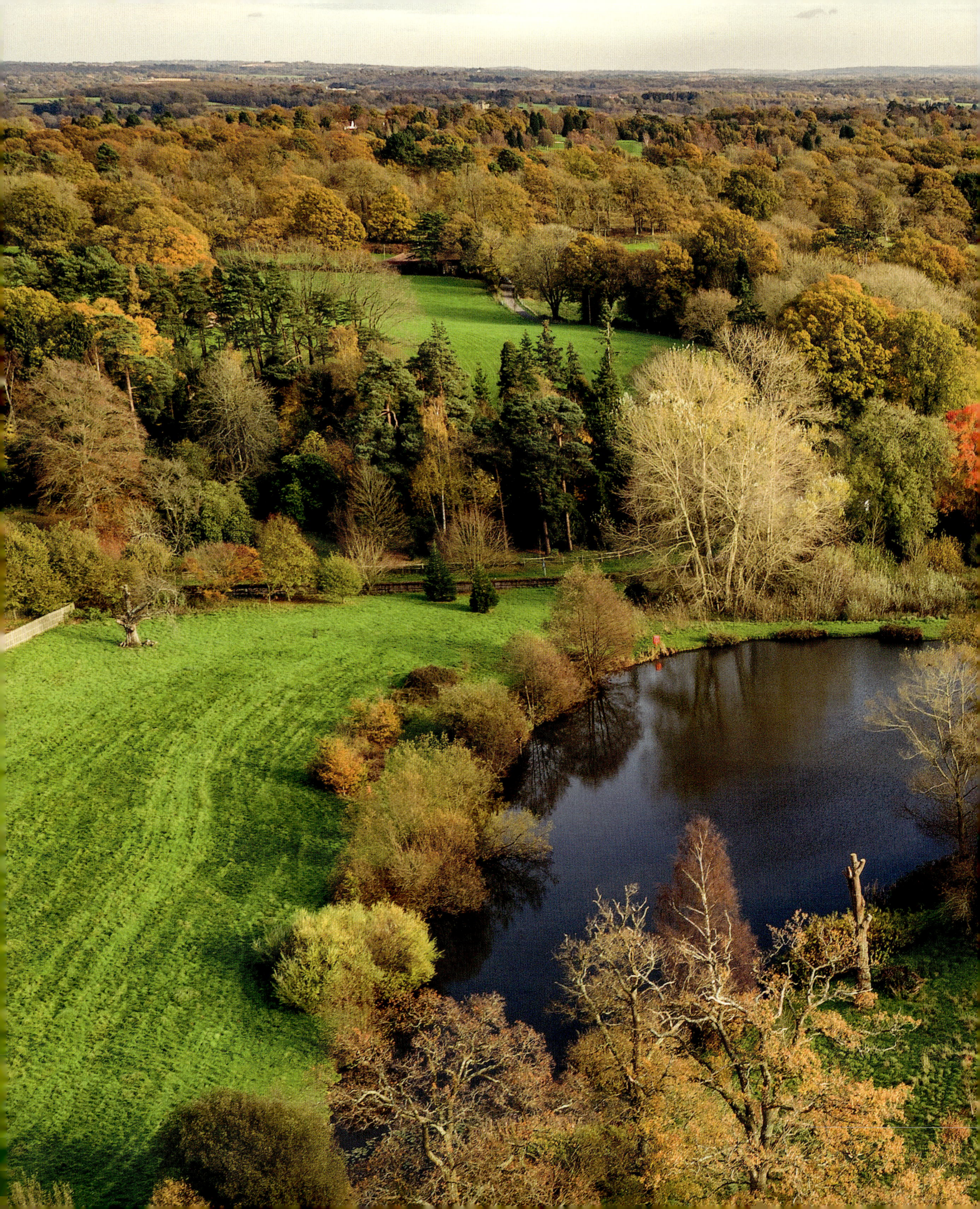

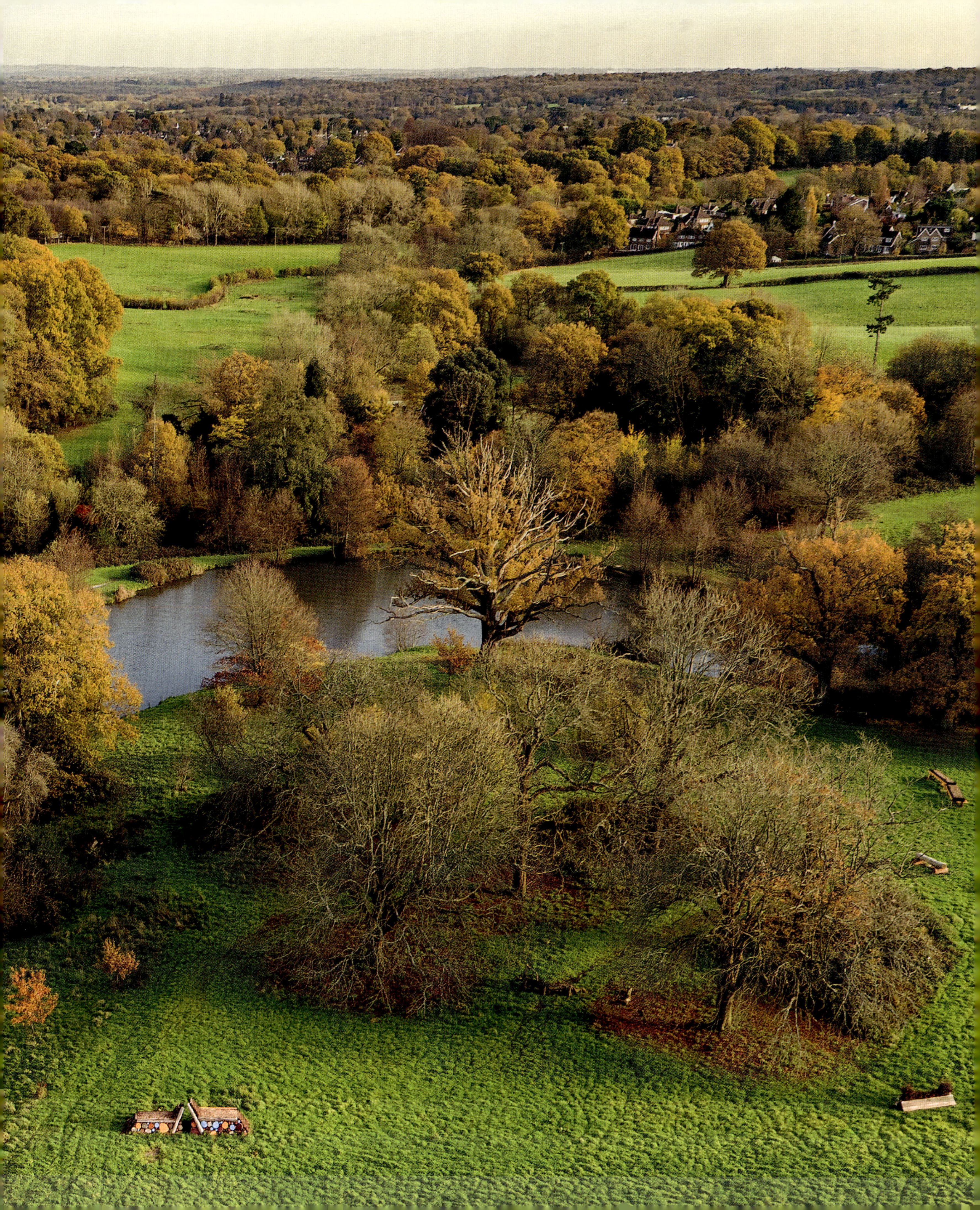

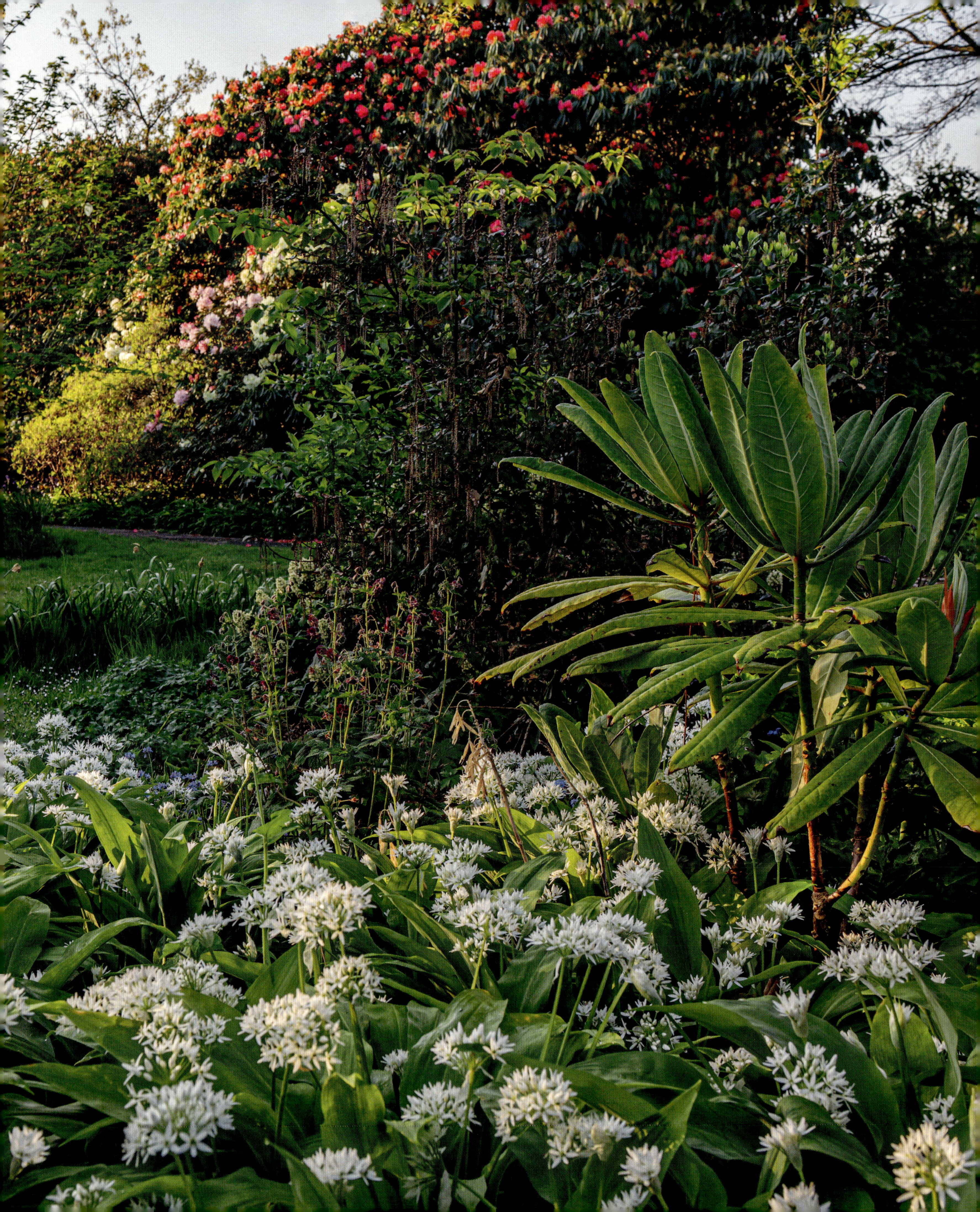

COLONEL STEPHENSON ROBERT CLARKE
The Great Project

'My first efforts at planting on Borde Hill date from the early nineties of the last century and were mainly devoted to shutting out unsightly views and to improving the landscape.' So wrote Colonel Stephenson Robert Clarke in his foreword to the *Catalogue of the Trees and Shrubs at Borde Hill, Sussex*, published by Oxford University Press in 1935. Colonel Clarke continues: 'Some ten years later I was encouraged by my friend, the late Mr H.J. Elwes, to combine with these objects the introduction of new and uncommon trees; and following these small beginnings additions have been systematically made to the collection.'

This is an unassuming description of a visionary project that led to the assembling of what the nurseryman Sir Harold Hillier described as 'probably the most complete private arboretum in the temperate region'. Its creator was a businessman, soldier, countryman, gardener, botanist and plant collector, ornithologist and traveller. A public benefactor, he helped build parish churches at Highbrook and at Shanklin on the Isle of Wight. He was known by his family and close friends variously as Stephie, Stevie, Stephy and even Steevy (his correspondents' spelling was cavalier). For simplicity, I shall call him Stephie.

Stephie was born on 28 June 1862, the eldest son of Stephenson and Agnes Maria Clarke. His childhood was spent at family homes in Tooting and Croydon, with weekends and holidays at Brook House in Sussex. He was educated at Winchester, where, according to his son Ralph, Stephie 'did not go in much for games, and did not play anything for his House, but he was even then keen on natural history and especially ornithology'. Stephie did not attend university, his father no doubt believing it more important that his eldest son should gain business experience. University was a luxury then for younger sons: Stephie's youngest brother, nineteen years his junior, Louis Colville Gray Clarke, studied at Cambridge and became a distinguished archaeologist. From 1937 to 1946, Louis was director of the Fitzwilliam Museum, to which he bequeathed drawings by Leonardo da Vinci, Correggio, Parmigianino and Rubens.

Instead, Stephie spent eighteen months working for a shipbroker near Rouen. According to his obituary in *Ibis*, the journal of the British Ornithologists' Union, Stephie 'said that much of his French was learned from a somewhat illicit acquaintance with French bird-catchers'. He collected birds throughout his life and served on committees of both the British Ornithologists' Union and the British Ornithologists' Club.

Stephie took pride in having been a real militiaman: in 1880 he was gazetted to the Royal Sussex Light Infantry Militia, before it became

Opposite: Davidias, wild garlic and rhododendrons in the Old Rhododendron Garden in May. This is where Stephie began planting rhododendrons in earnest in the early 1900s.

Above: Stephenson Robert Clarke (Stephie, 1862–1948) in his early seventies.

THE HISTORY

A drawing of Stephie's youngest brother, Louis Colville Gray Clarke (1881–1960), by Philip de László. Louis was director of the Fitzwilliam Museum in Cambridge from 1937 to 1946.

the 3rd Battalion, Royal Sussex Regiment. Military duties were combined with working in the family business; he was made a senior partner in 1890, aged twenty-eight, and in 1922 was elected chairman. He worked with other family members, including his brother Charles Bridger Orme Clarke, in building up the largest distributor, by road and sea, of British coal in the UK.

Like his forebears, Stephie joined the Coal Factors' Society in 1885 and the Clothworkers' Company in 1886 (he was master in 1924). A director of a South Wales docks and railway company, he also invested in railways and in telegraph, mining, gas and gold companies internationally. 'He clearly thought, if it's good business in the UK,' says his great-grandson Andrewjohn Stephenson Clarke, 'then it's good business elsewhere.'

Stephie married Edith Gertrude Godman at St Peter's, Eaton Square, in June 1890. Twenty-seven-year-old Edith was the daughter of Joseph Godman, owner of estates in Surrey and Sussex. Both came from large families, and the Godmans were also successful businessmen, Joseph's father having made his fortune with the Winchester-based brewer Whitbread. Edith's uncle was the naturalist Frederick Du Cane Godman, a founder of the British Ornithologists' Union, which Stephie joined in 1889. There were other links, too: Frederick's first wife was Edith Elwes, sister of H.J. Elwes, the galanthophile and horticulturalist who later encouraged Stephie at Borde Hill. Frederick and his second wife, Alice, collected rare orchids, alpine plants, rhododendron hybrids and magnolias at South Lodge near Horsham. Stephie and Alice exchanged plants and sat on RHS committees together. In the *Catalogue*, Stephie describes *Abelia engleriana*: 'This free-flowering species was given to me by Dame Alice Godman. Its pretty pink flowers carried on arching wands entitle it to be considered one of the most charming of this dainty genus.' The Godmans and the Clarkes understood one another.

A first son was born to Stephie and Edith in April 1891, but died within ten days. Their second son, Ralph Stephenson Clarke, arrived in August 1892. The following year, Stephie left his mother and siblings in what he called the 'dormitory' at Brook House. He bought Borde Hill, an estate of 25 acres (10 ha) around the house, with parkland of 610 acres (247 ha), and in 1894 sold Croydon Lodge, which had been owned by the family since the 1820s. Stephie later bought further land to unite the two properties, and beyond; at one point, he owned 20,000 acres (more than 8000 ha) across Sussex as far as west Kent.

Stephie lived at the end of a period of imperial exploration. The Royal Geographical Society sponsored expeditions to search for the source of the Nile; it was discovered by John Hanning Speke in 1858, despite his having been wounded by Berber tribesmen. Stephie, too, was a man of action, one who valued his home landscape all the more for having faced perils abroad.

Sales details from 1893, when Stephie bought the Borde Hill estate.

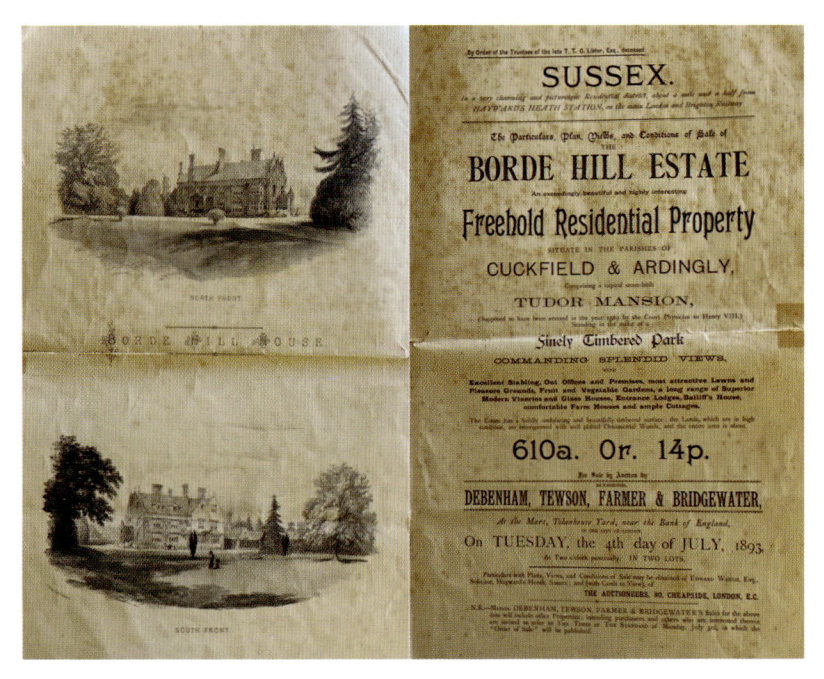

BORDE HILL GARDEN

Edith Gertrude Clarke (née Godman, 1862–1941), probably photographed at the time of her engagement to Stephie.

Sir Joseph Banks had launched the great age of plant hunting a century earlier as de facto director of the Royal Botanic Gardens at Kew. Understanding the political and economic uses of botany, he made Kew the centre of a worldwide network of botanical gardens. Explorers were dispatched to find plants of interest not only to botanists and collectors, but also to ordinary gardeners. The Horticultural Society of London (later the Royal Horticultural Society) sponsored David Douglas in the 1820s to visit America and Hawaii (where he perished in 1834 by falling into an occupied bull pit), and in the 1840s financed Robert Fortune in China. Estate owners followed suit: the Duke of Devonshire, encouraged by his head gardener, Joseph Paxton, sent an undergardener on expeditions in the 1830s to India and Burma (now Myanmar). Between 1842 and 1885, the Hookers, father and son, as successive directors of Kew, built on Banks's work, shipping off plant hunters to the Far East, Africa, the Americas, the Caribbean and the Azores. The son, Joseph Dalton Hooker, travelled through India and the Himalayas in 1847–51. The first westerner to reach remote northern areas of the Himalayas, he was imprisoned by the Rajah of Sikkim. On his release, Hooker returned home with twenty-five previously unknown species of rhododendron, triggering a craze for the spring-flowering shrubs in Britain. His introductions included *Rhododendron barbatum* and *R. falconeri*, both grown at Borde Hill.

Plant hunting was no longer just the preserve of botanical gardens: nurseries, such as Veitch of Chelsea, had become involved. In 1899 Harry Veitch commissioned Ernest Henry 'Chinese' Wilson (1876–1930) to travel to China to collect seeds of the handkerchief tree (*Davidia*), which Veitch wanted to grow commercially. Wilson was eventually successful, proving his rare talent for finding plants that would succeed in British gardens. Another plant hunter, George Forrest, had his first and most perilous mission to China and Burma, in 1904–1907, underwritten by a Liverpool cotton broker, Arthur K. Bulley, who had set up his own nursery, A. Bee & Co., in 1903. Both collectors subsequently enjoyed Stephie's support.

Nurseries were driven by the appetite for new plants among the gardening public. During the nineteenth century, gardening had become the pastime of a broader cross-section of society, inspired by John Claudius Loudon (1783–1843). His books, encyclopaedias and influential *Gardener's Magazine* demystified the subject and encouraged those with small spaces to garden. Joseph Paxton (1803–1865), head gardener at Chatsworth and designer of the Crystal Palace, followed suit, launching *The Gardeners' Chronicle* in 1841 to show that estates such as Chatsworth could offer lessons for amateur gardeners.

Towards the end of the century, a splenetic Irish writer, William Robinson (1838–1935), advocated breaking with formal Victorian gardening. He urged gardeners to choose plants for the soil and aspect, rather than shoehorning hothoused exotics into over-elaborate carpet bedding schemes. '[T]he process which is

Ernest Henry 'Chinese' Wilson (1876–1930) collected many plants that Stephie would later grow at Borde Hill.

THE GREAT PROJECT
31

commonly called "bedding out" presents to us simply the best possible appliance for depriving vegetation of every grace of form, beauty of colour, and vital interest', he wrote in *Alpine Flowers for English Gardens* (rev. edn, 1875). This and other books, including *The Wild Garden* (1870) and *The English Flower Garden* (1883), were known to Stephie, as was Robinson himself. Robinson visited Borde Hill on several occasions in the 1930s from his home at Gravetye Manor, a few miles away. 'We liked the face of the house and the fine landscapes beyond, and we thought we saw some new friends among the hardy flowers and some very fine trees', he wrote to Stephie in September 1930. 'We also enjoyed your flower borders and the long walks. Your gardner [*sic*] was most obliging.'

Stephie took Robinson's mantra ('right plant in the right place') to heart: a major reason for buying Borde Hill was its range of soils and aspects. All Stephie's *Catalogue* notes reflect his concern with planting overseas introductions in conditions most akin to their native habitat. *Erica arborea*, for instance, from southern Europe, northern Africa and the Caucasus, 'has proved quite hardy here and blooms with great freedom'. *Cornus controversa*, from Japan, was tried in two situations: No. 142, in the soil near the kennels, grew better than No. 285, planted south of the kitchen garden. 'When suited this tree grows quickly and flowers freely', Stephie noted. 'In the first week of June 1933 No. 142 was quite the handsomest object in the garden.'

Gertrude Jekyll (1843–1932), like Robinson, believed 'It is not enough to cultivate plants well;

William Robinson (1838–1935) was a major figure in British gardening from the 1870s. A Sussex neighbour of Stephie's, he visited and admired Borde Hill Garden.

they must also be used well', as she wrote in *Wood and Garden* (1899). Her books, including *Wall and Water Gardens* (1901) and her paean to a vanishing age, *Old West Surrey* (1904), were also in Stephie's library. The influence on Stephie of these two gardeners can be seen in a description of Borde Hill in a 1902 issue of *Country Life*, a magazine to which Jekyll regularly contributed: 'Here is natural flower gardening at its very best, and nothing can surpass the charm of those long borders of hardy flowers, which are gay with successive blooms from early spring until the last winds of autumn have blown.' This could indeed be a portrait of Jekyll's own garden at Munstead Wood, where she planted hardy perennials for an extended season of interest, with a focus on the plants' intrinsic beauty.

The influence of the plantswoman Gertrude Jekyll (1843–1932) was felt in the style of Stephie's first flower gardens at Borde Hill. Jekyll is pictured here in her garden in Surrey in the early 1920s.

This was the auspicious background against which Stephie bought Borde Hill. An adventurer at heart, he embarked on gruelling, months-long safaris and plant-hunting trips in America, Africa and India, so understood the impetus of Ernest Wilson, Reginald Farrer, George Forrest and Frank Kingdon Ward to hunt for plants in dangerous territories. It is no surprise that Forrest wrote often and frankly to Stephie, sensing a kindred spirit in this veteran of game-hunting expeditions.

By the early 1890s, the Victorian predilection for serried rows of carpet bedding was in full retreat and Stephie's style of gardening was becoming the fashion. He started around the house and then, spurred on by H.J. Elwes,

BORDE HILL GARDEN

moved out into the parkland to establish his collection. The estate effectively runs east to west along three ridges, with the house on the narrow central ridge. The southern ridge, as outlined in the *Catalogue* foreword, is broadly two different types of clay with Tunbridge Wells sand. The soil around the house was more challenging, as Stephie wrote (and as the gardeners still find today): 'I have found it necessary to remove large quantities of surface clay and to replace this with topsoil from the Park and humus from the woods.' The northern ridge, where Stephie planted his Pinetum, is also clay, but Warren Wood and other wooded areas to the west of the estate are a mixture of rich loam and clay.

Stephie bought a simple garden with a few good native trees, the usual shrubberies and a walled kitchen garden. An early project, in 1898, was to reshape the area around the house. He laid out the South Lawn, flanked by two centuries-old oaks, and built a ha-ha so that lawn and parkland merge seamlessly. Gradually, he replaced the shrubberies either side of the lawn with newly introduced rhododendrons and other shrubs and specimen trees.

The existing formal Victorian garden, transformed in the spirit of the Arts and Crafts movement, was described in the 1902 *Country Life* article. 'The east garden, with its rose arch, has a radiant vista through a realm of floral loveliness', wrote the author in prose as flowery as the garden itself. 'There are roses clustering on arches and walls, exhaling their fragrance in the sun, queenly lilies rising from the border, tall hollyhocks, spiked veronicas, and the towering red lychnis, contrasted with the dark blue monk's-hood, phloxes in all their gaiety, gorgeous peonies, and the lofty spires of varied larkspurs, foxgloves.' The article also noted the alpines in the rock garden and on the garden terrace, 'with its rugged stone wall affording friendly rootage to many plants that flourish in such situations'. The alpines lover William Robinson told Stephie in April 1932 that 'I was delighted with your little stone walls.'

Early encouragement came from Henry John Elwes (1846–1922), also an ornithologist. After resigning his commission in the Scots Guards in his twenties, Elwes devoted himself to naturalism and country pursuits. In 1870 he retraced Joseph Hooker's journey through the Sikkim Himalayas and into forbidden Tibet, Hooker's *Himalayan Journals* in hand. Near Smyrna, Turkey, in 1874 he discovered a snowdrop the size of a tulip, subsequently named *Galanthus elwesii*. This was the foundation stone of one of the UK's best snowdrop gardens – Colesbourne in Gloucestershire, where Elwes also planted exceptional trees.

Elwes collaborated on an erudite seven-volume work on the trees of Great Britain and Ireland with the Irish botanist and plant collector Augustine Henry. Henry briefed Ernest Wilson when Wilson was sent by Veitch to China to find the handkerchief tree, *Davidia involucrata*. From that expedition, Stephie planted *Rhododendron houlstonii* (*R. fortunei* subsp. *discolor* Houlstonii Group), as well as a Davidia. Stephie contributed to Wilson's later expeditions, and was to plant many other of his introductions at Borde Hill: *Acer griseum*, *Berberis julianae* and *Ilex pernyi* are all listed in the *Catalogue*, as are *Camellia cuspidata*, marked as 'one of Wilson's original plants', and '× *Ilex wilsonii*', according to Stephie, 'one of the handsomest and most thriving of the hardy hollies'.

For these new trees and shrubs, Warren Wood was planted up in 1905, followed by Stephanie's Glade in 1910. Stephie also created a walled kitchen garden by the stables, and planted conifers along Borde Hill Lane.

In 1912 Stephie extended the house to the south and east, and built a new entrance on the north front, above which his initials were carved, echoing those of Stephen Borde over the west porch. A family photograph taken about this time shows Edith and Stephie sitting on a bench, with their three grown sons and teenaged daughter behind, and the youngest, Robert, born in April 1904, perched on an arm of the bench. Mother and daughter are dressed

The distinctive Elizabethan chimneys of Borde Hill House can be seen in this picture from a 1902 issue of *Country Life*. The article described Stephie's garden as 'natural flower gardening at its very best'.

THE GREAT PROJECT
33

Right: Stephie with his wife, Edith, and their five children (from left to right), Edith, John, Ralph, Edmund (Eddie) and (on the bench arm) Robert.

Below: Despite being in his late thirties, Stephie volunteered to fight in the Second Boer War (1899–1902). This statuette dates from that conflict.

in simple white blouses with dark, ankle-length skirts, while all four sons wear tweed jackets, ties and waistcoats, and the colonel a tweed suit, a stick in his right hand. To us, it all looks very formal, but this was casual, off-duty clothing for late Edwardians.

When the Second Boer War broke out in 1899, Stephie, already thirty-seven, volunteered, along with three of his brothers, and was mentioned in dispatches. On his return home in 1902, his carriage was hand-drawn from Horsted Keynes station to Brook House. 'It was quite a gesture from the estate workers,' says his great-grandson Andrewjohn, 'as they would have been pulling the carriage uphill for the last stage.'

Stephie commanded the 3rd Battalion of the Royal Sussex Regiment from 1906 to 1912, retiring with the substantive rank of lieutenant colonel and honorary rank of colonel. In 1911 he was awarded the Companion of the Order of the Bath for his military service.

In the large reception room at Borde Hill House hangs a portrait of Stephie by Philip de László. Stephie wears the red tunic of his regiment and a medal on his chest, and has a greatcoat slung loosely round his shoulders and a pair of white gloves in his right hand. He has a neatly clipped moustache and a die-straight parting through well-brushed hair. He appears a man of energy, determination and presence, yet his warm brown eyes have a slightly distant look, as though he is gazing beyond military life to his other interests.

While in Africa, Stephie made field notes on birds in the Orange River Colony and Natal, and published them in 1904 in *Ibis*. In 1906 he visited Wyoming, where he combined hunting with collecting plants and trees. The trees from that expedition were planted at Brook House, in more suitable soil than at Borde Hill. Two trips followed, again without his wife, to the then British East Africa in 1909 and 1912, the later trip in the company of his brother Goland and a large local support team of porters, gunbearers and a cook. On that trip, on the east coast of Kenya, near Malindi, Stephie discovered a bird that was subsequently named the Clarke's weaver. He travelled to Rhodesia/Zimbabwe in 1920, Uganda in 1923–24, and India between November 1925 and March 1926.

Stephie, an inveterate recorder and letter writer, kept sharply observant notes of the native flora. In October 1909, in British East Africa, he recorded: 'We wondered to see in this Equatorial forest so many plants familiar to us at home, Blackberries, Raspberries, Violets, Bracken, etc., but there were also many tropical forms, Coleus thyrsoideus, a Thunbergia (possibly Alata), ferns I had seen wild in St Helena, a Parochetus, climbing asparagus, etc.' He demonstrated the physical toughness that helped him understand professional plant hunters: two days later, he and his party 'commence a march of at least 50 miles without water'.

At home, Stephie served as a magistrate from 1912 and, in 1915, as High Sheriff of Sussex. A lifelong Conservative, he was chairman of the Cuckfield Association from 1908 to 1936. He was too old to fight when the First World War broke out, but his two eldest sons, Ralph and Edmund, served and were both wounded.

Plant hunting continued, despite the hostilities. In China, Reginald Farrer was barely aware of the war, alerted only by the increased prayerfulness of Buddhist monks as he searched for primulas and meconopsis. George Forrest embarked on his fourth expedition to the China/Burma borders in 1917, Stephie's contribution being £50 a year and a down payment of £40. The first extant letter from Forrest to Stephie dates from July 1918. Forrest discusses Stephie's interest in rhododendrons, mentions that he will be able to supply *Anemone rupicola* seeds and, aged forty-five, regrets not having fought: 'In May I wrote to Mr Chittenden [at RHS Garden Wisley, the expedition's second-largest shareholder] stating that, when the age was raised for active service, I should like to return home to join up ... I can have no peace of mind to work on here, now I know others of my own age have been drawn into the conflict.'

In the event, Forrest remained in the Far East until 1920 and later embarked on further expeditions sponsored by Stephie. The latter's support for Forrest and other plant hunters, including Wilson, Farrer and Kingdon Ward, made an important contribution to British horticulture. Stephie benefited not just collectors like himself, but also the gardening public, whose interest was stimulated by the vast range of newly available plants.

A portrait by Philip de László of Stephie in the uniform of the 3rd Battalion, Royal Sussex Regiment, hangs in the main reception room in Borde Hill House.

THE GREAT PROJECT
35

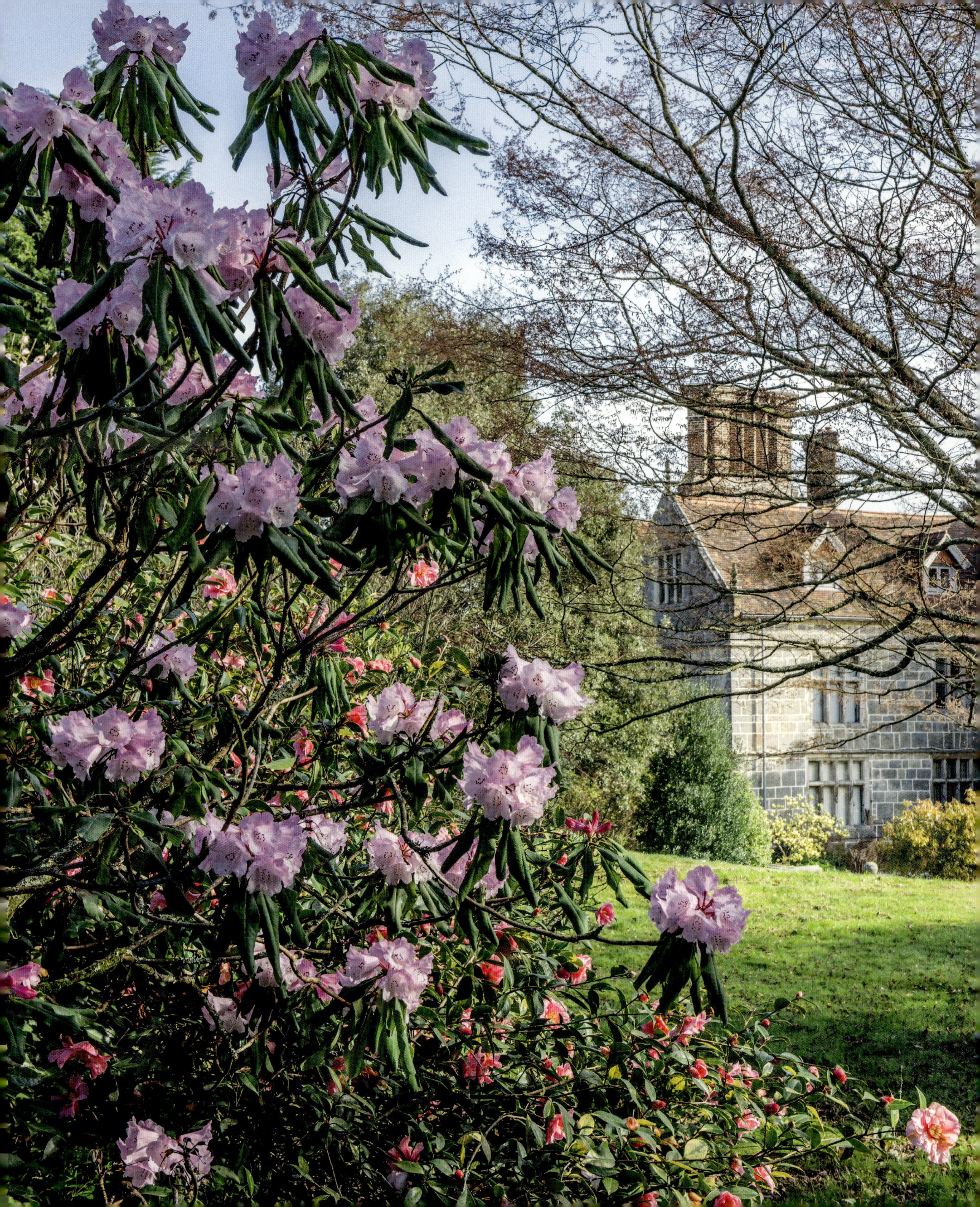

COLONEL STEPHENSON ROBERT CLARKE
The Colonel and the Collectors

Plant hunting has always been hazardous, involving treks through hostile and uncharted territory. For the early twentieth-century collectors, hearing from their sponsors was a lifeline, as Reginald Farrer (1880–1920) told Stephie when writing from Upper Burma in 1919: 'I was delighted, today, to find your letter waiting for me, on my way down country.' He mentions a magnolia species, one of his final sendings: 'I am sure you will spare no pains or methods known to science: could you also, from time to time, keep me advised as to your results with them ... as nothing so revives a collector's heart.'

Stephie contributed about £20,000 (in today's money) to George Forrest's four expeditions between 1917 and 1932 in Burma and China. Forrest (1873–1932) trained as a pharmacist and thereby gained medicinal knowledge of plants. He worked at the Royal Botanic Garden Edinburgh before his first, dramatic expedition to China (1904–1907). On the Tibetan border, Forrest encountered warlords (lamas), who murdered and disembowelled two French plant-hunting missionaries. Forrest went on the run for eight days, largely barefoot, jettisoning his boots to hide his footprints; at one point, a sharp bamboo spike pierced his foot. Eating nothing but a few ears of wheat, he still noticed 'several species of meconopsis, all of them surpassingly lovely, miles of rhododendrons and acres of primulas ... These mountains have, rightly in my opinion, been called the flower garden of the world.' Finally reaching safety, he wrote, 'I shall carry the marks of what I have come through till the day of my death. I am utterly changed.'

Forrest told Stephie of further challenges in 1921, of couriers being robbed in the pass between the Yangtze and the Mekong. In 1922 he reported heavy fighting between 'the Junnan & Kwangsi troops: another missionary Dr Howard Taylor of the CFM has been captured by the brigands outside Junnanfu, & Dr Sheldon of the American mission at Batang was waylaid by the armed robbers & murdered'. He concluded with mild understatement: 'It is very disturbing and certainly not conducive to good work.'

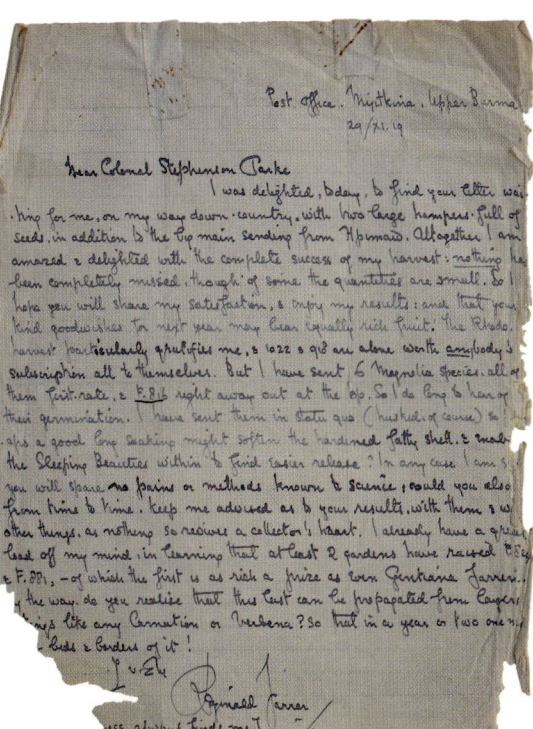

Opposite: Rhododendrons and camellias on the West Bank in May.

Far left: The introductions of the plant hunter Reginald Farrer (1880–1920) led to the early twentieth-century fashion for rock gardening.

Left: Farrer wrote to Stephie from Upper Burma the year before he died.

THE HISTORY

George Forrest (1873–1932) travelled to the Far East on seven plant-hunting expeditions between 1904 and 1932.

Despite the difficulties, Forrest was meticulous: he ensured all seeds and specimens were correctly dried, labelled and packaged for sending, and trained up a trusted team of local collectors. Often tetchy, Forrest complained about Frederick Chittenden, director of RHS Garden Wisley, in a letter to Stephie in 1919: 'I get ... practically no news from Wisley, Mr Chittenden's notes being of the briefest ... Surely they cannot expect me to know what has or hasn't done well, & if I were to collect on broader lines, & thus duplicate species I expect the Wisley people would be the first to shout.'

Frank Kingdon Ward (1885–1958) was also a target, as Forrest wrote in 1929: 'The idea of sending seed home from the East in Thermos flasks is not original ... though, like much else, [Kingdon Ward] takes credit for it ... Besides, in sending home seed *in bulk* ... as I have always done, it is not a workable scheme.' Forrest's competitiveness was provoked in 1930 on discovering that Kingdon Ward, bound for the Irrawaddy–Salween divide, 'seems to have planned on much the same lines as myself. Good luck to him! Only I hope we don't meet in the East.'

This proved to be Forrest's final expedition: he died from a heart attack in January 1932 at Tengyueh (now Tengchong) in western Yunnan. A poignant extract from Forrest's last letter was forwarded to Stephie by the Royal Botanic Garden Edinburgh: 'If all goes well I shall have made a rather glorious and satisfactory finish to all my past years of labour.' There are records at Borde Hill of seventeen sendings of seeds from that expedition, the last of which included *Decaisnea fargesii*, listed in the 1935 *Catalogue*. Another Forrest introduction at Borde Hill was *Rhododendron maddenii* subsp. *crassum*, marked as 'outstandingly excellent' in a list drawn up in the 1970s by Stephie's rhododendron-expert grandson, Robert.

During the 1930s, Kingdon Ward travelled almost annually to Burma and Tibet, and was a British government spy as well as a plant hunter. From Rima, Tibet, in April 1933, he

Stephie contributed to several of Forrest's expeditions, and the men corresponded regularly from 1918 until Forrest's death. This letter was written from Forrest's home in Edinburgh in October 1929 as he planned his final expedition to China.

BORDE HILL GARDEN

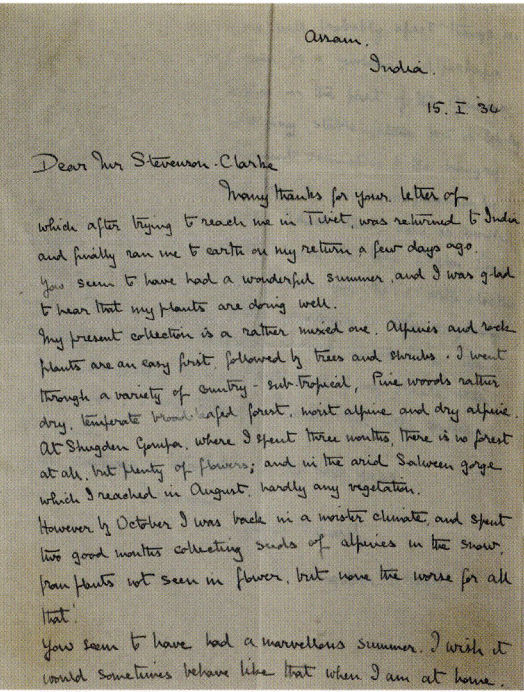

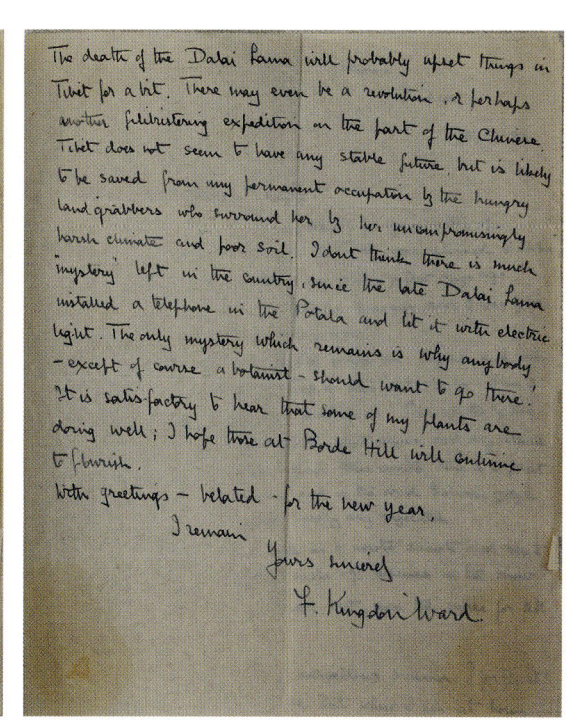

Above: Frank Kingdon Ward (1885–1958) travelled almost annually to Burma and Tibet in the 1930s.

Above, right: In January 1934 Kingdon Ward described the turbulent political situation in Tibet in a letter to Stephie.

was 'faced with the usual problem of transport and food supply in a not thickly populated country … The murder of my mail runner rather jammed things.'

The following January, Kingdon Ward described the political situation to 'Mr Stevenson-Clarke' (sic): 'The death of the Dalai Lama will probably upset things in Tibet for a bit. There may even be a revolution, or perhaps another filibustering expedition on the part of the Chinese. Tibet does not seem to have any stable future … I don't think there is much "mystery" left in the country, since the late Dalai Lama installed a telephone in the Potala and lit it with electric light. The only mystery which remains is why anybody – except of course a botanist – should want to go there.'

Among Kingdon Ward's hundreds of introductions from the expeditions Stephie sponsored in the 1930s was a cotoneaster, listed as *Cotoneaster conspicua* in the 1935 *Catalogue*. There were many rhododendrons, including *wardii*, *imperator*, *leucaspis*, *auritum* and *pemakoense*, all listed by Robert as still growing at Borde Hill in the 1970s, with the last being noted as 'excellent'.

Another plant collector supported by Stephie was the celebrated nurseryman Clarence Elliott (1881–1969), from whose Six Hills Nursery at Stevenage emerged the eponymous *Nepeta* 'Six Hills Giant', now a staple of British gardens. Stephie bought gentians from Elliott in 1925, and the two men were still corresponding about *Alstroemeria violacea* in 1944. 'I found it growing in one place only, on coarse scree on a sharp hillside in Coquimbo', wrote Elliott, who had visited this region of northern Chile on his 1927 expedition, to which Stephie contributed £50. Distribution of Elliott's plant material was handled by the Royal Botanic Garden Edinburgh, but Stephie and Elliott also had a personal understanding, as Elliott wrote, 'If I can secure you two specimens of *Jubaea spectabilis*, I will probably ship these direct to you.'

Stephie helped fund Elliott's expeditions to north-west America in 1931 and to the Alps in

As well as acquiring plants from collectors, Stephie bought plants from nurseries all over the world. This invoice from a Pennsylvanian nursery, dating from 1923, displays his interest in trees.

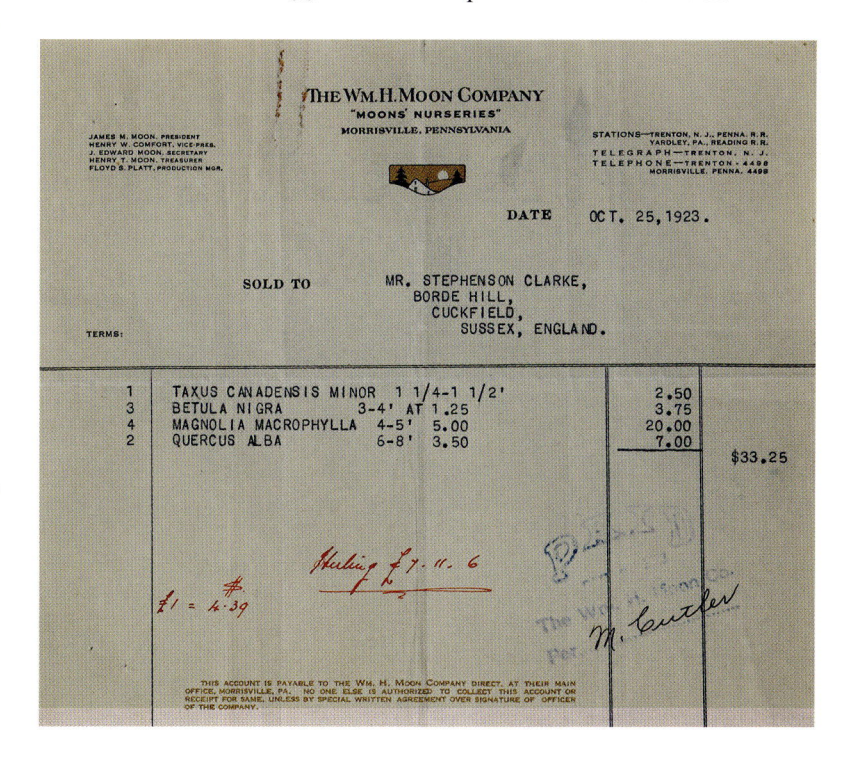

THE COLONEL AND THE COLLECTORS

39

1933, as well as those of Edward K. Balls (1892–1984) to Persia (now Iran) in 1932 and of Harold Comber (1897–1969) to Argentina (1925–26), the Andes (1926–27) and Tasmania (1930s). The son of James Comber, head gardener at nearby Nymans, Comber battled with the language, weather and trying conditions. 'We burst two tyres on the heavily laden Ford camion and had to sleep by the roadside that night under 3" of snow', he wrote from Argentina. 'The weather here at Zapala is fierce, 80 degs. F in the shade one day … then next a piercingly cold wind off the snow-clad Cordilleras raising a dust storm.' Comber planned 'a dash even into Chile for Roble seed', but 'my man, an ex-police sergeant, dare not cross into Chile, having once been involved in a fight with the Chilian police, and is liable to be shot at sight if recognised by them.'

Comber's letter was copied to Stephie by Henry McLaren (later 2nd Baron Aberconway, 1879–1953). Aberconway bred rhododendrons and magnolias at Bodnant in North Wales, and was president of the Royal Horticultural Society between 1931 and 1953. Like many of Stephie's correspondents, he co-sponsored interwar plant-hunting expeditions.

Lord Aberconway (1879–1953), seen here with Queen Elizabeth II and Prince Philip at the Chelsea Flower Show in May 1952, was president of the Royal Horticultural Society from 1931 to 1953.

At Borde Hill are volumes of Stephie's own letters, covering the last three decades of his life (earlier volumes were lost when the estate office was destroyed by a falling tree in the storm of 1987). Bound in two-monthly periods with at least 500 pages per volume, the letters were typed by his two full-time secretaries, Miss W.M. Bacon on the Isle of Wight and Miss Leggett at Borde Hill. Stephie also wrote other letters by hand.

Plants were always the main topic. When the Army requisitioned Borde Hill in the 1940s, Aberconway commiserated: 'My dear Colonel Clarke, I am so very sorry to hear about the exactions of the Military Authorities. They are most inconsiderate, and you have all my sympathy.' Then, without drawing breath, he was straight on to camellias: 'I am much interested in hearing that you propagate them from leaf cuttings: I will try the same thing.' The letter is signed 'Aberconway'. The formality of Stephie's relationships, even with someone who was a fellow RHS committee member for nearly twenty years, is striking to a modern ear.

Stephie profited from exchanges with many other estate-owning collectors, as they did from their correspondence with him. In Sussex he was surrounded by notable gardeners: Sir Edmund Loder (1849–1920), who collected rhododendrons, azaleas, camellias and exotic conifers at Leonardslee and after whom *Rhododendron* 'Loderi Sir Edmund' was named. The garden was later tended by his grandson Sir Giles Loder (1914–1999), a member of the Borde Hill Garden Council until the late 1980s.

Colonel Leonard Messel (1872–1953), the owner of Nymans, was a collector and breeder of magnolias (and James Comber's employer). A letter of 1931 from Stephie to Messel reveals the dynamics of plant exchange: 'Some time ago you talked of exchanging two "Magnolia officinalis" seedlings with me for two "Magnolia hypoleuca". The "hypoleuca" that I have reserved for you are nice young plants about 3 feet high, and ought to have a shift this autumn; but if you do not want them, Kew would like to have one.'

During the 1920s, Stephie also swapped letters, plants and ideas with Lionel de Rothschild (1882–1942), who from 1919 created the gardens at Exbury on Southampton Water. Rothschild described himself as 'a banker by hobby – a gardener by profession'. Both men were closely involved with their gardeners on their breeding programmes. In June 1926 Stephie wrote by hand to thank Rothschild

BORDE HILL GARDEN

Lionel de Rothschild (1882–1942) created the great rhododendron garden at Exbury on Southampton Water. He and Stephie both contributed to Forrest's plant-hunting expeditions.

J.C. Williams (1861–1939), owner of Caerhays in Cornwall, was a founder of the Rhododendron Society in 1916. He gave Stephie plant material from which Stephie's gardener, Walter Fleming, bred the award-winning *Camellia* × *williamsii* 'Donation'.

'for the preliminary determination of species of [Kingdon Ward's] rhododendrons which will be very useful … With regard to Magnolia Tsarongensis my gardener thinks that next spring we should try to march it on Hypoleuca & if we are successful I will send you a plant.' In October 1929 Rothschild wrote to 'Dear Stephenson Clarke' about Kingdon Ward's seeds that 'came back in thermos flasks and I think that is one of the reasons why they germinate so well' (backing Kingdon Ward over Forrest).

Stephie corresponded frequently with J.C. Williams (1861–1939), who had inherited Caerhays in Cornwall aged eighteen and later became George Forrest's chief sponsor. Williams bred daffodils, then collected acers, camellias, magnolias, michelias, oaks and rhododendrons from Forrest and from Ernest Wilson. So eager was Williams to discuss gardening that he wrote to Stephie on Christmas Day 1931: 'As regards rhodos I have turned from the small ones to those with the largest leaves, & after living here for 70 years I am beginning to find a few places which may please them, anyhow as time moves on I find more real pleasure in fine foliage than in big blooms.'

Other Cornish correspondents were J.C.'s cousin P.D. Williams at Lanarth, also a daffodil breeder, and George Johnstone (1882–1960) at Trewithen. Their letters were detailed and practical. In one, Johnstone asks Stephie for advice: 'What exactly do you mean by "leaf cuttings"? I take it to be a leaf with a bud in the axil but I wish you would send me a sample in an envelope so that I may know.' They also discussed staff problems, with Stephie writing to Johnstone in 1936, 'I am afraid I cannot help you with a gardener, the fact of the matter is that I am very selfish about gardeners, if I have one who is useful I dislike losing him very much.'

Stephie was an early member of the Rhododendron Society, established in 1916 by J.C. and P.D. Williams, along with Charles Eley, another frequent correspondent of Stephie's, and the rhododendron collector John Guille Millais, son of the Pre-Raphaelite painter Sir John Everett Millais. All were Veitch Memorial Medallists, and their descendants remain involved in growing rhododendrons today. The great-grandsons of J.C. Williams, Charles Eley and Stephie still run their family gardens, while Millais's great-nephew David owns the UK's leading rhododendron nursery and sits on the Borde Hill Garden Council.

The letters between these 'amateurs' convey their professionalism. Stephie's work and collections were held in the highest esteem by major botanical gardens, to which he donated seeds and plants. For more than twenty years he wrote to Sir William Wright Smith (1875–1956), Regius Keeper of the Royal Botanic Garden Edinburgh from 1922 to 1956. In December 1924 Smith congratulated Stephie on his success with Forrest's magnolia No. 21722: 'You have had much better fortune than we regarding this number as none of the seeds generated with us. You must have given them more sensible

THE COLONEL AND THE COLLECTORS

treatment.' A decade later, Smith thanked Stephie 'very much indeed for the plants of Gentiana pneumonanthe (Styrian form) and Hydrangea longipes – both welcome'.

There were similar interactions with RHS Garden Wisley and with Kew. R.L. Harrow, director of Wisley from 1931 to 1946, wrote in June 1936 to say, 'I am very glad to have the opportunity of seeing the specimen you sent us of *Magnolia tsarongensis* of W.W. Smith. The flower enables me to see for the first time this beautiful plant.' Stephie was asked to contribute plants for the creation of the Rock Garden at Wisley, while a letter in 1942 to Charles Raffill, assistant curator, confirmed that Stephie supplied Kew with a small plant of the newly raised *Camellia* 'Salutation'.

Even during the Second World War, Stephie enjoyed a special relationship with Kew: William Macdonald Campbell, curator from 1937 to 1960, sent Stephie in December 1942 'a young plant of Magnolia Sprengeri which, as you know, is the true pink form. It is certainly one of the most beautiful Magnolias in cultivation … I would ask you not to circulate the fact that you obtained the plant from us as we should be unable to meet the demands that would be likely to arise if this was common knowledge.' In 1944 Stephie supplied the Cambridge University Botanic Garden, to which he gave financial support, with a 'nice plant of Asteranthera ovata'. He also exchanged plants with the head gardener at Osborne House on the Isle of Wight: Mr G. Nobbs sent cuttings of *Quercus coccifera* to Stephie in August 1931; three months later, Nobbs wrote to thank Stephie for 'the nice plants of Pinus Montazuma [*sic*] and Azara lanceolata'. Royal gardens also benefited from Stephie's plant swaps.

Stephie's correspondence was international: in 1932 Mr K. Wada of Hakoneya Nurseries in Japan asked Stephie to spare him seeds of more than fifty rhododendrons, including *hookeri*, *forrestii*, *griersonianum*, *wardii* and 'any of beautiful species which form a shapely bush'. The geneticist at the Missouri Botanical Garden offered plant material in 1935, while the botany department at University College Dublin requested information about *Fitzroya* in 1937.

An omnivorous collector, Stephie bought plants from nurseries across the United Kingdom and abroad. There are invoices from Guernsey, Newry, Wimborne, Woking, St Albans, Carlisle, Gloucestershire, Bagshot, Tunbridge Wells, Dover and Elstree. In another file are invoices from South Africa, North Carolina, Georgia, France, The Netherlands, Japan, Kenya, Darjeeling, Canada and New Zealand.

Files are filled with almost monthly letters and invoices from 1930 onwards from Hillier & Sons at Winchester. Most were signed by Edwin Hillier, whose son Harold would later describe Stephie as 'the greatest amateur all-rounder in the gardening world of the twentieth century'. Just one invoice from November 1930, for £23 13s., lists '3 *Tsuga sieboldii*, 2 *Pinus sabineana*, 2 *Picea polita*, 1 *Pileostegia viburnoides*, 1 *Pistacia mutica*, 1 *Abies kawakamii*, 1 *Acer trifolium*, 1 *Quercus cerris* 'Variegata', 1 *Cornus kousa* 'Chinensis', 2 *Cupressus macnabiana*, 2 *Clematis luxurians* 'Alba', 1 *Enkianthus albiflora* and 1 *Enkianthus palibinii*'.

Even with nurseries, it was two-way traffic. In a letter to Edwin, Stephie offered 'some seedlings from the Chinese mountains of *Rhodoleia championii* and *Luculia gratissima*. Would you like some to try?' Stephie also suggested that Edwin use trees from Borde Hill for grafting in his nursery. Jean Hillier wrote in her history of the family and the nursery that 'this was a generous offer from a collector who valued the propagation of rare plants above keeping them to himself'. 'I have placed an order with your Mr Fleming for some trees you so kindly offered', wrote Edwin to Stephie in thanks. Stephie's generosity to nurseries such as Hillier ensured his influence spread far beyond the confines of his immediate circle.

Edwin Hillier (1865–1944) established his family's business as one of the leading tree nurseries in the UK. Stephie often bought from Hillier, but also gave him plant material from which to graft.

This correspondence continued throughout the Second World War with occasional references to difficulties caused by the conflict; for example, Hillier's having to clear beds of saplings for vegetable crops.

Plants poured into the garden at Borde Hill for more than forty years, leading to the extension of the garden into both the North and South Parks. To the east of the house, Stephie created the Azalea Ring, where he also planted *Magnolia campbellii* and *Emmenopterys henryi*, both introduced by Forrest in the 1920s.

Stephie reclaimed land from the North Park in 1925 to create the Garden of Allah. There, he planted a magnificent *Liriodendron chinense*, raised from seed collected in central China in the early 1900s by Ernest Wilson and bought from Veitch in 1913. When this flowered for the first time in 1927, Wilson, then keeper of the Arnold Arboretum at Harvard University, wrote to Stephie: 'I am very, very interested to learn that you have flowered the Chinese Tulip Tree. So far as my knowledge goes this is the first record under cultivation … I congratulate you.'

Species rhododendrons flourished in Gore's Wood (1934), to the south-west of the house and the highest point of the garden, so untouched by spring frosts. Among the oak and beech of Warren Wood, Stephie planted rare rhododendrons, junipers and pines, including a Wilson introduction, *Picea likiangensis*. Beyond, in Stephanie's Glade, he planted another Wilson introduction, *Fagus engleriana*.

A Pinetum was planted up in the North Park, partly in response to the threat that the graceful Victorian brick viaduct might be replaced by a more unsightly metal structure. In the event, it was not, but the viaduct was hidden from view until much of the Pinetum blew down in the hurricane of October 1987.

Stephie was extending his garden at Borde Hill as Lawrence Johnston worked at Hidcote Manor in Gloucestershire and Vita Sackville-West created first Long Barn and then Sissinghurst Castle in Kent. But Stephie's aesthetic was different. Both Johnston's and Sackville-West's gardens feature a series of enclosed, often colour-themed rooms. Stephie, however, allowed his plants' requirements to dictate their placing, which is why the garden at Borde Hill, even near the house, has the feel of naturalistic woodland. To walk in spring through the Azalea Ring or the Long Dell is to be transported to a verdant Chinese hillside.

Devoted though Stephie was to trees and shrubs, he also cared for flowers, as he pointed out in an article in 1938 in the *Journal of the Royal Horticultural Society*: 'My oldest and best-beloved garden friend told my wife that after fifty years study of my character and disposition he thought that I did not really care for flowers. I know that he was wrong.' He collected and hybridized nerines and alstroemerias, and also assembled a valuable collection of orchids that was sold at auction after his death: the thirteen-page catalogue listed over 450 species and cultivars.

August 1935 saw the publication of the *Catalogue of the Trees and Shrubs at Borde Hill, Sussex*, a project instigated by Ralph. 'Your son has made a very sensible suggestion and I shall be most pleased to undertake the task of making a catalogue of what I know is a very interesting collection', wrote the prospective compiler, Albert Bruce Jackson, to Stephie in February 1930. Jackson (1876–1947), a Kew-based botanist and dendrologist, worked closely with Stephie for five years on a volume that ran to 275 pages and almost 400 species. Stephie described the process to his brother Louis in Cambridge: the *Catalogue* 'is now completed … Although I say "completed" we had to fix a date for the final admission of shrubs, and that was 1933 … and in my endeavours to keep the collection up to date there have been a good many additions since then, which I shall be able to put in M.S. in an interleaved copy.' This copy, with handwritten notes, is in the Borde Hill Archive.

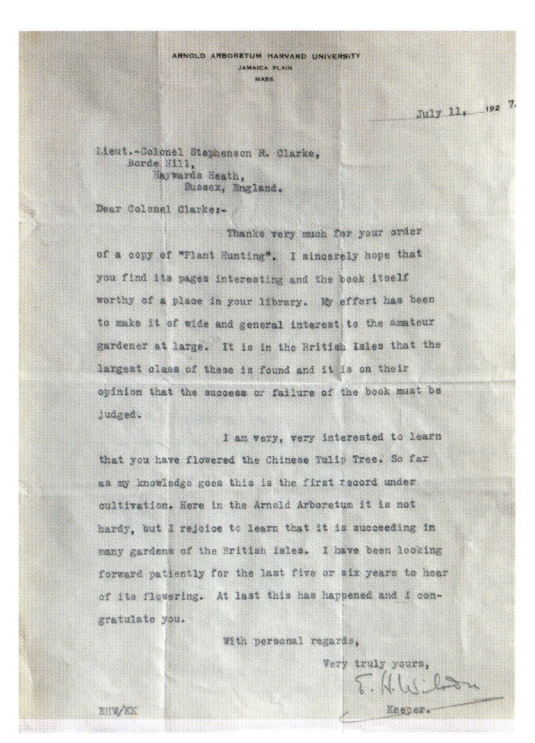

Ernest Wilson, by then keeper of the Arnold Arboretum at Harvard, wrote to congratulate Stephie in July 1927 on his being the first gardener in Europe to flower *Liriodendron chinense*.

THE COLONEL AND THE COLLECTORS

Despite fine species collected by Wilson, Forrest, Kingdon Ward and the Austrian-American plant hunter Joseph Rock, rhododendrons were excluded, as Stephie explained: 'Unfortunately, owing to a confusion in the labelling of seedlings, of which large numbers have been raised here, it will not be possible to identify many of these plants until they flower, which in some cases may mean a lapse of years.' Forty years later, Stephie's grandson Robert would attempt to catalogue them fully.

Dozens of letters were exchanged by Stephie and Jackson between September 1934 and February 1935 about page proofs and alterations, discussing, for example, the distinction between *Mahonia bealei* and *M. japonica*. Stephie added notes to Jackson's descriptions based on his own experience of cultivating the plants. Some are dryly funny. For instance, Stephie described *Fortunearia sinensis*, an introduction of Wilson's from China, as 'rather a dull guest'.

Twenty-five gardeners, plus woodmen, worked at Borde Hill in the 1920s, with the most junior gardener employed to tap flowerpots with a small wooden hammer in order to check whether they needed watering. A workmen's time sheet, printed with 'Borde Hill Estate, Sussex', for the week ending 20 March 1926 shows that individual gardeners were paid £1 12s. for their week's work (accommodation was also provided for most gardeners). For the week ending 7 November 1931, the wage bill for fifteen gardeners was £30 10s. 7d. (including insurance). Walter Fleming, head gardener from 1928 to 1954, received £3 15s.

The son of a shepherd, Fleming was described as 'a huge silent Scotsman' by Stephie's grandson Robert. Fleming had previously managed a staff of twelve for eight years at a Wigtownshire estate, according to his letter of application to Stephie's private secretary in December 1927. He wrote that he had 'raised many thousands of seedlings from Forrest, Kingdon Ward and Professor Rock', and also that he had 'good experience in the cultivation of amaryllis and nerines'. Fleming was clearly the perfect candidate for head gardener at Borde Hill. He and his new employer had an instinctive understanding and corresponded almost daily when Stephie was away. In October 1936, for instance, Stephie gave Fleming instructions about new rhododendrons that had been supplied by John Waterer Sons & Crisp of Bagshot, Surrey: 'You had better plant "King George" in the garden, and the other four give to Hickcox, and go with him and find a place near where I marked for the Rhododendrons from Slocock [the Slocock family owned Goldsworth Nursery, also in

From 1923 onwards, Stephie's plants won dozens of Awards of Merit at RHS shows, including for *Camellia × williamsii* 'Donation' (1941; top) and *Alstroemeria violacea* (1930; bottom).

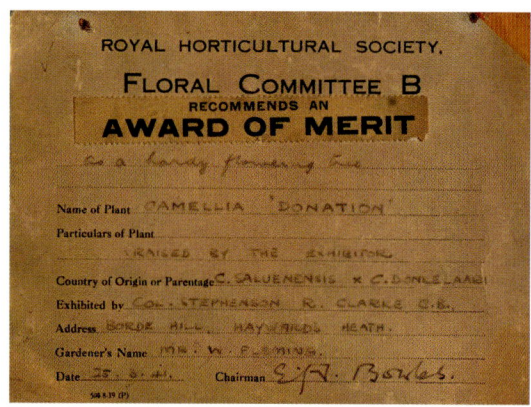

An early picture of *Camellia × williamsii* 'Donation', raised by Walter Fleming over the winter of 1937–38. It became a worldwide bestseller.

BORDE HILL GARDEN
44

Surrey]. The three Blue Peters had better be kept in one group.' Stephie's tone could be peremptory: 'Fleming, I have had a letter from Mr Bruce Jackson, and he thanks me for the plants but he says that you did not send him the "Cytisus Battandieri". Will you please send it to him at once.' Fleming wrote in detail about the garden, as in March 1940: 'Some of the Rhodos are coming on. Celophyton, praevernum, Sutchuenense & Fargesii all look promising and will be in bloom soon, some of the more forward blooms of almond time got caught last Thursday night [when] we had 12° of frost, I have now got a cover on, barbatums are not showing much this year.' The vagaries of the weather are the burden of Fleming's letters.

Crucially, Fleming proved himself a hybridizer of distinction whose award-winning cultivars include *Alstroemeria* 'Walter Fleming'. But his greatest coup was crossing *Camellia japonica* 'Donckelaeri' (now known as *C.j.* 'Masayoshi') with the pale-pink *C. saluenensis* in 1937–38. The result was *C.* × *williamsii* 'Donation', winner of an RHS Award of Merit in 1941 and a gold medal in 1952. Stephie named the new hybrid 'Donation' because he wanted to make it a gift to the nation; in the event, it proved a gift to Hillier, whom Stephie allowed to market what became a worldwide bestseller. Fleming also triumphed with another award-winner, *C.* 'Salutation'. Both still grow happily at Borde Hill.

'Donation' was the most celebrated of Stephie's and Fleming's RHS awards, but there were many more, as the boxes of certificates at Borde Hill testify. During the 1930s and '40s, Awards of Merit were won for an *Alstroemeria violacea*; several shrubs, including a stewartia and an olearia; a little low-growing perennial, *Scutellaria ovalifolia*; and *Richea scoparia*, grown from seed collected by Harold Comber in Tasmania.

Stephie was honoured personally in 1924 by an honorary degree from the University of Leeds. In 1936 he was awarded the RHS Victoria Medal of Honour, inaugurated in 1897 to commemorate Queen Victoria's diamond jubilee, and in 1944 he received the Veitch Memorial Medal for his part in advancing and improving horticulture.

On Whit Sunday 1927, Borde Hill was among the first gardens to open for the National Garden Scheme, founded to raise funds for the Queen's Nursing Institute by council member Elsie Wagg. She was one of Stephie's few female correspondents: they exchanged annual notes about the best day for Borde Hill to open for

In 1944 Stephie was awarded the celebrated Veitch Memorial Medal for his achievements in advancing and improving horticulture.

the charity, the one occasion the public were admitted. Otherwise, groups from national and international horticultural societies and botanical institutions came only by invitation; most visitors were personal acquaintances. A letter of thanks from the 6th Earl of Rosse, son-in-law of Leonard Messel and stepfather of Lord Snowdon, powerfully evokes the garden in 1937:

I had always heard so much about it, and expected a great deal, but found immensely more than I could have thought possible. It was a really thrilling afternoon, each corner we turned bringing us in face of some new wonderful rarity that one scarcely knew was in cultivation. I particularly loved the magnolias, the bold grouping of Berberis & Cotoneaster in the woods, and the fine specimens of rare conifers, Nothofagus, Meliosma, Chinese disidendum; in fact it seems perhaps invidious to choose any when there are wonderful examples of almost any hardy tree and shrub. We only unfortunately had time to take in a very few things, as it must require many weeks to begin to compute all the rarities in your collection. But it was an afternoon of sheer joy.

Social relations remained formal in the 1930s, with even close friends using each other's surnames. Typewritten letters from Stephie suggest a fond, if slightly remote relationship with his sons. One letter to Ralph expressed pleasure at the news that Ralph's

THE COLONEL AND THE COLLECTORS

sons, Robert and Simon, had received good reports from Eton. 'You and Becky must be very proud', he said, before signing himself 'Your affectionate father, Stephenson R Clarke'. In another letter to Ralph, written in April 1942, Stephie wrote more personally and concluded 'I am, with love': 'The garden here is marvellous just now, the Rhododendrons seem to be blooming all at once ... I wish that your dear Mother had been spared to see it.'

When Borde Hill was requisitioned by the Army in the Second World War, Stephie and Edith were allowed to move to the top floor of the house, rather than having to decamp. Thanks to representations by Stephie's friend Lord Aberconway to the requisitioning authorities, it was recognized that Stephie needed to keep an eye on a collection 'of value and importance to all horticulturalists'. But, despite being kindly and much loved, the ageing couple were becoming unapproachable, especially as conversation with Edith required negotiating her ear trumpet. They celebrated their golden wedding in June 1940, having suffered personal tragedies over the years: the loss of their first son within days of his birth, and of their youngest son, Robert, who died at Eton in 1920 aged just fifteen. This sadness is acknowledged in an anniversary letter from their staff at Borde Hill: 'We, your servants, cannot envisage the trials and sorrows that has beset you in all those years of active responsibility, but the *joys* along your path has been shared with us, so on this day there is a deep feeling of gratitude and heartfelt thankfulness.'

The loyalty felt by the Clarkes' staff is also apparent in condolences received by Stephie on Edith's death in April 1941 from Private Sharp, a former gardener stationed in Iceland. After expressing his sympathy, Sharp moved swiftly on to plants, in common with all Stephie's correspondents. In Iceland, Sharp had identified 'a nice dwarf Erigeron, a good blue geranium, a small spreading plant like × olisma & deep rose flowers'. From Stephie, he requested 'a small garden dictionary' for 'the long nights' and to 'help me know the Island plant life'. Two months later, Sharp sent two parcels of Icelandic plants to Borde Hill, including dwarf iris, a gentian, a saxifrage and mesembryanthemum. Stephie clearly inspired his gardeners with his own passion for plants.

Stephie had always shot and ridden to hounds, and spent most Julys at Fasnakyle in Inverness-shire stalking deer and fishing salmon. Even after Edith's death, he continued shooting. His son John recalled that 'after killing a Rt. and Lt. of very high driven partridges ... [Stephie] handed his gun to the Keeper Cram, and said, "I think this will be a good moment to give up shooting."' He was eighty-four.

At a regimental dinner, Stephie met Constance Gwendoline Bellamy, the widow of a fellow Royal Sussex officer, with two sons on active service. They married quietly on the Isle of Wight in April 1943 to some disapproval from friends and family. Stephie was touchingly grateful, therefore, for the support of his daughter-in-law Becky. His letter of thanks after the marriage was very different in tone from the gruff formality that often characterized his correspondence: 'My

Even in extreme old age, Stephie spent time out in his garden most days.

BORDE HILL GARDEN

Stephie with his second wife, Constance Gwendoline Bellamy (Gwennie), whom he married in 1943.

dear Becky, I very much appreciated your most kind letter. I am pleased indeed that you have affection for Gwennie; who was also delighted with your letter.'

A photograph in the drawing room at Borde Hill shows the much younger Gwennie sitting upright and smiling, with her elderly, full-bearded husband in an armchair at her side. During wartime, his sons away fighting, Stephie no doubt felt lonely after the death of his wife, his mainstay for fifty years. Gwennie looks as though she was a safe harbour for him at the end of his life, and was later remembered by the family with affection as 'Aunt Gwennie'.

Passionate about his collections to the end, Stephie was pushed daily around the estate in his wheelchair. He died at Borde Hill on 3 November 1948 and was buried at Highbrook Church. He left an incomparable legacy to be tended by future generations of his family.

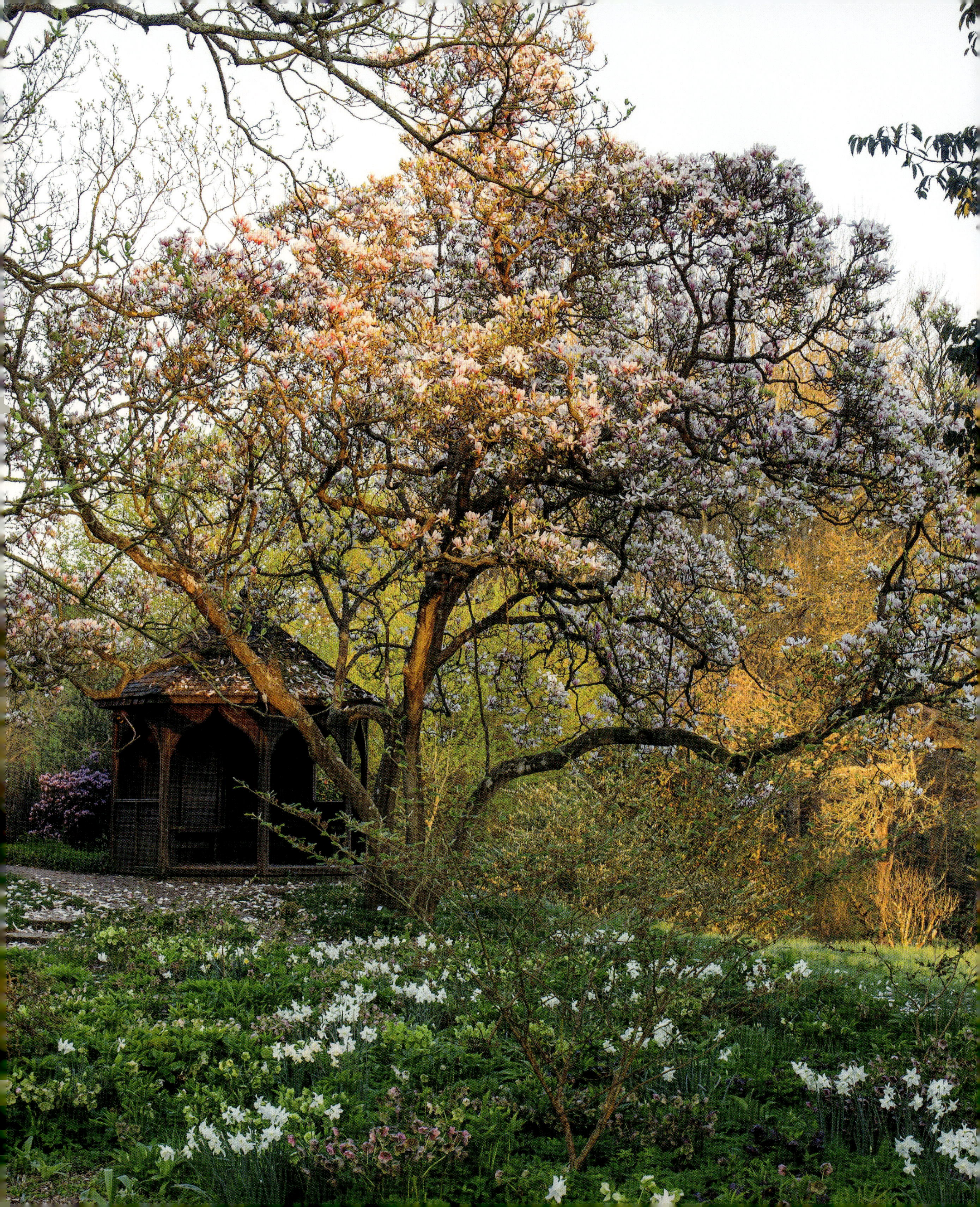

SIR RALPH STEPHENSON CLARKE
The Transitional Years

The Second World War took its toll on the garden, despite Stephie's unabated interest and Walter Fleming's continued efforts. Staffing became a problem as gardeners left for military service. More than 1300 military personnel were stationed between Borde Hill and Brook House, and lines of Nissen huts for a German prisoner-of-war camp were erected in the South Park (one German remained as a gardener after the war). Canadians posted there before D-Day built extensive sewage works, the remnants of which are still encountered when new trees are planted.

It fell to Ralph to repair the depredations of war, although he and his wife did not live at Borde Hill until Gwennie moved out in 1953. Ralph faced a challenge, especially as there were only four gardeners by the late 1960s. But he proved a worthy successor to his father, and took a particular interest in the tree collections, while Becky expanded Stephie's programme of hybridizing nerines and alstroemerias.

Ralph Stephenson Clarke was born at Brook House on 17 August 1892, the first surviving son of Stephenson and Edith Clarke, and the oldest of five. From Eton he won a scholarship to King's College, Cambridge, where he took a First in natural sciences. His education as a biologist underpinned his approach to Borde Hill and to the countryside in general.

The First World War broke out shortly after his graduation, and Ralph, his brother Edmund and younger brothers of their father all fought. Ralph rose to lieutenant colonel commanding the 98th Surrey and Sussex Yeomanry, and was awarded the Territorial Decoration with four clasps. He served in Palestine and Egypt, and was wounded in the chest at Gallipoli. During his time in the eastern Mediterranean, he collected seeds of *Platanus orientalis* var. *insularis* on the Greek island of Lemnos. Planted south-east of Warren Wood, Ralph's first contribution towers over the wood today.

Ralph remained a member of the Sussex Territorial and Auxiliary Forces Association, and was later honorary colonel of the 258th Sussex Yeomanry. The Second World War engulfed the family again: aged forty-seven in 1939, Ralph spent three years commanding a Royal Artillery anti-aircraft regiment. In August 1943 he was mentioned in dispatches 'in recognition of gallant and distinguished service in Persia-Iraq'. He also served in Sicily, where his first cousin Andrew Stephenson Clarke was killed in action in July 1943. Ralph's thirty-seven volumes of manuscript diaries covering the period were later given to the Imperial War Museum by his widow.

She was the former Rebekah Mary Buxton (known as Becky), whom Ralph had married in December 1921 at St Mary's, Theydon Bois,

Opposite: Ralph relished the calm atmosphere in the secluded Garden of Allah.

Below: Ralph Stephenson Clarke (1892–1970) as a young man.

THE HISTORY
49

Ralph and Rebekah (Becky) Buxton (1900–1985) on their wedding day at St Mary's in Theydon Bois, Essex, in December 1921.

near her parents' home, Birch Hall, in Essex. Becky came from a distinguished family. One ancestor was Sir Thomas Fowell Buxton, an MP, brewer, abolitionist and social reformer, while her great-grandfather on her mother's side was Alfred Fox, creator of Glendurgan Garden in Cornwall: gardening was in her blood. The couple honeymooned in Algeria before returning to Brook House, where their three children were born: Anne (1923), Robert (1925) and Simon (1926).

Ralph was a quiet, reflective man whose chief interests were hunting, politics and trees. Becky, by contrast, was fiery, vivacious and affectionate: Eleni Stephenson Clarke remembers her grandmother-in-law's kindness to her as a young bride. Becky loved pranks and arranging family games, and, as a member of the Victoria League for Commonwealth Friendship, hosted parties of overseas students.

In the mid-1930s Ralph and Becky became the third generation of Clarkes to be painted by family friend Philip de László, by then in his sixties. The portraits, in the dining room at Borde Hill, show Ralph as a dashing, dark-haired, moustachioed figure, similar to his father in de László's portrait of thirty years earlier, although less heavily built. Ralph is dressed for hunting, with a white stock, horn tucked into his jacket, and crop and gloves in his right hand. He looks to one side, but Becky's blue eyes focus directly on the viewer. Her shoulders are swathed in diaphanous chiffon and silk, while her fair hair is softly styled and her face lightly made up. With a single rope of pearls and pearl-drop earrings, she is the height of 1930s elegance.

Ralph, dressed for hunting, the third generation of Clarkes to be painted by Philip de László. László also painted Becky (far right) in fashionable 1930s evening dress.

BORDE HILL GARDEN

The children of Ralph and Becky (from left to right), Anne, Simon and Robert.

From 1920 Ralph was a director of Stephenson Clarke and Company until his election as a Conservative MP in July 1936, although his interest lay in understanding the industry rather than in making it his career. His younger brother John Philip Stephenson Clarke (1896–1969) was more involved: he became chairman of Powell Duffryn when that company acquired the share capital of Stephenson Clarke and Associated Companies in 1928.

A 1949 Conservative Party newsletter profiled Ralph as 'a modest man who hides a great deal of Parliamentary ability behind a quiet somewhat detached manner'. This ability had been revealed to MPs during debates on coal, fuel and power: 'What, some of them thought, could this Sussex country gentlemen know about the mines? Debates have shown them that Colonel Clarke knows a great deal, for he had long business associations with the distributive side of the industry. He also brings to industrial problems the keen and analytical mind of the scientist.'

Rooted in Sussex, Ralph became a Deputy Lieutenant in 1932 and a county councillor for East Sussex from 1934. He held his East Grinstead seat for nearly twenty years: he was knighted in the New Year's Honours of 1955 and stepped down at the general election in May.

As he told a rally at Sheffield Park in 1950, Ralph believed that 'the Conservative Party is devoted to the widest interests of the country as a whole, and that in their ranks the highest standard of service to the state can be given'. His love of the countryside, as well as his military experience, was integral to this. 'My experience as a Regimental Officer in both the Great Wars', he said in an election address, 'helps me to understand the problems of Service and ex-Service men and women.' He informed the Ramblers Association conference in Sheffield in October 1953:

I am one who is by nature and inclination a countryman … I have all my life been a natural wanderer. I never see a hill without wanting to know what is on the other side, or a wood without wondering what is in the middle of it. I have an urge to follow a river to its source, and I seldom come back from a walk without being late. Although I have had much opportunity at home and abroad to satisfy this desire, I have at the same time also not infrequently been constrained to live in towns, and therefore have learned to sympathise with the many who have an equal love of roaming the countryside but who have perhaps most of their lives undergone the same privation.

Ralph spoke often in the House, and was active in his constituency, being particularly well versed in road and transport problems.

Below: As a Deputy Lieutenant for Sussex, Ralph met Queen Elizabeth II on more than one occasion.

Bottom: In 1962, Ralph greets Princess Margaret and the Earl of Snowdon dressed in the robe and chain of the master of the Clothworkers' Company. Snowdon's grandfather Leonard Messel (1872–1953) was the owner of nearby Nymans and a gardening friend of Stephie's.

THE TRANSITIONAL YEARS

During Ralph's custodianship of Borde Hill, he arranged for the trees and shrubs in Warren Wood to be recatalogued. This map dates from 1958.

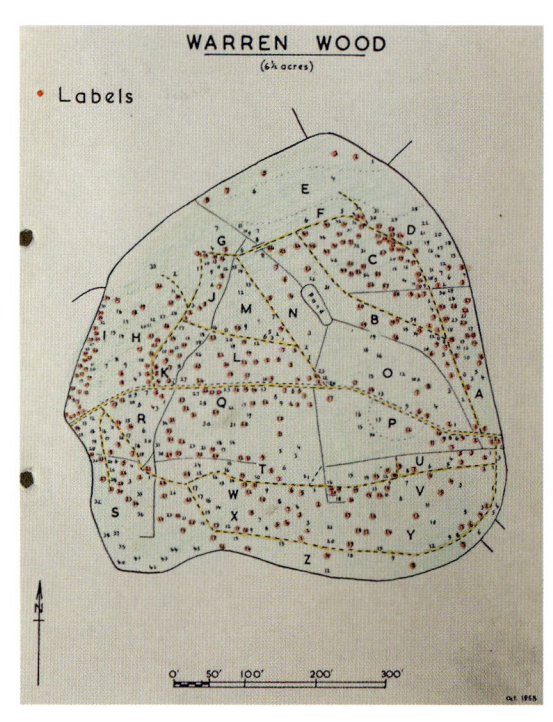

Even after retiring as an MP, he sat on transport committees, the Nature Conservancy Committee for England and the council of the Royal Agricultural Society of England.

Ralph alluded to his responsibility both to the estate and to his father in the same address to the Ramblers Association. He talked of 'landowners who regard their property in the light of a trust, and they really represent the majority'; their first objective was 'the preservation and enhancement of the natural beauty of the countryside'. He recognized Stephie's titanic endeavours at Borde Hill, as he said when Nymans was handed over to the National Trust by the Messel family. On that occasion, also in 1953, he spoke 'as a neighbour … and the owner of a garden which, in a humbler way, is not dissimilar to Nymans and which I watched grow up under my own father's care. I … call to mind the days and the hours of delight, disaster, success and failure that go into the making of any garden's history.'

Ralph gathered seeds on his travels in both wars. Six months before Stephie's death, Ralph wrote anxiously to his father, 'When you hear from Edinburgh about the names of my two trees I should be grateful if you could let me know, they came from a forest near Amadia in Northern Iraq.' This interest displayed itself in his attention to the tree collection and in his involvement with the Forestry Commission. According to his grandson Andrewjohn, when Ralph went out hunting, he would have pockets full of seeds in case he found somewhere suitable to scatter them.

In 1958 the trees and shrubs of the woods were recatalogued by the dendrologist Hatton Gardner: within the 6½ acres (2.6 ha) of Warren Wood there were 622 trees, conifers and shrubs, of which 323 were labelled. When the specimen woods were again catalogued in 1968, more than 200 exotic rhododendron species were listed. Ralph accepted that casualties were necessary to conserve the integrity and standard of the collection. 'To preserve alone is literally impossible. Nature is continually in process of change – development and decay', he said. 'Even trees have their allotted life.' A future head gardener, John Humphris, found Ralph rather less prepared to embrace 'development and decay' than these words suggest. When Humphris arrived in 1968, 'Sir Ralph didn't want anything changed. It was hard even to remove a sycamore seedling.'

Like Stephie, Ralph exhibited regularly at RHS shows. He won an Award of Merit in 1966 for the tree whose seeds he had gathered himself in Greece: *Platanus orientalis* ('as a hardy tree for ornamental effect'). Other AMs were given in the 1960s for *Hoheria angustifolia* ('as a half-hardy flowering shrub') and *Carya glabra* ('as a hardy tree for autumn effect'). Ralph also won awards for rhododendrons in RHS competitions throughout the 1950s and '60s.

The seedling and plant swaps continued with his father's friends, such as George Johnstone, who sent seedlings of *Magnolia macrophylla* var. *ashei* to Ralph in December 1949. Another exchange of letters discussed Johnstone's interest in the height of a *Magnolia sargentiana* var. *robusta*: Fleming measured it as 40 feet (12.2 m) high.

In August/September 1950 Becky corresponded with Francis Hanger, curator of Wisley, about her and Ralph's attempt to list all their rhododendrons. Hanger wrote, 'the hybrids in your garden may set a bigger problem, especially if no stud book has been kept as to the parents used'. Even a collector as punctilious as Stephie struggled with the promiscuity of rhododendrons.

The conversations started by Stephie continued: in December 1952 Becky asked Edwin Hillier's son, Harold, for seedlings of Forrest's 'Mollicamatta [sic] Magnolias, to take the place of what is probably our dying original one'. She also inquired about the price at which Hillier was marketing one- and two-year-old rooted cuttings of *Camellia* 'Donation'. The ship had sailed on that for the Stephenson Clarkes, the selling rights having been given to Hillier by Stephie.

Some years later, Harold Hillier contacted Ralph and Becky, having noted *Ribes sanguineum* 'Album' exhibited by Borde Hill at a show in Vincent Square, the RHS headquarters in London: 'I have lost this plant from my collection and I was wondering whether you would be kind enough to instruct your Garden Manager either to quote me for some unrooted cuttings for immediate delivery, or delivery next winter. Alternatively, to grow for me, say, 50 rooted plants.' Although never a commercial activity, the propagation and hybridization programmes continued to provide nurseries and other collectors with plants, in addition to supporting Borde Hill's own collection.

A letter from Stephie reveals that Becky was already showing visitors around Borde Hill by June 1937: 'I understand that you are bringing forty Australians here on Thursday next', he wrote. 'It is unfortunate that I cannot be here to receive them as we are having the Fiftieth Anniversary Dinner of the Regimental Club on that night. The Rhododendrons and Azaleas in the garden are pretty well finished but probably there will be some left in the Warren Wood.' In a manuscript note at the end of this typed letter, Stephie added with beguiling pride: 'There were competitions at the RHS today. I was the first with 8 shrubs.'

Becky's special interest was South African plants, and she went on plant-finding trips to South Africa and Morocco: at Borde Hill is a 1946 guide to Kirstenbosch, the National Botanical Garden of South Africa. She developed the nerine and alstroemeria collection, working initially on their hybridization with Fleming until his retirement in 1954, and then with Brian Doe, head gardener until the late 1960s. 'My mother's conception of gardening was energetic and contagious', wrote her son Robert. An article written by Doe in 1966 indicates the collection's extent: 'We grow over 10,000 bulbs in well over 100 varieties, mainly hybrids from such species as N. Sarniensis (the Guernsey Lily), N. Corusca, N. Undulata, N. Bowdenii, N. Fothergilli and N. Flexuosa. There is a tremendous colour range from deepest red to the palest pink and white.' He added: 'N. Corusca has played the biggest part in our hybridization programme, producing such fine hybrids as Angela Limerick [and] Miss

Brian Doe, head gardener at Borde Hill in the 1950s and '60s, was responsible for hybridizing many of the nerines.

Below: In the mid-1960s Ralph began opening the garden to the public two days a week from Easter to the end of August.

Below, right: An early map for visitors to Borde Hill. Today, the garden exists within the same boundaries, but has had further areas of interest added.

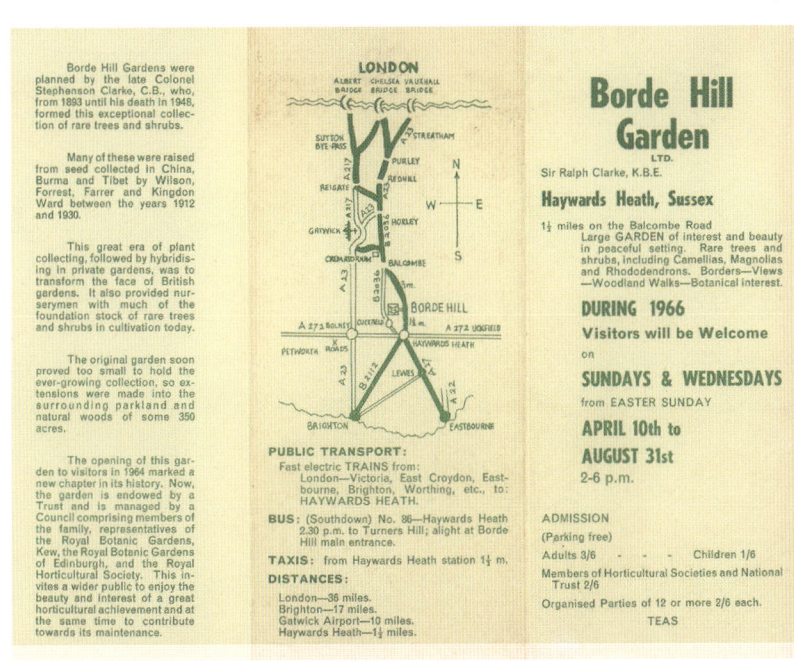

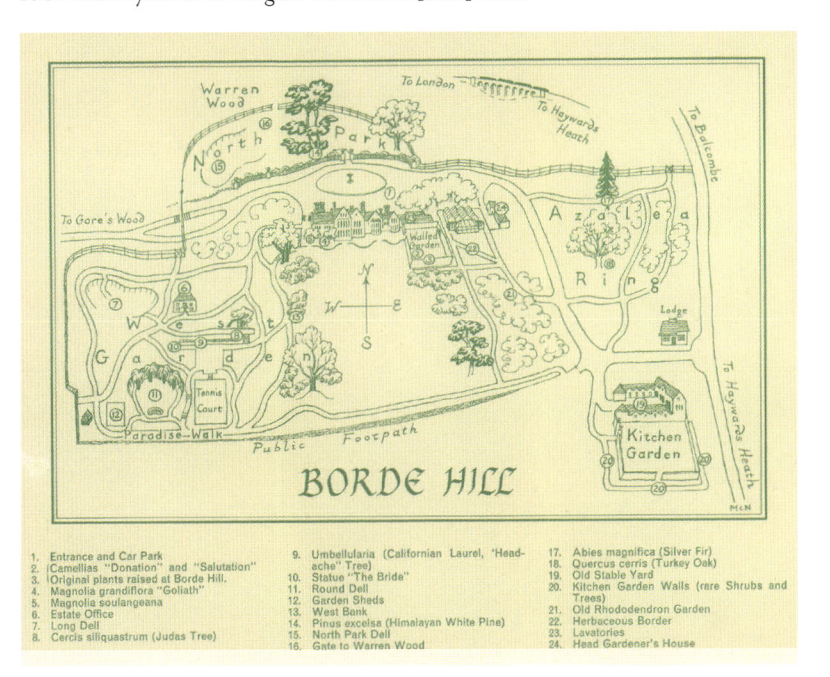

THE TRANSITIONAL YEARS

53

The statue of a bride by Antonio Tantardini, now in the main house, once stood in what is today the Italian Garden.

The gardening team in the 1970s, including John Humphris (far left) and Jack Vass (far right). Both started work at Borde Hill in 1968.

Willmott, both lovely shades of brilliant orange scarlet with well shaped heads.' Throughout the 1950s and '60s, Becky won RHS awards for her nerines, including an Award of Merit for 'Angela Limerick' in 1960, and gold, Banksian and Lindley medals for others. She became chair of the Nerine Society in 1968.

Becky corresponded with collectors, including Sir Frederick Stern (1884–1967), a leading horticulturalist and botanist, and an acquaintance of Stephie's, who advised her on lilies. His letter indicated that social life was loosening up: 'Do please call me Fred, all my friends do.' He added, 'As far as I know your soil, all lilies will flourish among your rhodos and azaleas … [A friend] has just sent me seed of some of his best hybrids which I enclose. I know nothing about them. It is a toss up if one gets a good lily from hybrid seed but it is quite exciting to see them flower.'

While the plant exchanges were never money-making, Becky did sell nerines and other seasonal plants from Borde Hill to such London florists as Pulbrook & Gould and Constance Spry. They were boxed up and sent by train from Haywards Heath several times a week. 'It was a good source of extra income for six or seven weeks in the autumn', recalls John Humphris.

Ralph was a keen sportsman whose deep knowledge of the Sussex countryside was derived in part from riding regularly to hounds.

Ralph in the mid-1960s with his spaniels in the herbaceous borders that later became Jay Robin's Rose Garden.

BORDE HILL GARDEN

Ralph established Borde Hill Garden as a charitable trust in 1965 and began opening regularly to the public. He had seen other Sussex gardens, such as Nymans (1953) and Sheffield Park (1954), handed over to the National Trust, but wanted Borde Hill to remain family-owned. Sir George Taylor (1904–1993), director of the Royal Botanic Gardens, Kew, was appointed as the trust's first chairman. Ralph planned that the garden council should always include representatives of the Royal Horticultural Society and of botanical gardens, such as Edinburgh and Kew, as well as nurserymen. In 2020 descendants of Stephie's friends were council members: Lionel de Rothschild of Exbury Gardens and David Millais of Millais Nurseries. The RHS was represented by Dr Tim Upson, director of horticulture, education and communities, and there were also botanists from the Cambridge University Botanic Garden and the Royal Botanic Garden Edinburgh. Ralph's vision was to enlist council members who had a real understanding of woody plants and sympathy with the ethos of Borde Hill, in order to formalize Stephie's lifelong sharing of plant knowledge.

The head gardener has always sat on the garden council, Brian Doe being the first. Doe, who died in 2021 at the age of eighty-nine, had previously worked at Wisley and was only in his mid-twenties when he became head gardener at Borde Hill. John Humphris, who joined Borde Hill in 1968, worked only briefly with Doe, although they remained friends, judging rhododendron competitions together until 2019. Doe, recalls Humphris, 'was very knowledgeable, very interested in propagating, and had a special interest in heathers, but didn't quite see the big picture of managing such an enormous collection'.

Doe left when he and Becky clashed, to be replaced in 1968 by Jack Vass, formerly Vita Sackville-West's head gardener at Sissinghurst Castle in Kent. Humphris describes Vass as 'one of the real old-fashioned, pre-war trained journeymen gardeners'. The two men worked well together and with Robert, in whose time the garden would win many rhododendron awards.

Ralph followed in the family tradition of being a Clothworker and was master of the company in 1962. He was also a farmer: he formed the Polled Sussex syndicate to breed a strain of hornless cattle, deep red in colour, long-living, adaptable and efficient producers of lean meat.

Leisure time was spent hunting (Ralph was master of the Old Surrey & Burstow Hunt), shooting and in the company of political friends, such as Harold Macmillan, who lived locally. Family parties for stalking, shooting and fishing took place every summer in Scotland, while, at Borde Hill, Ralph and Becky ran a big household. Even in the 1950s, the staff included a chauffeur, butler, cook, housekeeper, housemaids and Ralph's secretary, as well as the gardeners and woodmen on the estate (two of whom Andrewjohn inherited when he took over in 1988). It was a busy, clamouring life for a man by inclination private and introspective. Most years, Ralph withdrew to the silence of a Christian retreat for a couple of weeks' quiet contemplation.

Anecdotes abound about Becky and Ralph, one telling of the occasion when Ralph was in traction at Borde Hill after a hunting accident. Becky wanted him moved to another room, and hit on the idea of using undertakers. She omitted to mention that he was still alive, so, when they arrived with a coffin, Ralph looked up from his paper and shouted, 'Not yet!'

Ralph died aged seventy-seven on 9 May 1970 from pneumonia, his life shortened, his doctor believed, by being shot at Gallipoli in 1915. Like his father, he was buried at Highbrook Church.

Becky and Ralph on the terrace at Borde Hill House in the mid-1960s.

THE TRANSITIONAL YEARS

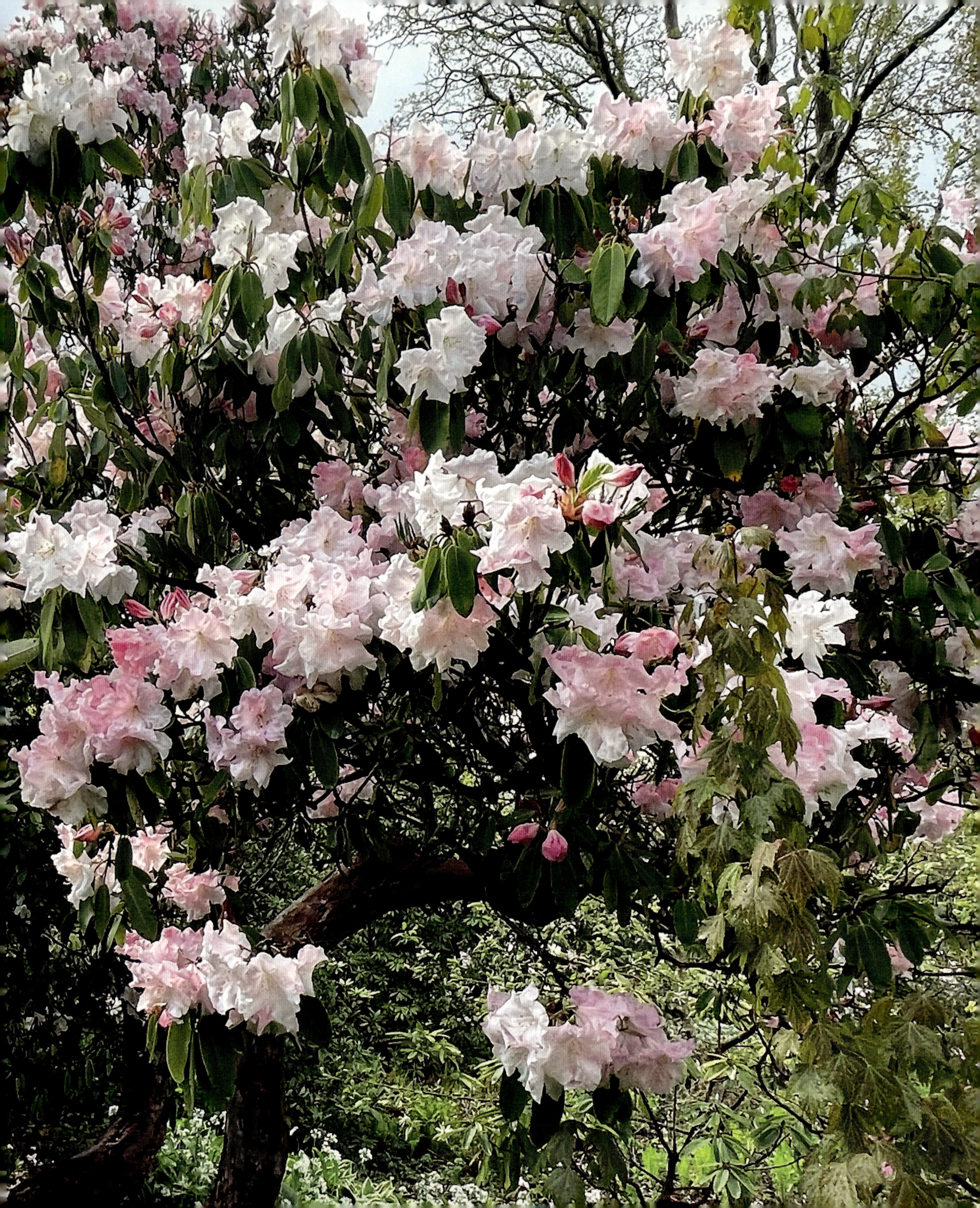

ROBERT NUNN STEPHENSON CLARKE
Resilience and Rhododendrons

In 1977 Robert wrote evocatively about Borde Hill in the *Yearbook of the RHS Rhododendron, Camellia and Magnolia Group*: 'It was, I found, a friendly garden with fine views and hidden reclusions and recesses but it yields up its secrets only slowly. Each of us is in a position for a given time – perhaps longer than each rhododendron, perhaps for a shorter lifetime. But the importance of life is in its continuation and its projection, not in its span alone.'
His words proved prophetic, for Robert was custodian of Borde Hill for just seventeen years before his early death in 1987. But during that time he achieved much, notably by enriching the rhododendron collection and establishing its national importance. He made the garden far more accessible to the general public, and award-winning entries in dozens of RHS competitions further raised its profile.

Robert Nunn Stephenson Clarke was born on 17 April 1925, the second child and elder of the two sons of Ralph and Becky Stephenson Clarke. He was at Eton when war broke out, and at the age of eighteen chose not to join the Army, as other family members had done: in July 1943 he was admitted as a midshipman in the Royal Naval Volunteer Reserve.

After the war, Robert read history at Trinity Hall, Cambridge, where his great-uncle Louis Clarke was a (by then elderly) fellow. Time in Paris led to his encyclopaedic knowledge of wine and to his becoming a master of wine in France. He was also secretary general (codename 'Fleurie') of the eccentric-sounding Society of Beaujolais, formed in 1960 'for the secret and confidential investigation of restaurants … in Europe, and the collection and editing of information gleaned'. He wrote guidebooks to good eating: *Ici on mange bien* and *A Parisian Table*. He later worked in shipping insurance at Lloyd's of London, before joining the family business. His particular interest was railways at a period when, as he wrote, 'to see a truck marked "Stephenson Clarke" was a common sight on railway journeys'. His son Andrewjohn says Robert 'knew the west European railway timetable by heart. Engines would be hired to tow our coal wagons, so he needed to minimize the duration of hire by slotting into gaps in passenger traffic on each line. My father applied his active mind and first-class memory to this work.' Robert later directed these same abilities to the study of rhododendrons.

In April 1949, at Highbrook Church, Robert married Juana Nidia Gereth Bickersteth-Wheeler (known as Nidia), the only daughter of a former military attaché to Chile and Paris, and Blanca Emilia, his Chilean wife. Nidia had an eventful girlhood. On Lt Col. John Bickersteth-Wheeler's retirement, the family moved to Jersey,

Opposite: Rhododendron 'Loderi King George' in the West Garden. Robert developed a passion for rhododendrons, creating new hybrids and attempting to catalogue Borde Hill's vast collection.

Above: Robert Nunn Stephenson Clarke (1925–1987) during the Second World War in the uniform of the Royal Naval Volunteer Reserve.

THE HISTORY
57

Robert and his bride, Juana Nidia Gereth Bickersteth-Wheeler (1928–2013), on their wedding day in April 1949 at Highbrook Church.

from which they escaped just before the German occupation in 1940, taking only what they could carry. As they headed for Weymouth in a collier, thick fog kept the ship in the Channel, and they thereby avoided the overnight bombing of the harbour, in which they would almost certainly have died.

Robert and Nidia had three children: Marylynn (1950), Roland (1953) and Andrewjohn (1955). For a time, the young family lived in Northumberland, in a house that had belonged to the Clarkes for generations. When the business was finally sold in the late 1950s, some family members, but not Robert, remained as directors until the final Clarke involvement petered out in 1982. Robert and Nidia settled at Hoathly Hill, on the Brook House estate. There, in the 1960s, he set up Highbrook Enterprises, to organize private, tailor-made tours of British stately homes and gardens for Americans recruited on his lecture tours of the United States. This business, if never very profitable, combined many of Robert's passions: visiting historic places and talking about them, and eating and drinking well. In the archive at Borde Hill are fantastically detailed notes in Robert's tiny, meticulous handwriting on cities in the UK, Scandinavia and other parts of Europe. Key places of interest and architectural details are all itemized, along with the best hotels, restaurants and cafés. In style and shape, these lists closely resemble his rhododendron records. 'That was Robert to a T', according to his future head gardener, John Humphris. 'He would sit up half the night listing things.'

Although rather different from his quieter, more reserved father, Robert shared Ralph's sense of duty and responsibility. In an address to Borde Hill's gatekeepers in the 1970s, Robert

Robert and Nidia's children, Andrewjohn (left), Marylynn and Roland.

BORDE HILL GARDEN
58

described the Clarkes as never having 'belonged to the Jet Set, nor gained a reputation of wasters. They have always put back into life the greater part of what they receive ... Perhaps it can be said that they have always been rather shy of walking into the limelight of the upper crusts.'

From his mother, Robert inherited a twinkle in his eye and a fondness for practical jokes. He excelled at crosswords and writing cryptic poems, using the latter to set elaborate treasure hunts around Sussex. He enjoyed shooting, like his father and grandfather, and was an energetic member of the Eton Ramblers Cricket Club. In the 1950s he assembled an amateur cricket team that played on the pitch Stephie had made at Brook House.

Robert and Nidia were divorced in 1967, after which Nidia and the three children moved to London. Robert remarried and bought a house on the Isle of Wight for his new wife. That marriage, too, ended in divorce, and in 1972 he married the twice-widowed Maria Williams, whom he met through Highbrook Enterprises.

By then, Robert had been living at Borde Hill since his father's death in May 1970. He recognized the challenges: 'I am the third generation to enjoy [the garden] and at times to suffer the enormous problems it offers, if it is to be maintained.' Despite Ralph and Becky's efforts, areas were becoming overgrown, while Stephie's rhododendrons had seeded themselves liberally thanks to the rich soil and what Stephie had described as 'good air drainage'. Plants were still growing through the woods marked with the original collector's numbers, as, with an increasingly small team of gardeners, it had been hard to find time to identify and name them fully.

Robert set to with a will to establish the estate on a firmer financial basis. He converted part of the house into flats to reduce overheads (having first considered, but then rejected, plans to demolish the east wing). He was not a farmer, so he sold his father's herds and concentrated instead on running the estate, in Andrewjohn's words, 'as a benevolent and benign landscape'.

Becky lived on for a while at Borde Hill, but she and Robert clashed, as they had always done, their battleground now being the garden. Eventually, she bought Brook House from Robert and divided her time between there and her family home in Essex. Despite their disagreements, Robert built on what Becky had achieved, carrying on her cut-flower business, as well as continuing to hybridize nerines.

Robert was a meticulous list-maker, filling pages with his small, neat handwriting. Here, he itemizes in detail different varieties of rhododendron.

Clearance of wilder areas around the estate's perimeter began under George Catt, recruited as garden manager by the garden council chairman, Sir George Taylor, before Ralph's death. Catt oversaw the systematic labelling of trees and shrubs, assisted by Robert's cousin Desmond Clarke. Desmond, a dendrologist responsible for updating W.J. Bean's authoritative guide *Trees and Shrubs Hardy in the British Isles* ('Bean's Trees and Shrubs'), was also on the Borde Hill council. In the early 1970s the National Trust received funding to list all its important trees, this funding being dependent on the inclusion of Borde Hill's trees and shrubs. The rhododendrons proved a special challenge, for the seed is very small and the plants had reproduced almost too freely at Borde Hill. 'The stronger grew and smothered the weaker', as Robert observed in garden notes written in the mid-1980s.

Although Robert had no direct involvement with the garden in Ralph's lifetime, he had already acquired compendious knowledge of rhododendrons and camellias. There were no half measures with Robert, so, spurred on by Jack Vass, his study of rhododendrons became all-absorbing. As Stephie had done fifty years earlier, Robert established contacts with experts and fellow enthusiasts, including representatives of the Rhododendron Species Foundation. They met during Robert's visits to Washington State and Florida to find large-leaf species missing from the collection, which were subsequently planted in Gore's Wood. Robert recruited to

RESILIENCE AND RHODODENDRONS

the council the rhododendron experts Thomas Hope Findlay, head gardener at the Savill Garden in Windsor Great Park, and Alan Hardy of Sandling Park, a noted rhododendron garden in Kent. He became friendly with Ted Millais, owner of Millais Nurseries and nephew of Stephie's friend John Guille Millais, one of the founders of the Rhododendron Society in 1916. Another regular visitor was Peter Cox, whose father, Euan, had travelled with Reginald Farrer in Burma in 1919. The Coxes established Glendoick Nursery near Perth, Scotland, in 1953, and Robert obtained many wild-collected plants from them.

When planting, Robert was concerned, like Stephie, to do so in the right places. In his 1983 chairman's report, he told the council, 'I am particularly keen to carry on the burden of Gore's Wood myself and treat it as a devoted hobby. Before the freeze-up we had already planted out over 200 rhododendrons there. I am sure that this cold winter will prove that their survival capacity there is far greater than in the Garden area. The soil here was so much better than in the Garden that we did not have to use any peat.'

Robert began hybridizing intensively, working first with Jack Vass and then with John Humphris. He often selected species for grafting, although the actual grafting was mostly done by the gardeners. Robert was constantly on the lookout for new plant material, as Humphris remembers: 'Robert didn't much like driving, so I would drive him in the Volvo to Wisley, Exbury and the Valley Gardens at Windsor. We would meet the head gardener, look round the collections, then get cutting material, bag it up and take it back to Jack Vass, who would pot up the cuttings. There was a wonderful competitiveness between Robert and the Rothschilds at Exbury.'

Robert exhibited frequently at RHS shows held in the society's halls near Vincent Square: showing in dozens of different classes every year brought Borde Hill to the full attention of the horticultural world. Walter Fleming had germinated thousands of seeds, including groups of single species, and planted them in Gore's Wood. The gardeners and Robert would select the best examples to put up for awards five days before a show, keeping the picked rhododendron sprays in the cellar or a cold room, so they would be perfect on the day. The old Volvo was pressed into service again, its back seats removed to accommodate the rhododendrons. The gardening team went up to London at six in the morning to prepare the stand, and in the evening Robert took everyone out to dinner.

According to Humphris, 'It was hard work, but fascinating. I learned so much about exhibiting from Robert and from Jack. Every

Liriodendron chinense, first flowered by Stephie in 1927, continued to impress, winning an RHS Award of Merit in June 1980.

Robert with Jack Vass, head gardener at Borde Hill from 1968 to 1979.

BORDE HILL GARDEN
60

In 1975 Jack Vass was presented with the prestigious A.J. Waley Medal for his work with rhododendrons. Vass is seen here with Robert and Maria and with members of the Borde Hill Garden Council and the gardening team.

time you cut something for a show, you labelled it. You labelled it when you were packing up and then again at the show, so you really got to know the plants.'

Awards came thick and fast: Awards of Merit were won by *Rhododendron metternichii* in 1976 and *R. phaeochrysum* in 1977, with five more for rhododendrons in the following year. These included *R. iodes*, its citation being 'Collected by George Forrest, raised by Colonel S.R. Clarke, and shown by Mr R.N.S. Clarke', and the intense-pink *R. sutchuenense* (Wilson No. 1232), called 'Seventh Heaven' by Robert. He also won the RHS Roza Stevenson Challenge Cup in 1983 for *R. davidsonianum* (Wilson No. 4239) and many RHS awards for camellias.

There were awards, too, for Vass and Humphris. Both won the prestigious A.J. Waley Medal, presented by the Royal Horticultural Society to a working gardener in charge of large-scale rhododendron cultivation.

In his grandfather's memory, Robert set up the annual Stephenson R. Clarke Cup for an exhibitor in the RHS Ornamental Tree and Shrub Competitions. Winners in the 1980s included Lord Aberconway at Bodnant, Sheffield Park, and the Kleinworts from Sezincote in Gloucestershire, all gardens or descendants of garden owners known to Stephie.

Although rhododendrons were Robert's abiding passion, he exhibited in other classes, too. Borde Hill's conifer collection was also outstanding, so George Catt was keen for the garden to be represented at a conifer conference organized in 1970 at the RHS halls by Sir Harold Hillier and Roy Lancaster. To supply good foliage and cones, Humphris climbed every tree on a list drawn up by Catt. Conifers from Borde Hill also won Awards of Merit in 1978 (*Cupressus guadalupensis* and *Fitzroya cupressoides*) and in 1979 (*Pinus wallichiana*). Other prize-winning trees

Vass was a skilled hybridizer and spent hours at work in the greenhouses.

RESILIENCE AND RHODODENDRONS

Robert and his third wife, Maria Williams, on the sundial lawn by the north front of Borde Hill House.

and shrubs included *Liriodendron chinense*, the tree flowered first by Stephie in 1927.

Competitive though he was, Robert, like Stephie, wished to see plant material shared around. In 1986, for instance, he drew up a long list of rhododendron species for grafting with collectors' numbers from Wilson, Farrer, Forrest and Kingdon Ward. 'I am sending this list to a few people who may be interested', he wrote. 'If anybody would like to take graftings of these rare rhododendrons at Borde Hill they would be welcome in the Spring. It would have to be on a fair "keep and exchange" basis … It is essential that everything is done to try and retain these rare rhododendrons in circulation.'

Robert approached his hobby with his grandfather's steely professionalism. He published a thirty-six-page alphabetical catalogue of rhododendron species, 'explaining the changes in reclassification based on an insight into the Collection at Borde Hill and other observations'. In this catalogue, and in another A4 hardback notebook in the archive, are minutely observed comments on individual rhododendrons. About 'Glischroides Series Barbatum subspecies Glischrum', for example, he writes: 'Attains almost 15ft at Borde Hill where it bears in two places F26455 and F26428 numbers – about 10 examples of the species in all … Only perhaps a variety of R. glischrum, but earlier flowering at Borde Hill – having dark matt green leaves vividly veined beneath … a reticulated network of veins formed by fine hairs and bristles. Flowers in loose trusses 6–10 [inches] long –

Greenhouses and borders on the east side of Borde Hill House, before this area was transformed into Jay Robin's Rose Garden in 1996.

BORDE HILL GARDEN

campanulate white or creamy white flushed rose & crimson blotch. Bristly & glandular species.' (The two numbers beginning with 'F' are those given by George Forrest, who collected these specimens.)

Among the same notes, Robert showed himself to be pugnacious. 'In my view R. galactinum is not given the rating in the RHS handbook it deserves', he wrote. 'A prejudice that is contagious to judges.' This pepperiness chimes with comments in his 1983 chairman's report: 'I wonder if the Rhododendron World has yet learnt what fair exchange really means – there is still too much taking and not much giving ... In 1983 I have not been entirely pleased with the gardening world, I find it quarrelsome. That is not the world to preserve in a great collection.'

Robert was a collector and hybridizer, but was also conscious that public footfall was needed to sustain both garden and collections. He saw Borde Hill's being a family garden, rather than publicly owned, as a selling point: 'I would like to see this Garden sold more as a private garden that was created by private people', he told the Borde Hill Garden Council in 1983. 'It is not a garden that can fall back on Government gifts or borrowing, it must find its way mainly through private enterprise – the spirit of the Garden itself is connected with that being.'

Robert aimed to balance these two imperatives, as Andrewjohn would do in his turn. Botanists visited to look at the tree and shrub collection, but other attractions were required for the general public. Robert began developing the formal garden, as well as improving the infrastructure. To the south of the house, he made the dilapidated tennis court into the Bride's Pool (so called because of the Antonio Tantardini statue that stood there), refigured the Round Dell, planted up the Old Potting Sheds and replanted the West Bank terrace – all of which gave more interest during summer and early autumn.

In the mid-1970s Robert started selling plants from Stephie's walled kitchen garden. He put in a new car park, made a public entrance away from the house and wrote a proper garden guidebook. The openings continued low-key, however, with a sentry box manned by volunteers, such as Robert's secretary. Another was a retired British Museum curator, who built models from matchsticks on slow afternoons. Robert monitored every detail closely, urging that he must be 'kept in touch with everything that is important; that nothing important [should be] hidden from me'.

Robert, in his early sixties, was full of plans. He proposed a water feature for the South Park that would also provide a source of water for the garden. With an eye to opening up Borde Hill in other ways, he intended that his elder son, Roland, a successful three-day eventer, should host equestrian events in the park.

On the night of 15–16 October 1987 a hurricane tore through southern England. At Borde Hill, it uprooted the Pinetum, destroyed the estate office (and many valuable documents) and caused widespread devastation across the estate. A month later, on 17 November, aged just sixty-two, Robert died in hospital after a long illness. Fortunately, he did not see the devastation of the hurricane. His younger son, Andrewjohn, would pick up the pieces and lead the estate into the twenty-first century.

Borde Hill lost hundreds of trees in the hurricane of October 1987.

RESILIENCE AND RHODODENDRONS

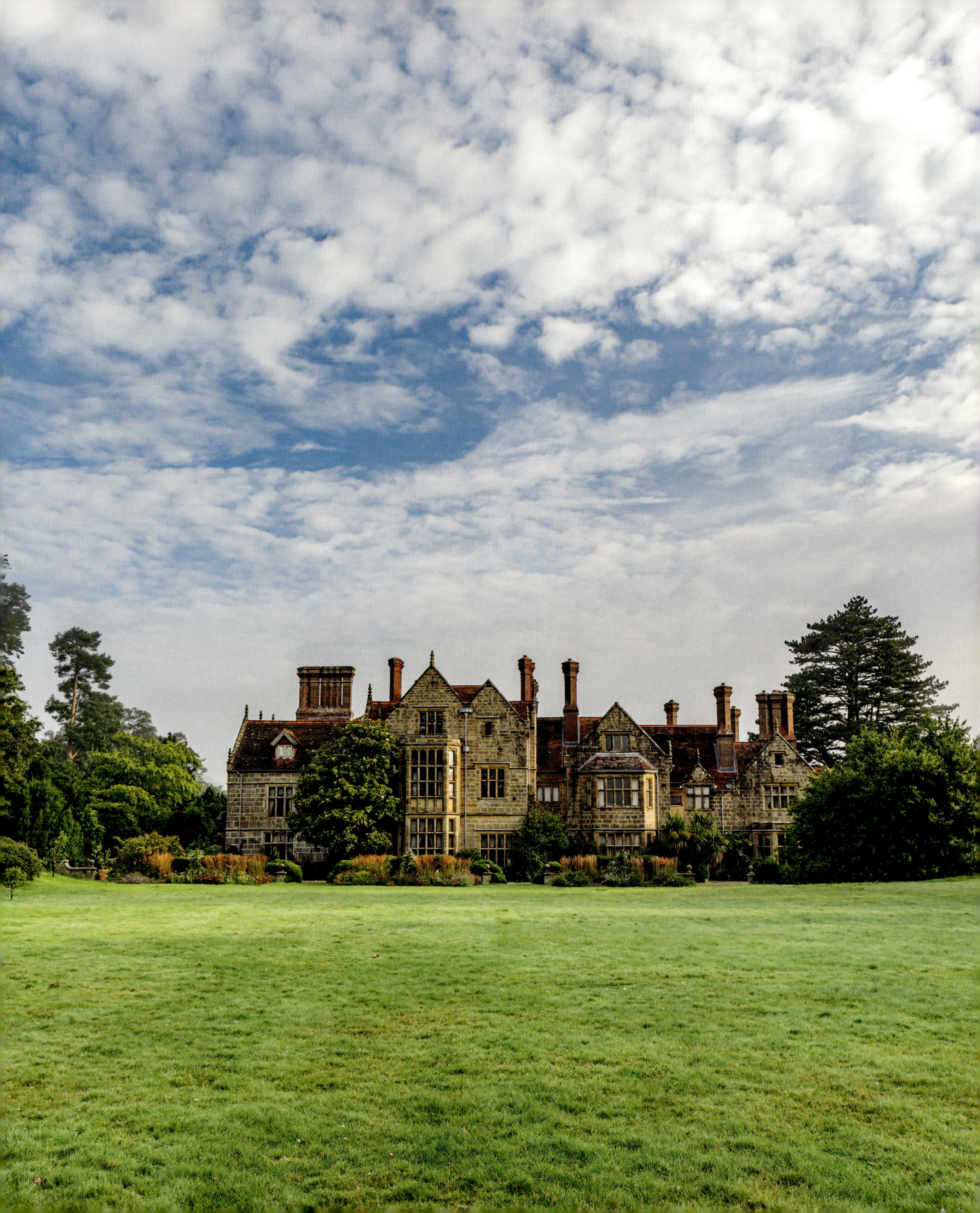

ANDREWJOHN STEPHENSON CLARKE
Consolidation and Reinvention

South-eastern England awoke to widespread destruction on 16 October 1987. At Leonardslee, High Beeches, Sheffield Park and Nymans, acres of woodland had been flattened overnight. For months afterwards, the sound of grinding chainsaws filled the Sussex and Kent air as wreckage was cleared. On the brighter side, Robin Loder said there were trees he would never have dared touch but whose felling opened up glades of the rhododendrons, azaleas and camellias for which Leonardslee was famous. At Borde Hill, although the Long Dell and the Pinetum were ravaged, and there were other losses through the woodlands, the collections were wide and deep enough to recover: in the early twenty-first century the estate would be claiming seventy champion trees (tallest trees or those with the biggest girth in the British Isles; see pp. 192–93).

But it was an unpropitious moment for a London-based IT consultant with two young children to take on the estate, especially as he had had little preparation for the role. The Stephenson Clarkes' generations-long tradition of primogeniture meant that Andrewjohn was shocked to discover on the reading of the will that Robert had planned that he, and not his older brother, Roland, would inherit Borde Hill. There had been clues: for some years, Robert had been including Andrewjohn in discussions about the garden and estate management, and he had appointed him to the garden council. But Andrewjohn says, with quietly self-deprecating humour, the penny had not dropped that Roland's political views and attendance at CND demonstrations suggested that he was not perhaps ideally suited to settling down as a Sussex landowner. Roland, a kindly elder brother when the boys were at school, seems to have accepted their father's decision without acrimony. As Robert had projected, he ran three-day events in the South Park, thereby helping his brother to build the reputation of Borde Hill not just as a garden and collection, but also as a major recreational venue in Sussex.

Andrewjohn and his wife, Eleni, found themselves in a similar position to others inheriting important gardens in the late twentieth century. They moved to Borde Hill in 1988, just as, for example, Anne and Johnny Chambers stepped into Anne's mother's shoes at Kiftsgate Court Gardens in Gloucestershire. Both couples recognized that the only way their houses and gardens could survive under family ownership was by being put on a proper

Opposite: The south front of Borde Hill House, with borders along the terrace designed by James Alexander-Sinclair.

Below: Andrewjohn Stephenson Clarke and his wife, Eleni, in Jay Robin's Rose Garden.

THE HISTORY

commercial footing. That would be their challenge and, ultimately, their achievement.

Andrewjohn Patrick Stephenson Clarke was born three months prematurely on 26 November 1955. As his mother was wheeled through the corridors of St Margaret's Hospital, Marylebone, she overheard a nurse say, 'This woman is having a miscarriage.' Nidia fought back, exclaiming, 'No, I'm not. I'm having a baby!' Not expected to live, the tiny boy was baptized John by the only available clergyman, a Catholic priest. But Andrewjohn survived and flourished (he would eventually be over 6 feet/1.8 m tall). When he came to be baptized according to the rites of the Anglican church, his parents discovered that the same name could not be used – hence his compound forename.

Andrewjohn and his siblings spent their childhood at Hoathly Hill, and only occasionally visited Borde Hill. 'But I was always conscious of its being very much a family home. I loved the space and the multitude of paths and places to play with my siblings and cousins.' Theirs was a country childhood: Andrewjohn and Roland hacked to kindergarten on their ponies kept at Brook House, across the estate from their home. Andrewjohn walked the hounds and beagles for his grandfather's hunt, and also rode out with Ralph, although he describes himself as 'a poor member' in comparison to his sister and brother, both more accomplished riders.

During holidays on the Isle of Wight, the children would rush down to the shore to spot the distinctive black-and-white funnels of Stephenson Clarke colliers, still sailing the Channel in the 1950s and early '60s. Ralph, Becky and all their descendants also congregated in Scotland for summer house parties involving fishing, shooting, stalking and other country pastimes. The children attached themselves to an adult and participated in that adult's pursuit for the day. A Cambridge undergraduate or postgraduate was sometimes employed to look after the younger ones and give their parents a holiday. It was preferable if the student had a taste for mountaineering, since that was another activity during sporting holidays that Andrewjohn remembers as 'all being quite jolly'.

When Robert and Nidia divorced in 1967, Nidia and the three children moved to Kensington. Andrewjohn saw less of his father, although, as a teenager, he helped select sprays of rhododendrons for exhibitions. There was also a memorable weekend while Andrewjohn and Roland were at Eton. Robert's near-obsessive interest in railways long outlived his professional involvement. One Saturday morning, he picked up his sons for a thirty-six-hour exeat. 'He hustled us to the car, announced he had our passports and that we were off to Belgium to see a branch line due to close', says Andrewjohn. 'We shared a three-bedded room in a hotel, but my father snored so loudly, Roland ended up sleeping in the bath.'

After Eton, Andrewjohn studied civil engineering at King's College London. He bought a blue notebook from the stationer Ryman, with lined pages facing blank pages. 'Being naturally careful with money, I organized it so I worked from one end in one subject and from the other end in another', says Andrewjohn. 'When I started going through the family archive, I discovered my grandfather's Cambridge notebooks, and found that he had done just the same thing for zoology and botany, and in the same design of book.' A touching bond across the generations.

At KCL, Andrewjohn met a geology student, Eleni Charalambos Pari, and they were married in May 1979 at Eleni's home in Paphos on Cyprus. A subsequent celebration was hosted by Nidia at Birch Hall, Becky's family home. Their daughter, Jay Robin, was born in September 1982, followed twenty months later, in May 1984, by a son, Harry Ralph. Andrewjohn was working with Shell International when Robert died, having moved from engineering to management and IT

Andrewjohn (left) and his older brother, Roland, photographed while at Eton in the late 1960s.

consultancy. This freelance portfolio career gave him the flexibility to devote time to Borde Hill, although Eleni, who acquired a deep and abiding love of the garden, handled much of the day-to-day management, and marketing and publicity.

Robert had been sharply aware of the difficulties facing the next generation, for whom landholdings alone would not supply the income to support the garden and its collections. In his 1983 chairman's report, he said, 'It is hardly the time yet to introduce sons to this Garden simply because they are engaged in building their own lives at a time when it is very hard to find profitable jobs and there is so much competition.'

Yet, stealthily, Robert had begun to familiarize Andrewjohn with the estate, walking him round the garden and telling him about the rhododendrons. Had he not died prematurely, Robert would possibly have made his objectives clearer to the son who, being fond of country pursuits, was more likely to succeed. Andrewjohn freely admits he is less of a plantsman than were his predecessors, but he is no less passionate about the survival and embellishment of the garden and its collections.

Theirs was to be a very different existence from that of their forebears. Even in Robert's time, there was still a butler at Borde Hill, but Andrewjohn and Eleni run house and estate with minimum help. Gradually, Andrewjohn changed Borde Hill from a traditional family estate into one operated proactively using advisers and modern management techniques. The house is at the centre of a portfolio of activities – public gardens, residential and commercial properties, and tenanted beef and sheep farmland – all of which must work together. Borde Hill's management became two-tiered, with a board of trustees responsible for the overall running of the estate and the garden council attending to the horticultural side.

Andrewjohn's initial task, however, was to clear the devastation caused by the hurricane, and then make the most of the opportunities it afforded. The Pinetum's loss opened up the view of the railway viaduct obscured some sixty years earlier, while the felling of trees in the Long Dell introduced more light and gave other plants the chance to prosper. In 1989 a report was commissioned from the eminent dendrologist Alan Mitchell. It recognized that 'Borde Hill is one of the most comprehensive collections of trees and shrubs in the world … The chief aim in rehabilitating Borde Hill after … the gale of October 16th, 1987 must be to retain, preserve and enhance the huge wealth of species, and especially of rare eastern Asiatics, within the framework of the original scheme.' New planting continued across the estate, with advice from garden council members including David Millais of Millais Nurseries, Lionel de Rothschild of Exbury Gardens, and Jim Gardiner. The last is the council's longest-standing member: he joined in the early 1990s, and was chair from 2009 to 2016. A former curator of RHS Garden Wisley and director of horticulture at the RHS, Gardiner is now a vice president and was awarded the Victoria Medal of Honour in 2020.

Improvements to both the planting and the garden's infrastructure have been continuous since 1988. Other studies have been commissioned, including a conservation, repair and development plan from Lear Associates in 2002, while in 1997 a Heritage Lottery Fund grant enabled the restoration of two Victorian greenhouses. In the early 1990s the stables next to the former walled kitchen garden were turned into a restaurant and café, and a new visitor centre was built. In the South Park, Robert's plan was honoured, the lake being named Robertsmere in his memory. Later, Harry's Lake was added, both lakes being used for coarse fishing.

Spearheaded by Eleni, a major success has been the reinstatement of flower gardening, an aspect highlighted in the 1902 *Country Life* article, which described the house as 'lying in the midst of as fair a flower garden as we could

The Bride's Pool, seen here with original planting by Robert and John Humphris, before Andrewjohn and Eleni commissioned Robin Williams senior to redesign it as the Italian Garden in 1997.

In 2004 Borde Hill Garden won the Historic Houses Association/Christie's Garden of the Year Award, an award voted for by members of the visiting public.

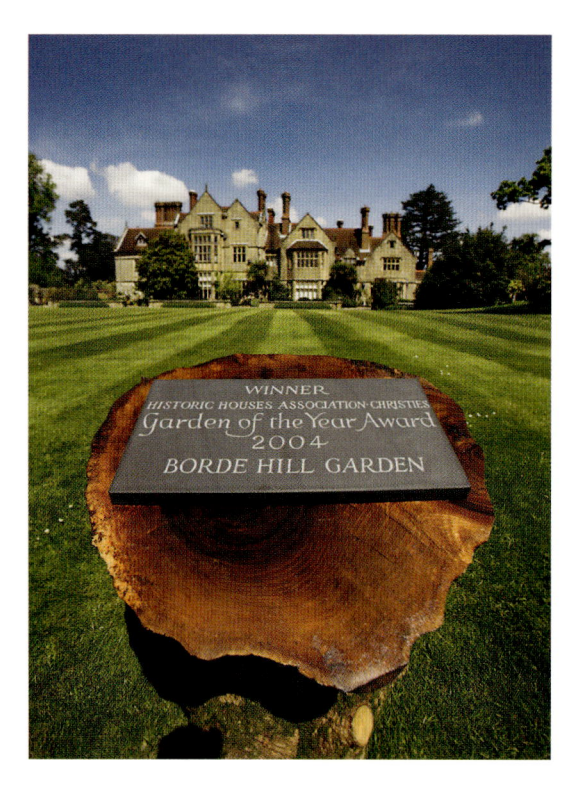

Jim Gardiner, VMH, former curator of RHS Garden Wisley and RHS director of horticulture, is the longest-standing member of the Borde Hill Garden Council.

desire'. Stephie's interest was in collecting rather than in laying out formal gardens, as Robert noted in a 1980s chairman's report: 'If [my grandfather] knew any landscape gardeners in those days it is not apparent in his work. He was, above all, a plant collector, not a garden designer.' For the first time, a strong element of design was injected into the gardens around Borde Hill House, in step with the zeitgeist: in the 1990s the RHS began placing far greater emphasis on the design of show gardens at the Chelsea, Hampton Court and Tatton Park flower shows.

Jay Robin's Rose Garden was designed in 1996 by the RHS gold medallist Robin Williams senior. Planted with more than 500 David Austin English roses, the garden replaced two 1960s herbaceous borders on what was once Stephen Borde's orchards. The following year, Williams redesigned Robert's Bride's Pool as the Italian Garden, with terracing and a formal structure of box parterre beds. The Old Potting Sheds became a shelter for southern hemisphere species. Further work by RHS award-winning designers included the Mid-Summer Border by Dr Tony Lord in 2011, the borders around the house by James Alexander-Sinclair in 2014, the redesign of the Round Dell by Sophie Walker in 2017, and, in 2020, Chris Beardshaw's replanting of the Italian Garden and Paradise Walk.

In 2018 Gardiner Grove was planted by and in recognition of Jim Gardiner and to mark the 125th anniversary of Stephie's purchase of Borde Hill. Gardiner has been visiting Borde Hill since 1977, when he came as a staff member of the Royal Botanic Garden Edinburgh to take rhododendron cuttings for grafting. This magnolia grove links Warren Wood, the Garden of Allah and the Long Dell, and adds to Borde Hill's wealth of magnolias. Hybrids of Asiatic and American species have been planted within their genetically similar groups so that, by growing close together, their differences and similarities are immediately apparent. Gardiner Grove is part of a long-term strategy, as it will be more than ten years before the trees start making an impact on the landscape.

Year-round interest has now been created in what was once primarily a spring and early-summer garden. The designed areas sit well within the woodlands and parklands, providing varied places for visitors to explore. Other developments have boosted the visitor's experience, including a biennial sculpture exhibition and sale, which began in 1999. Sculptures by both local and international artists are strategically placed to show them to their best advantage, and also to highlight surrounding planting. Some were specifically commissioned for the garden, including the kinetic stainless-steel water sculpture *Aquapoise*, by Angela Conner, in the Italian Garden pool.

Borde Hill remains very much a family home, and the Stephenson Clarkes encourage

Council member David Millais is owner of Millais Nurseries and a descendant of John Guille Millais, one of the founders of the Rhododendron Society in 1916.

They have built up visitor numbers to around 60,000 a year, with a further 40,000 people coming annually to the restaurant and café in the former stables. Although Borde Hill functions very differently from when the garden's founder was alive, at the heart of every endeavour is the determination to preserve his vision. Andrewjohn and Eleni have expanded networking connections with journalists, horticulturalists and related organizations. They have co-opted council members who are keen to help reinvigorate propagating activities, among them Jim Gardiner, Tim Upson and David Millais. The garden writer and television journalist Stephen Lacey is also on the council, advising on planting as well as media coverage. Eleni has raised the profile of the garden both nationally and internationally, and is an adept photographer whose pictures are used regularly on social media. Both she and her husband are deeply involved in the horticultural world, working within the same sphere of influence as Stephie did: there are regular contacts with Messels, Loders, Eleys, Williamses and Millaises, all descendants of Stephie's correspondents.

other families to enjoy what it has to offer. They have made a small area for children, Harry's Playground, near the Azalea Ring within the formal garden, and activities are run throughout the season from Easter egg hunts to Halloween trails. Jim Gardiner admires Andrewjohn and Eleni's achievements: 'They have a very good understanding of what visitors want from a garden visit.'

Local participation continues to be important: from 2012 to 2013 Andrewjohn was High Sheriff of West Sussex, as his great-grandfather had been a century earlier. Having taken a year out to concentrate on the role, Andrewjohn decided not to return to his consulting work but to focus exclusively on Borde Hill.

Andrewjohn and Eleni at Borde Hill with their children, Jay Robin and Harry.

CONSOLIDATION AND REINVENTION

69

Chris Beardshaw, a Chelsea gold medallist, redesigned the planting in the Italian Garden in 2020. He extended the season by planting such long-flowering perennials as *Salvia* Mystic Spires Blue.

The collections remain the bedrock for all the other activities, and Andrewjohn and Eleni work with modern-day plant hunters. Sophie Walker, who redesigned the Round Dell, introduced new woody and herbaceous plants from Crûg Farm Plants in North Wales. The nursery's owners, Bleddyn and Sue Wynn-Jones, have searched for plants worldwide over the last thirty years, travelling among other places to Jordan, Taiwan, Nepal and Korea.

Borde Hill has always attracted head gardeners of high calibre. Since the late 1990s, they have included Harvey Stephens, who previously worked at the Botanical Garden of Moscow State University. After leaving Borde Hill, he became head gardener at the Savill Garden in Windsor, and he is presently working for the Duke of Westminster at Eaton Hall in Cheshire. From 2008 to 2021, Andy Stevens was head gardener, joining after eight years with Robin Loder at Leonardslee. Stevens was succeeded by Harry Baldwin, who trained and then worked as a taxonomist at Kew. As head of horticulture, he leads a team of three full-time gardeners, two part-timers, and volunteers. Between them, they maintain 35 acres (14 ha) and oversee some of the collections in the wider 200 acres (81 ha) of parkland open to the public. Day-to-day upkeep carries on with little hindrance from or inconvenience to visitors, but bigger jobs are left until the closed season.

Plant material continues to be shared with botanical gardens and nurseries. Seedlings of the flowering tree *Meliosma alba*, for instance, were sent by Stevens to Pan-Global Plants at Frampton-on-Severn in Gloucestershire to ensure that rarer plants are successfully repropagated.

In the 2020s, few great gardens created in the first decades of the twentieth century are still in the hands of the families who made them. Caerhays and Trewithen in Cornwall are, but many more, including Nymans and Sheffield Park, have been handed over to the National Trust, or sold, as in the case of Leonardslee. That Borde Hill has survived in its original ownership is because of the dedication of four generations of Stephenson Clarkes. All, in turn, have reflected their own age. Stephie, like many other hobbyist gardeners, had the wherewithal to build a personal paradise. His son Ralph resisted the pressure after the Second World War to bail out, and instead protected the garden with a charitable trust. Robert put Borde Hill in the limelight by exhibiting often and successfully at the then very frequent RHS shows. For Andrewjohn, the way forward from the late 1980s was to run garden and estate as a business, and, encouraged by the upsurge of interest in garden design, he gave Borde Hill more contemporary appeal.

Andrewjohn and Eleni's children, Jay Robin and Harry, in the Jay Robin Rose Garden.

In future years, house, garden and estate will be in the hands of Andrewjohn and Eleni's children, whose aim is also to preserve and augment the collections and to keep Borde Hill as a family estate for generations to come. Jay Robin and Harry have identified complementary roles for themselves. Jay, who has worked in marketing and public relations for more than fifteen years, takes a particular interest in the house, garden and woodland, while Harry, a product designer with architectural experience, looks after the wider estate. It has been 'a natural and obvious progression', says Harry. 'We are keen to continue our family's legacy and remain guardians of the collection, while innovating for the future', adds Jay.

Jay and Harry will work in the context of twenty-first-century priorities, including climate change and biodiversity. Their messaging will emphasize the importance of nature for physical and mental well-being, and will urge visitors to share their passion for the natural world. Collaborating with Natural England, they want to plant more trees and grow the collection to encourage biodiversity. Sustainability will be at the heart of their programme for managing the houses and farms on the estate: Harry's barn conversion is heated entirely by renewable energy, and he plans that other estate buildings should follow suit. Woodchips laid down as mulch and paths are all sourced locally, and the mansion and adjacent lodges are heated by biomass.

This notable garden, created by a far-sighted gardener well over a century ago, will soon be run by a fifth generation of Stephenson Clarkes. They share Stephie's values and his resolve, while acknowledging that adaptability is key to the garden's viability. The future of Borde Hill is in safe hands.

CONSOLIDATION AND REINVENTION

The Garden

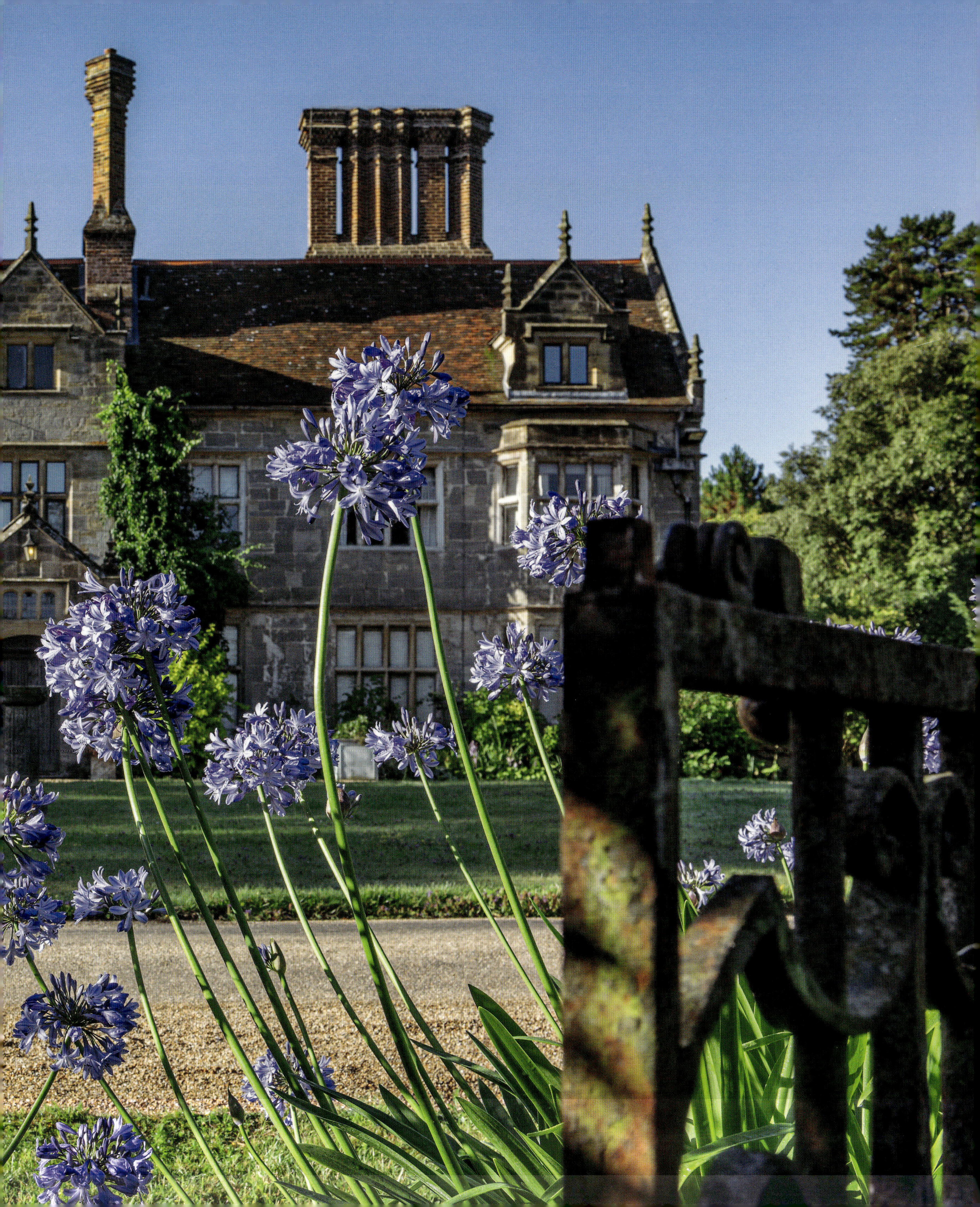

Introduction to the Garden

Spring comes early to Borde Hill. In February, as the gates reopen to visitors, snowdrops and hellebores brighten the dark days of late winter, while fragrant hamamelis scents the air. A month later, garden and parkland are dominated by the flowers of magnificent magnolias planted over the course of almost a hundred and twenty years. They are among the glories of the garden, and, together with other flowering trees and shrubs planted by Stephie over the first five decades of the twentieth century, once provided the main period of interest here, in spring and early summer. But all gardens must change and evolve, and Borde Hill has done just that. Developing it into a garden for all seasons, open from February to the end of October, has been the work of the current generation, Andrewjohn and Eleni Stephenson Clarke. They have introduced the design previously absent in this plant-led garden, and have planted perennials, annuals and bulbs throughout the formal garden around the house. Jay Robin's Rose Garden, the Mediterranean Garden, the White Garden, the Mid-Summer Border, Paradise Walk, the Italian Garden and the Round Dell have all been either created or redesigned under their guidance.

But Andrewjohn and Eleni have always remained acutely conscious of Stephie's legacy, as the garden tour over the following pages will show. Framework is given to the Stephenson Clarkes' new plantings by Stephie's ha-ha, the banks of rhododendrons and other shrubs that line the South Lawn, by the Garden of Allah to the north, and by the Azalea Ring to the east. A new Mediterranean Garden has been planted within the Victorian greenhouses, the propagation hub in Stephie's time. There are pleasant walks through Warren Wood and Stephanie's Glade, and through the South Park, although some areas of surrounding woodland are not accessible to the general public. Another important feature of the garden is the unrivalled collection of champion trees in private hands. These are the largest trees by girth or height in the British Isles, as listed on the Tree Register (TROBI).

During a walk around Borde Hill, its ever-changing vistas and rich, unusual planting make even the most casual of visitors constantly aware of the history of this unique garden.

A wrought-iron gate, surrounded by euonymus, camellias and hydrangeas, frames a late-autumn prospect of the West Bank.

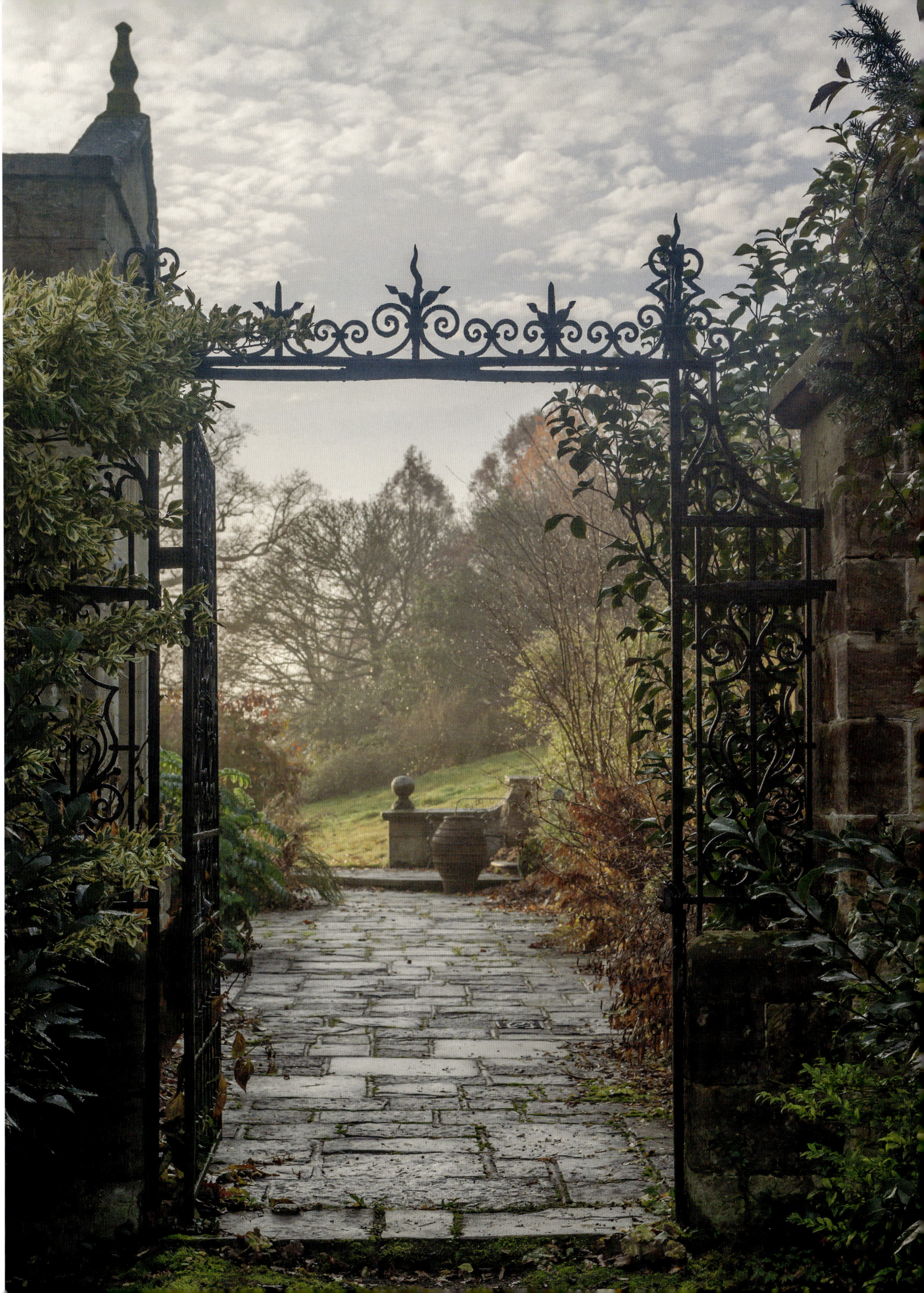

Old Rhododendron Garden

Among the first of the magnolias to put out its rich-pink flowers along leafless branches is the tall 'Goddess Magnolia', *Magnolia sprengeri* var. *diva*. This splendid tree was collected by Ernest Wilson in central China for the Veitch nursery in Chelsea and planted here in the 1910s. It soars above the entrance to the Old Rhododendron Garden, where visitors begin their garden tour.

Walking through a picket gate from the garden shop, you plunge straight into deep-green shrubberies at the core of Colonel Stephenson Robert Clarke's project. The Old Rhododendron Garden is so called because it was here in 1906 that he began his rhododendron collection in earnest. Spurred on by his friend Henry Elwes, Stephie turned a conventionally pretty country garden into one of national importance. On the site of former orchards, Stephie initially planted rhododendrons introduced to the United Kingdom from China by the nineteenth-century plant hunters Robert Fortune and Joseph Dalton Hooker.

The larger rhododendrons here are mostly hybrids of Himalayan species, in creamy whites and shades of pink, carmine and red. These include *Rhododendron arboreum*, *R. griffithianum*, *R. thomsonii* and *R. barbatum*, the last having dark, glossy leaves and crimson-scarlet flowers in early spring. *R. barbatum* was brought back by Hooker in the early 1850s after his imprisonment by the Rajah of Sikkim, and helped to launch the Victorian craze for rhododendrons. The first Chinese rhododendron to be introduced to Britain, *R. fortunei*, is also planted here, with its trusses of large mauvy-white flowers.

On the left is a grassy glade, cut through the Old Rhododendron Garden in the early 1970s and named after Jack Vass (head gardener, 1968–79), who propagated many of the rhododendron hybrids here.

But rhododendrons are not the only feature of this densely planted and wood-like area. As important to Stephie were the magnolias introduced to the UK by the early twentieth-

In May hybrids of Himalayan rhododendron species, including white *Rhododendron* 'Palestrina' and cerise *R.* 'Hinode-giri', fill Jack Vass Walk with glorious colour.

BORDE HILL GARDEN

THE GARDEN

The 'Goddess Magnolia', *Magnolia sprengeri* var. *diva*, in the Old Rhododendron Garden is the visitor's striking introduction to Borde Hill.

BORDE HILL GARDEN
78

Magnolias are an important feature of the Old Rhododendron Garden. On the left is *Magnolia dawsoniana* and, on the right, *M. sargentiana* var. *robusta*.

Right: The dark-pink-centred flowers of *Magnolia dawsoniana* are surrounded by layers of pink-tinged petals.

Far right: The pure-white blooms of *Magnolia* × *soulangeana* 'Brozzonii'.

Right: The tissue-paper blooms of *Magnolia dawsoniana*.

Far right: The unfurling flower of *Magnolia sargentiana* var. *robusta*.

century plant collectors. In the May 1938 issue of the *Journal of the Royal Horticultural Society*, he wrote that he had planted 'many favourite trees, especially Magnolias; amongst these are *Magnolia Sargentiana*, now in bud'. *Magnolia sargentiana* var. *robusta* (to give it its full name) has goblet-shaped rose-pink flowers. Wilson, who collected it in western China, tried unsuccessfully to germinate the seeds in the cold conditions of the Arnold Arboretum at Harvard, Massachusetts, where he was keeper. Instead, the tree was propagated at Chenault's Nursery in France, and was planted here after 1918. In the *Journal* article, Stephie was noting its first flowering at Borde Hill, when the tree had reached a height of 25 feet (7.6 m).

Stephie also refers to the nearby *Magnolia dawsoniana*, whose multi-stemmed branches regrew from suckers after the original tree fell down. Its star-shaped white flowers, just flushed with pink and as delicate as tissue paper, are perhaps the loveliest of all magnolia flowers.

Other magnolias here include *M. sieboldii*, *M.s.* subsp. *sinensis* 'Grandiflora' and *M.* 'Susan'. The last, a cross between *M. liliiflora* 'Nigra' and *M. stellata* 'Rosea', has lily-shaped reddish-purple flowers that appear in mid- to late spring.

The sense of being in an Asian woodland is heightened by other trees and shrubs planted through the Old Rhododendron Garden. These include several acers (*Acer cappadocicum* 'Aureum' and *A. rubrum* for striking autumn colour) and three different species of oak: *Quercus robur*, *Q. ilex* (the evergreen holm oak) and *Q. cerris*. There are stands of bamboo, along with a *Cornus kousa* and the serrated-leaved *Hoheria* 'Borde Hill', a shrub with small pure-white flowers in summer.

Over the years, there has been further lower-level planting through the Old Rhododendron Garden. Many of the rhododendrons are now underplanted with epimediums, early-flowering woodland plants that flourish in dappled shade, and with *Brunnera macrophylla* 'Jack Frost', remarkable as much for its white-iced leaves

Magnolia sargentiana var. *robusta* in full bloom.

Above: Jack Vass Walk, named after the head gardener in the 1960s and '70s, features a selection of evergreen rhododendrons.

Far left: Rhododendron oreodoxa var. *fargesii*.

Left: Rhododendron arboreum 'Barchard's Variety'.

as for its pale-blue flowers. In the open glades are sheets of daffodils in March, before the buttercup-yellow flowers of the Molly-the-Witch peony (*Paeonia daurica* subsp. *mlokosewitschii*) open in April and the pure-white *Viburnum* × *burkwoodii* 'Anne Russell' is sweetly fragrant.

In May the air is scented by wild garlic (*Allium ursinum*), interplanted with forget-me-nots and followed later in the month by the creamy-pink flowers of *Paeonia* 'Picotee' and then by *Geranium* 'Brookside'. Above is the honey locust tree, *Gleditsia triacanthos* f. *inermis* 'Sunburst', which turns a glorious gold in autumn. The nearby smoke bush, *Cotinus coggygria* 'Royal Purple', becomes a soft haze of tiny purple flowers, and its dark stems then give winter interest.

By the path to Jay Robin's Rose Garden stand three *Davidia involucrata*, covered in spring with white handkerchief flowers. Planted by Andrewjohn and Eleni, these young trees are descendants of the tree that Harry Veitch sent Wilson to search for in China in the early 1900s.

Above: Wild garlic, scattered through drifts of forget-me-nots (*Myosotis*), scents the air of the Old Rhododendron Garden in May.

Left: Paeonia 'Picotee' is an early single peony hybrid.

OLD RHODODENDRON GARDEN

Jay Robin's Rose Garden

Jay Robin's Rose Garden, created in 1996, was inspired by the description, mentioned on p. 33, of Stephie's rose garden in the *Country Life* article of 1902: 'The east garden, with its rose arch, has a radiant vista through a realm of floral loveliness. There are roses clustering on arches and walls, exhaling their fragrance in the sun.' As this garden had vanished several decades before Andrewjohn and Eleni took over responsibility for Borde Hill in 1988, they chose to reintroduce that quintessential English element here. Replacing double herbaceous borders, the new rose garden was the first of many design projects the couple would tackle over the next three decades, and it perfectly captures the spirit of the *Country Life* feature. Named after their (then) fourteen-year-old daughter, the garden was designed by Robin Williams senior (1935–2018), a gold-medal winner for Chelsea Flower Show gardens and a holder of the RHS Veitch Memorial Medal.

Within a framework of walls and yew hedging, Williams devised an intriguing geometrical layout, setting the garden at an angle to Borde Hill House. A straight, grass-edged path drives into Jay Robin's Rose Garden from the Old Rhododendron Garden. At forty-five degrees to this thoroughfare is another brick path, this one flanked by four box-framed triangles of roses, three with a lollipop bay at their centres. The diagonal line of this path carries the eye over the roses towards the roofline, which is framed by a line of topiary yews against the wall of a former kitchen garden. The effect of Williams's design is that the Elizabethan chimneys are immediately noticeable as you walk into the garden, and make a spectacular backdrop to the vibrant planting.

Opposite: The Elizabethan chimneys of Borde Hill House are the imposing background to the rich planting of Jay Robin's Rose Garden. Change is a feature of the garden at Borde Hill: the Bird of Paradise fountain has now been replaced.

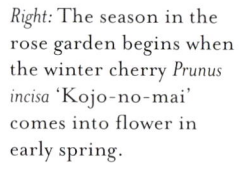

Right: The season in the rose garden begins when the winter cherry *Prunus incisa* 'Kojo-no-mai' comes into flower in early spring.

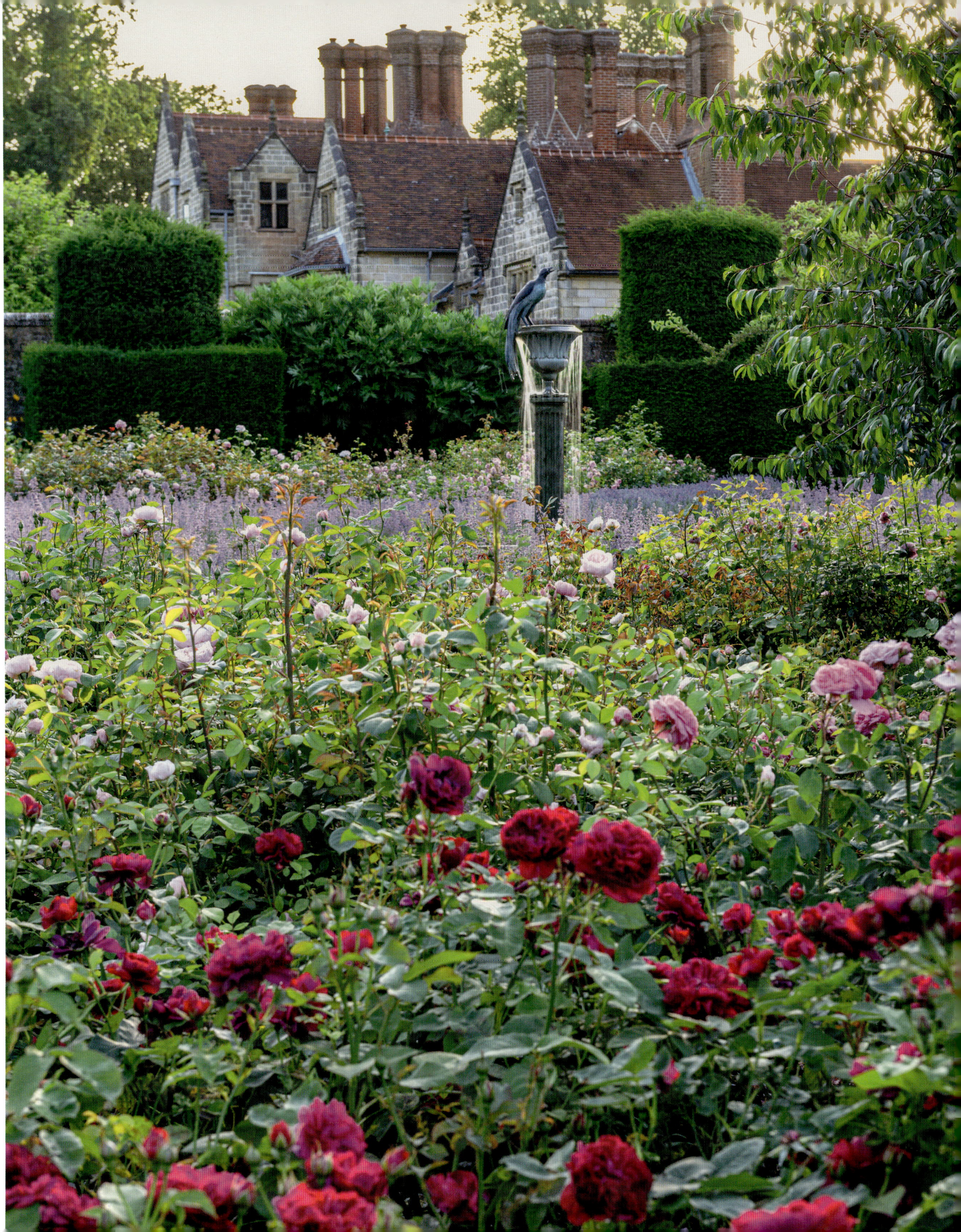

Above: A multi-stemmed, shiny red *Prunus serrula* is the centrepiece of one of the sections of Jay Robin's Rose Garden. In this bed the roses gradate from pale pink through to warm reds.

Left: An astrolabe surrounded by *Rosa* 'The Fairy'.

BORDE HILL GARDEN

Right: David Austin shrub roses in shades of apricot and pale and deep pink are highlighted by the central circle of soft-blue *Nepeta* × *faassenii*.

Right, bottom: Rosa Imogen is a lightly scented shrub rose from David Austin.

The yews are more than a century old. Once cut into parallel layers, they are currently being slowly pruned into octagons to match the chimneys.

At the heart of the rose garden is an arresting fountain statue of Aphrodite, installed in August 2020. Sculpted by Brendon Murless, the life-size copper filigree figure is studded with roses and has a face cast in copper resin. Her head thrown back, she holds up a bouquet of roses from which water bursts forth spectacularly. *Nepeta* × *faassenii* is planted around the central pool, with *Lavandula angustifolia* 'Loddon Blue' along the edges of the paths between the beds. The lavender is a long-lasting dwarf variety that is pruned hard after flowering. The rose beds are arranged around the fountain and were designed by Williams on a colour wheel of whites, creams and yellows through to dark reds. Ornamental trees among the roses add a further dimension. At one end, a crab apple, *Malus sargentii*, has white spring flowers and waxy bright-red fruits that are a magnet for birds in autumn. In a circle of grass within a rose bed is a Tibetan cherry, *Prunus serrula*, the striated red bark of which gleams in sunlight or in rain.

Some 500 roses, mostly repeat flowerers from David Austin and all chosen for their fragrance, were planted initially through the four beds, so as to make the garden a sensuous feast from June through to October. Over the years, there have been losses and additions, although some highly scented shrub roses – among them pale-pink Brother Cadfael and 'Fritz Nobis', rich-pink Gertrude Jekyll and dark-red Chianti – remain from the original planting.

In 2020 there were 105 rose varieties in the garden and about 750 individual roses in all. As one in ten probably now needs replacing, about seventy-five roses are likely to be changed each year. Recent introductions include the shrub roses Buttercup (yellow), Winchester Cathedral (pinky white), Olivia Rose Austin (mid-pink), Darcey Bussell (crimson pink) and L.D. Braithwaite (crimson). The planting of the warm-apricot Lady of Shalott has helped to intensify the colour mix in the garden.

Against the yew hedge between the rose garden and the adjacent Mediterranean Garden are two lines of posts, divided by an arch covered with *Rosa* 'Sander's White Rambler'. Suspended from post to post are swags of newly introduced rambling roses, including fragrant light-pink 'Albertine', small-flowered mid-pink 'Blush Rambler' and salmon-pink 'Paul Noël', with Rambling Rosie (a white-centred red rose from

JAY ROBIN'S ROSE GARDEN

From left to right: Rosa Port Sunlight; *R.* Lady Emma Hamilton; *R.* Kathryn Morley.

From left to right: Rosa 'Felicia', a hybrid musk raised in 1926 by a clergyman, the Reverend Joseph Pemberton; the rambler *R.* 'Paul's Himalayan Musk'; *R.* Harlow Carr.

From left to right: Rosa Gertrude Jekyll; *R.* Golden Celebration.

BORDE HILL GARDEN

Peter Beales) and blush-pink The Albrighton Rambler from David Austin. The last three, unusually for ramblers, are repeat flowerers. On the posts between the swags are David Austin climbers: The Generous Gardener and James Galway (both pink), with apricot-coloured Wollerton Old Hall. These sweetly scented roses are underplanted with dark penstemons.

Another recent introduction is *Rosa* Frank Kingdon Ward, a hybrid of *R. gigantea* bred in India in 2012. This prickly, vigorous climber is a nod to the plant hunter who introduced so many plants to Borde Hill, and is planted against the wall by the yew topiary. Also in this bed are a spectacular tree peony, *Paeonia* 'Anne Rosse', with ruffled yellow petals, and other herbaceous perennials.

Running alongside the main path is the Blue Border, beyond which is the Shady Garden, a quiet, green contrast to the exuberant colour in the border and rose garden. In this grassy semicircle, on either side of the wooden Bride's Shelter, Harvey Stephens (head gardener in the 1990s) planted the rare *Picrasma quassioides*, a deciduous tree native to the Himalayas and appropriate for Borde Hill, given the provenance of so many of its shrubs and trees. Nearby, underplanted with *Liriope muscari*, is a *Maackia amurensis* from north-eastern China, probably introduced to the UK by one of the Victorian plant hunters. It is a member of the pea family and has white panicles; its sister, a champion by girth, is by the car park.

With a dark cotinus at one end and *Pittosporum tenuifolium* 'Irene Paterson' at the other, the Blue Border has changed considerably from Robin Williams's original plan. Its development in the winter of 2019–20 was partly influenced by a talk given by the Dublin-based garden designer Helen Dillon and heard by the former head gardener Andy Stevens. 'Everyone sat up when she mentioned her blue border', he says. 'That made me think it would be a good idea for Borde Hill.' Stevens designed four metal girdles, which spread out at the top, to replace tapering wooden obelisks that were rotting away; these wider girdles work better for winding climbers, and are planted with blue clematis and coral-pink *Rosa* 'Compassion'.

The new planting scheme for the border was designed by the rest of the garden team. It is now edged with a bee attractor, germander (*Teucrium* × *lucidrys*), which has also been used elsewhere in the rose garden to replace blight-affected box. A Mediterranean plant growing in rich Borde Hill soil, it needs pruning twice a year. The planting within the border, in shades of blue from sapphire through to deep purples, prolongs the season of interest in the rose garden. Lower wands of *Salvia nemorosa* 'Caradonna' and *S.n.* 'Ostfriesland' alternate with spires of dusky-purple *Delphinium* 'Pagan Purples' and with various asters, aconites and the tall, brush-like white flowers of *Actaea simplex* (Atropurpurea Group) 'Brunette'. Other planting includes hardy geraniums, deep-blue *Lobelia siphilitica* and *Thalictrum* 'Elin' for height and impact.

This is one of the most labour-intensive areas at Borde Hill. The beds are mulched annually and weeded by hoeing (fine in summer, but more difficult when the clay soil becomes waterlogged in autumn), while the roses are given a granular feed twice a year and a foliar feed later in the season. A new approach to the pruning regime is being trialled to create a slightly different look, stimulated by the visit of a garden team member to Alnwick Castle garden: the aim is to make the roses higher in the middle around the lollipop bays and lower at the edges. The process will take three or four years, with more mid-season pruning needed to achieve the desired shape.

Jay Robin's Rose Garden has been a great success, for, as Borde Hill council member Jim Gardiner says, it is 'a quality garden, laid out effectively in its space and very attractive to visitors'. This is borne out on a summer's day: everyone is naturally drawn to the rose garden by its colour, aspect and, above all, its almost overwhelming fragrance.

An aerial view reveals the strong geometrical structure devised for Jay Robin's Rose Garden by Robin Williams in 1996.

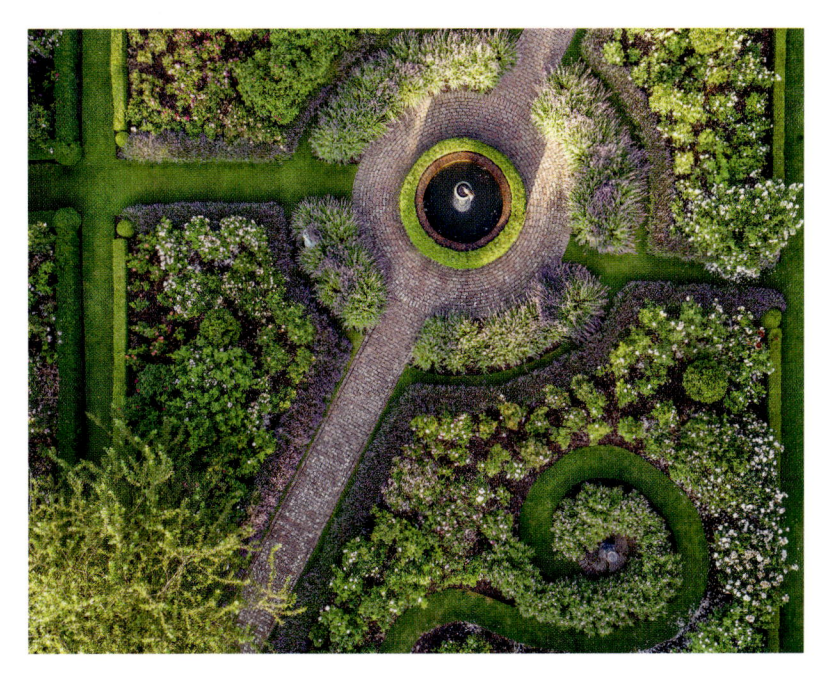

BORDE HILL GARDEN

In early-morning mist, Jay Robin's Rose Garden is particularly magical, with the soft light intensifying the blue of the lavender (*Lavandula angustifolia* 'Loddon Blue'). The fountain statue of Aphrodite was installed in 2020.

Mediterranean Garden and Victorian Greenhouses

Below: An arch smothered with *Rosa* 'Sander's White Rambler' leads from Jay Robin's Rose Garden into the Mediterranean Garden.

Passing from Jay Robin's Rose Garden under the arch of *Rosa* 'Sander's White Rambler' and through a yew hedge, you walk into the Mediterranean Garden, also designed by Robin Williams. This was once the site of a Victorian greenhouse that housed orange trees and South American plants, including a puya, before being badly damaged by the hurricane of 1987. When the new design was implemented, the waist-high brick walls of the greenhouse were retained, while panels of pale-blue trellising replaced the windows.

Effects here are derived from the shape and colour of foliage as much as from flowers. Over the entrance arch runs *Vitis* 'Brant', with dark-green leaves that turn a mix of scarlet, russet, gold and pink in autumn. A simple terracotta amphora stands in the middle of the courtyard on ground laid with flagstones and embedded gravel. It overflows with scarlet ivy-leaved pelargoniums, and is surrounded by smaller pots, also planted with pelargoniums and with *Senecio candicans* Angel Wings. The senecio is easy to propagate, and its silvery-grey foliage makes it a useful background plant elsewhere in the garden. Here it contrasts well with the bright pelargoniums.

Structural plants around the edges of the garden include a pencil cedar, *Trachycarpus fortunei*, pineapple broom (better known as *Cytisus battandieri* but now called *Argyrocytisus battandieri*) and the loquat tree, *Eriobotrya japonica*, with large stripy leaves and curvy branches. Through the trellising runs another vine, the purple-leaved *Vitis vinifera* 'Purpurea'. A deciduous jasmine, *Jasminum × stephanense*, runs over one wall; this has pinnate leaves and star-shaped pinky-white flowers. In pots are a pomegranate (*Punica granatum*) and waxy-leaved evergreen *Pittosporum tobira*.

Around the little courtyard grow sun-loving, drought-resistant plants, including agapanthus, olives and orange in pots, spiky blue-flowered perovskias (*Salvia yangii*) in late summer, and the glaucous *Melianthus major*, with saw-toothed leaves and occasional brick-red flowers in spring after a mild winter. Rosemary and helichrysum release aromas of the Mediterranean in high summer.

What is now the Mediterranean Garden was once one of a range of Victorian greenhouses, listed in the 1893 sales particulars; they became the powerhouse of Borde Hill's garden in the 1920s and '30s. The team of twenty-five or so gardeners spent much of their working lives here, caring for peach, apricot and fig trees and for ornamental plants both for the house and for summer displays in pots around the formal garden. One or more of the greenhouses would have housed Stephie's orchid collection (the sales catalogue of 1949 listed over 450 species and cultivars); in others, the gardeners would have been busy propagating, grafting and crossing plants introduced from overseas or from gifts from Stephie's gardening friends. It was here that Walter Fleming grew the legendary and award-winning *Camellia × williamsii* 'Donation', having crossed *C. japonica* 'Donckelaeri' (now called *C.j.* 'Masayoshi') with the pale-pink *C. saluenensis*, the latter a gift from J.C. Williams at Caerhays.

Although this area is no longer the beating heart of Borde Hill, there is a numinous quality to these wonderful old greenhouses, and their names evoke the endeavours once carried out here: the Africa House, the Deep House and the Peach and Melon Houses. Some have been replaced by aluminium-framed buildings, while the original cast-iron winding gear, floor grates, glass and pipework of the Africa House (which

Opposite: Vitis 'Brant' runs over the entrance arch to the Mediterranean Garden, which was created from a derelict Victorian greenhouse. A terracotta amphora is planted with red pelargoniums and surrounded by other pots of pelargoniums and the silver-leaved *Senecio candicans* Angel Wings.

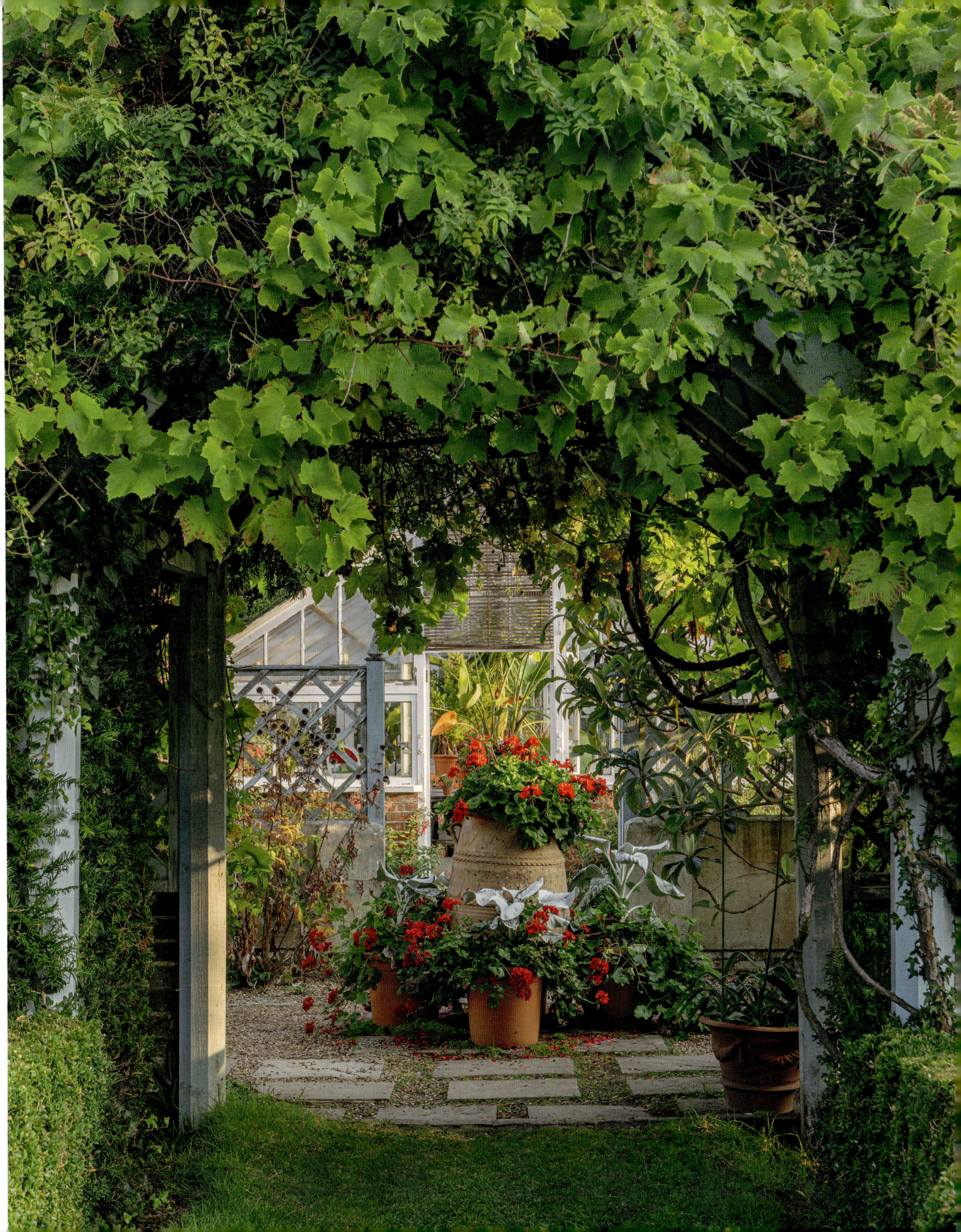

BORDE HILL GARDEN

Opposite, top left: The Africa House, one of the greenhouses restored between 1997 and 1999, is still used for overwintering tender plants.

Opposite, top right: Although now rusted with age, the intact winding gear of the Fig House is a monument to Victorian engineering.

Opposite, bottom: During the biennial summer exhibition, sculptures are displayed in the Africa House. In 2021 these included abstract circles by Rosie Jones and a figure by Christine Baxter.

Left: The Peach House.

housed Becky's nerine collection) and Peach House were restored in 1997–99 with a Heritage Lottery Fund grant. Others, such as the Fig House, are glassless, but the good-quality Victorian cedar frames are still intact, as are the decorative ironwork and the winding gear.

Some have vanished altogether: the oldest greenhouse, the Deep House, is now derelict, while the low brick walls of the former Melon House enclose a rose garden designed by Charles Quest-Ritson. The roses are all Gold Standard roses, tested for their health, floriferousness and scent by the British Association of Rose Breeders, which donated the selection to Borde Hill in 2010. They range from patio to rambler roses and include floribunda roses Belmonte and 'Lucky' (both pink) and yellow Maid of Honour. Among other plants featured here are perovskias, nepeta and *Pittosporum tenuifolium* 'Purpureum', with drums of *Cephalotaxus harringtonia* 'Fastigiata' for evergreen structure.

There is a quiet sense of activity. Fuchsias, agapanthus, *Verbena bonariensis* and phygelius spill out from the brickwork footings of the greenhouses. The Africa House is still used for overwintering and for tender South African plants such as nerines and strelitzias, while plant exhibits and historical information are displayed in the Peach House. In an aluminium greenhouse tucked away in one corner are tender, fragrant rhododendrons from Burma, acquired by Robert Stephenson Clarke (and now needing less protection than they did forty years ago, thanks to warmer winters).

Bushes of *Paeonia* × *lemoinei* 'Souvenir de Maxime Cornu' flourish along a wall in the greenhouse area. Different blooms vary in colour from yellow to peach.

MEDITERRANEAN GARDEN AND VICTORIAN GREENHOUSES

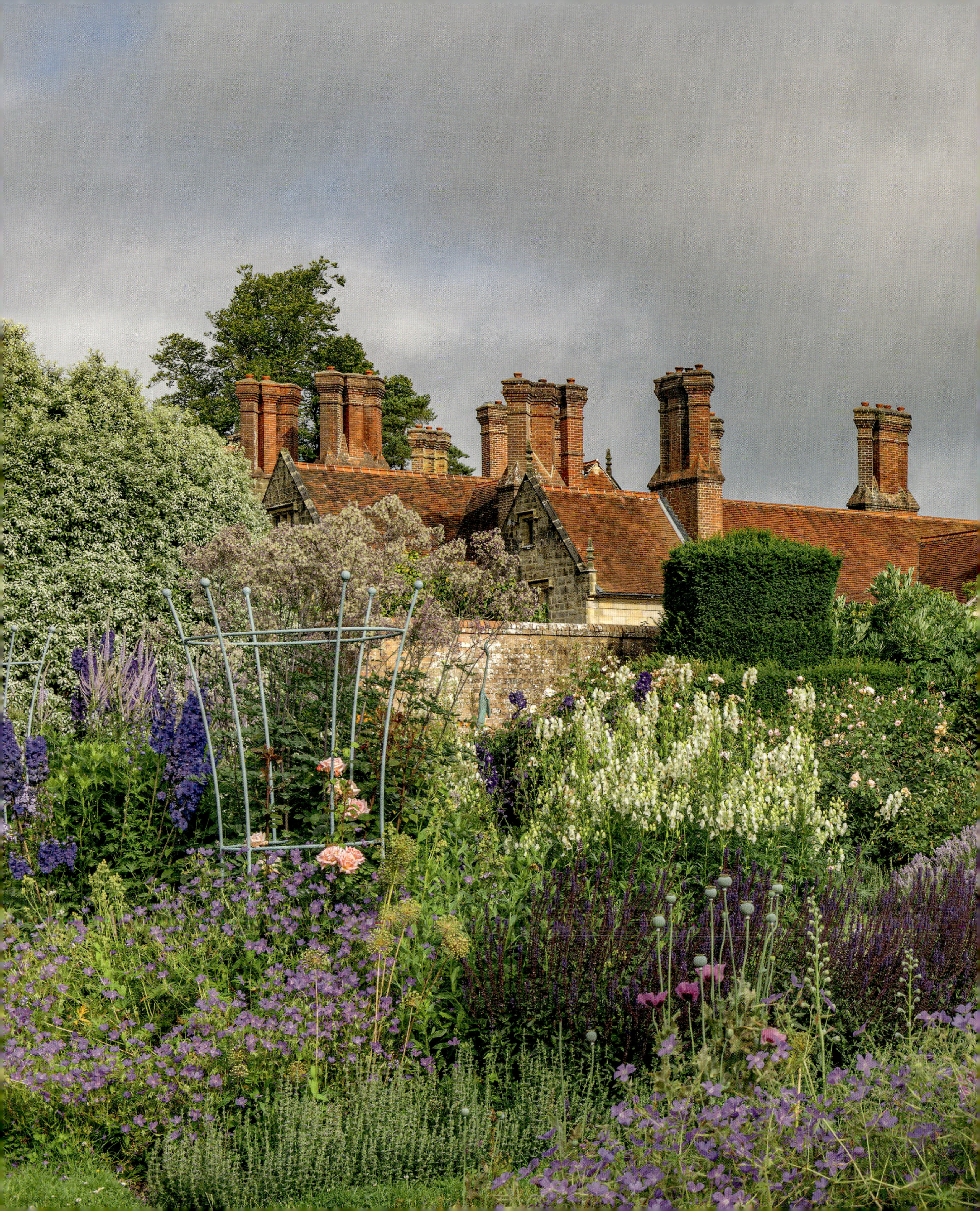

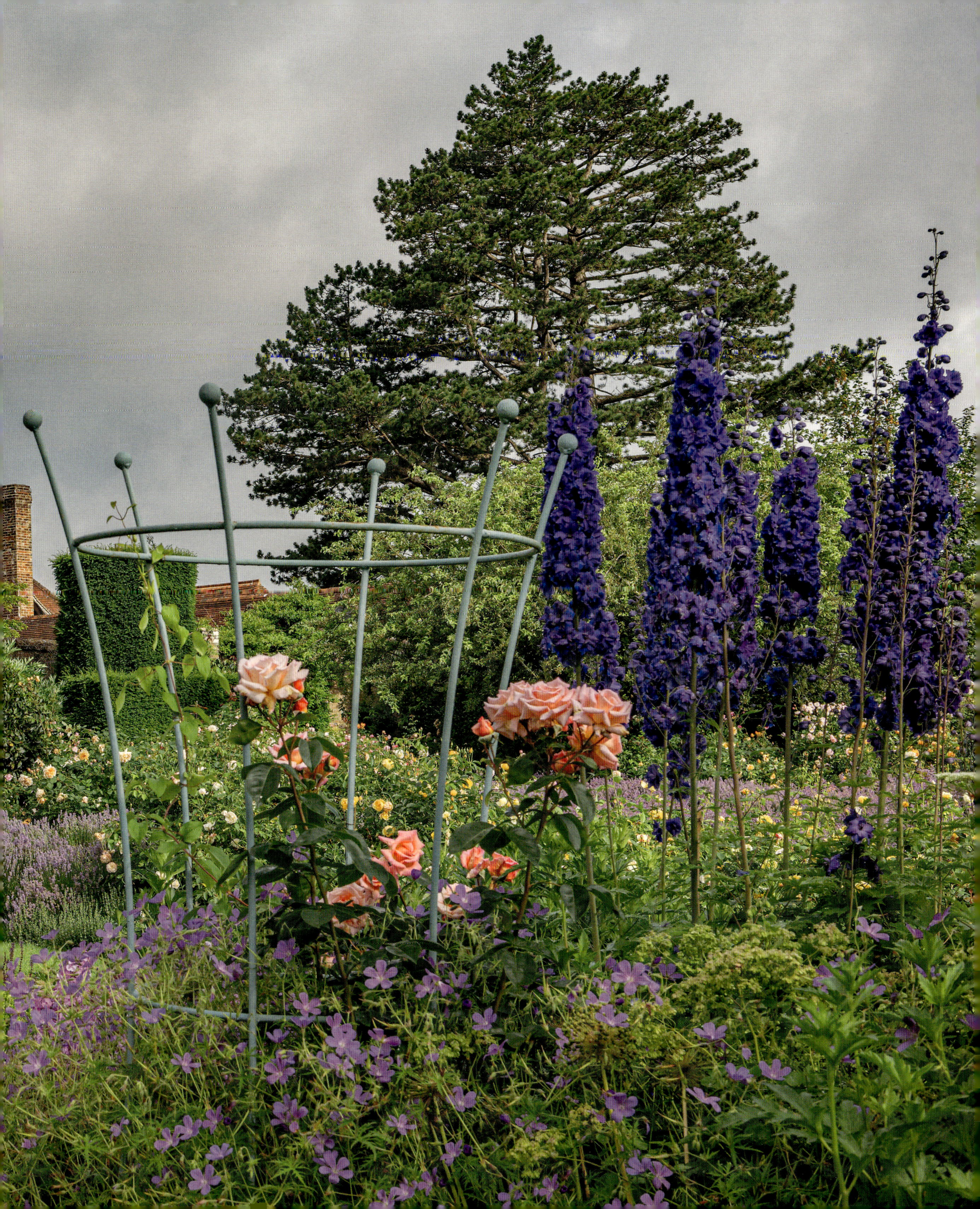

White Garden

The red-brick path through Jay Robin's Rose Garden and the Blue Border leads into the White Garden, an intimate, bosky corner tucked away between yew hedging and walls. Like the Mediterranean Garden, it marks another change of tempo after the dazzling profusion of the roses. These pleasing variations in pace have been skilfully introduced by the Stephenson Clarkes in their redesigns, creating an intriguing journey of exploration through the formal gardens around the house.

Here, eucalyptus, a box tree, *Pittosporum tobira*, *Ligustrum quihoui*, *Hoheria* 'Glory of Amlwch' and the lily of the valley tree, *Crinodendron patagua*, provide the framework for other planting. Along the wall is trained star jasmine (*Trachelospermum jasminoides*), sweetly scented in June. Also on the walls are various clematis, including the early *Clematis* 'Miss Bateman', which has large pink-tinged white flowers with purple centres. *C.* Samaritan Jo, from Raymond Evison on Guernsey, has star-shaped purple-edged silvery flowers that appear from early summer to late autumn. In early spring the pale-pink flowers of Walter Fleming's award-winning *Camellia* 'Salutation' (a cross between *C. reticulata* and *C. saluenensis*) appear above the

Pages 96–97: The Blue Border, beside the rose garden, carries the season through into late summer with *Delphinium* 'Pagan Purples', *Salvia nemorosa* 'Caradonna', *S.n.* 'Ostfriesland', hardy geraniums and *Thalictrum* 'Elin'.

Below: In late summer the delicate flowers of *Anemone* × *hybrida* 'Honorine Jobert' are highlights of the White Garden.

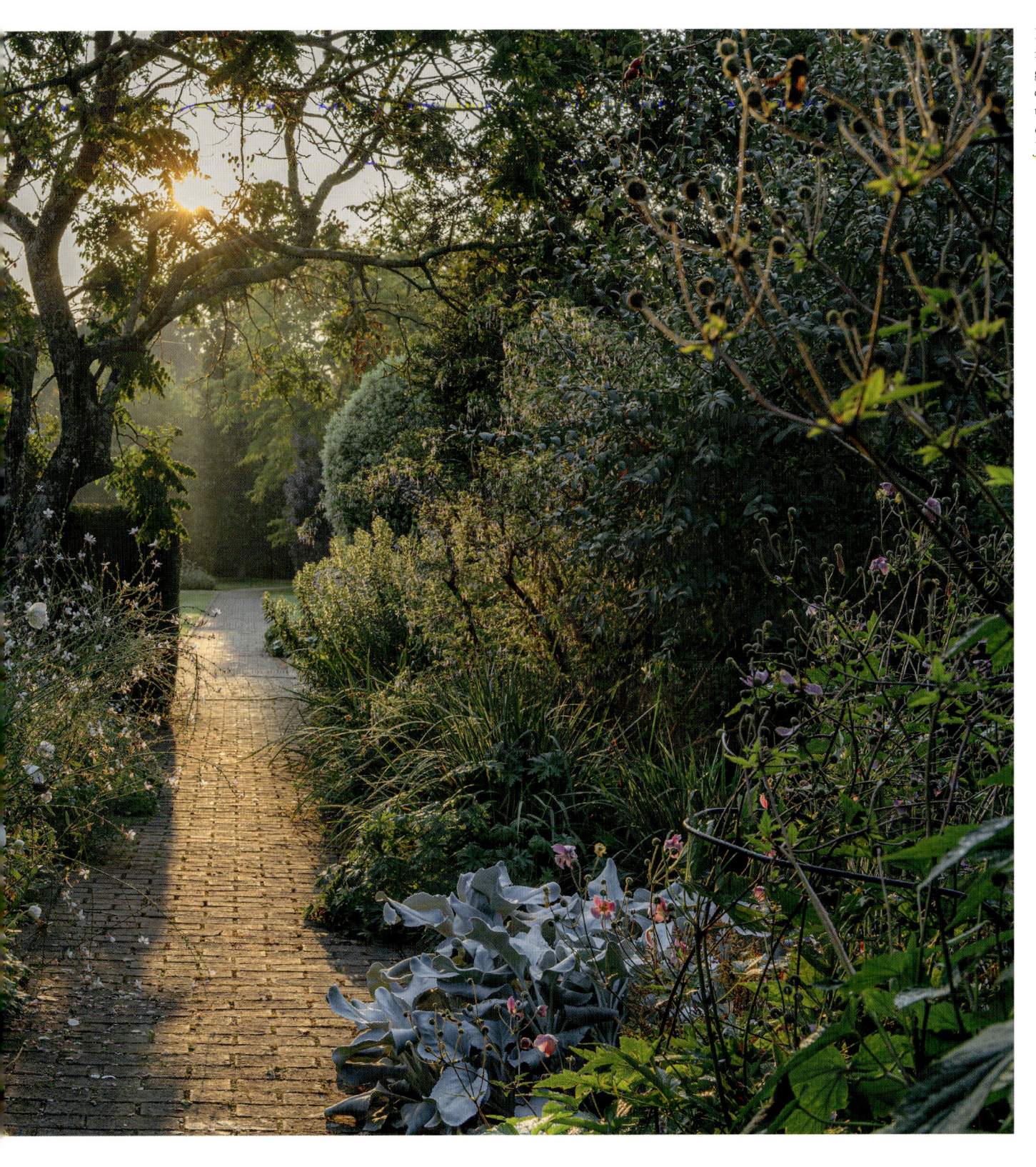

Early autumn sunshine illuminates the silvery-grey leaves of *Senecio candicans* Angel Wings in the White Garden and dew on the lawn of the Jay Robin Rose Garden.

BORDE HILL GARDEN

Opposite, top: A graceful pinky-white *Fuchsia magellanica* overhangs dainty, late-flowering *Oenothera lindheimeri*.

Far left: Hydrangea arborescens 'Annabelle'.

Left: Astilbe Younique White, or false goat's beard, flourishes in the slightly damp conditions of the White Garden.

A corner of the White Garden in August, with the long-flowering *Hydrangea arborescens* 'Annabelle', *Hoheria* 'Glory of Amlwch' and *Clematis recta*.

Opposite, bottom, from left to right: Camellia saluenensis, one of the parent plants of *C.* 'Salutation'; the award-winning cross *C.* 'Salutation', bred by Walter Fleming, can be seen over the wall from the White Garden; a white tree peony.

wall from what is now the house tenants' garden.

Plants tumble out across the paths, creating a relaxed feeling of abundance. Highlights at the corners are the silvery-grey leaves of *Senecio candicans* Angel Wings, a link with the Mediterranean Garden. White hardy geraniums, irises (including 'White Swan') and *Paeonia rockii* in May are followed in July by white agapanthus and the bolder flowers of *Lilium regale*, a plant originally discovered in China in the 1910s by Ernest Wilson. During his search, he broke his leg and was left for the rest of his life with what he called his 'lily limp'.

White veronicastrums, achilleas, phlox, sanguisorba, the blowsy-headed *Hydrangea arborescens* 'Annabelle', *Aruncus dioicus* and tall, daisy-like *Vernonia arkansana* 'Alba' flowers together take the season in the White Garden forward to the autumn. The beds then are full of asters, fuchsias, single and double white anemones, white autumn crocuses and the dainty gaura flowers (*Oenothera lindheimeri*) on wispy long stems.

WHITE GARDEN

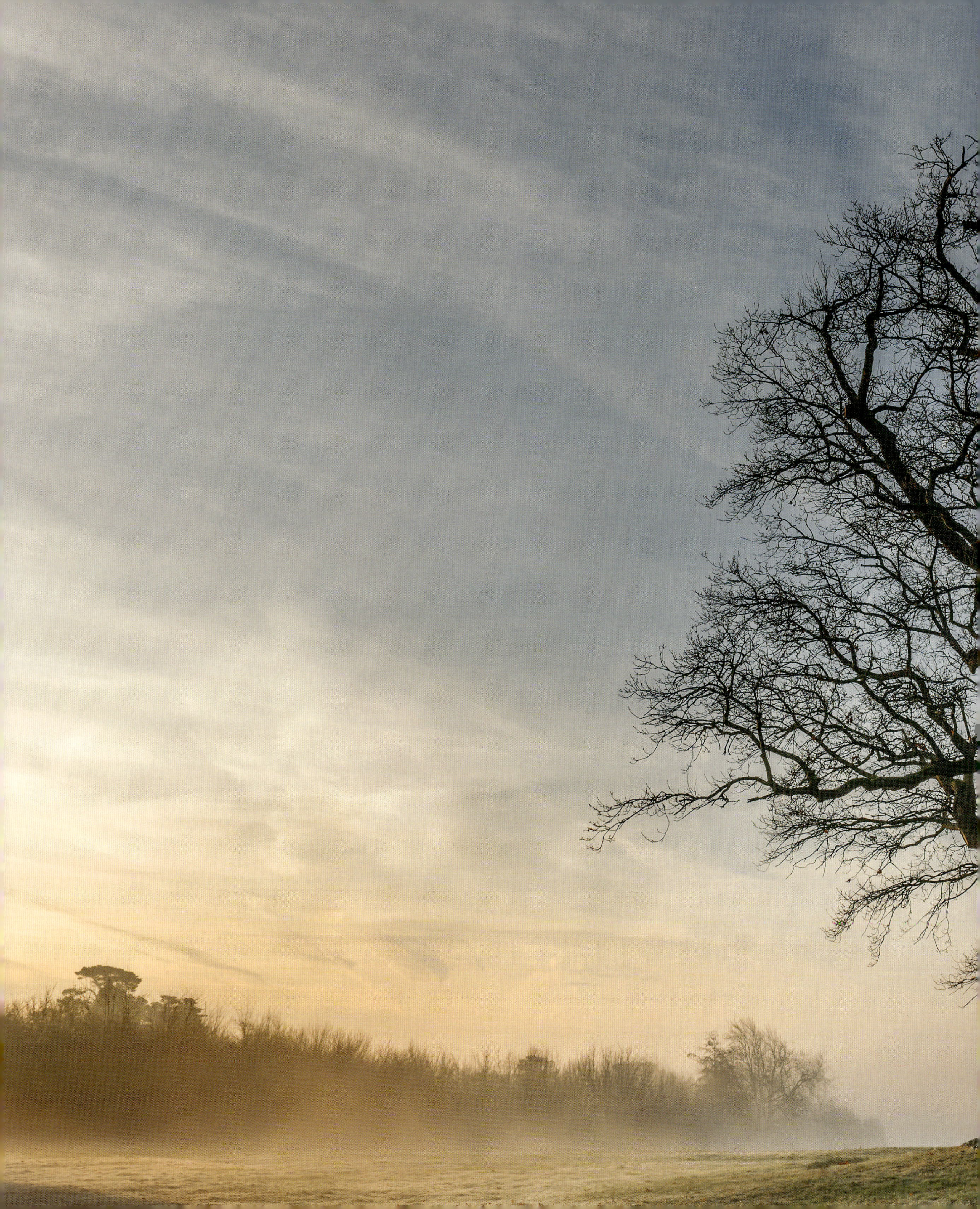

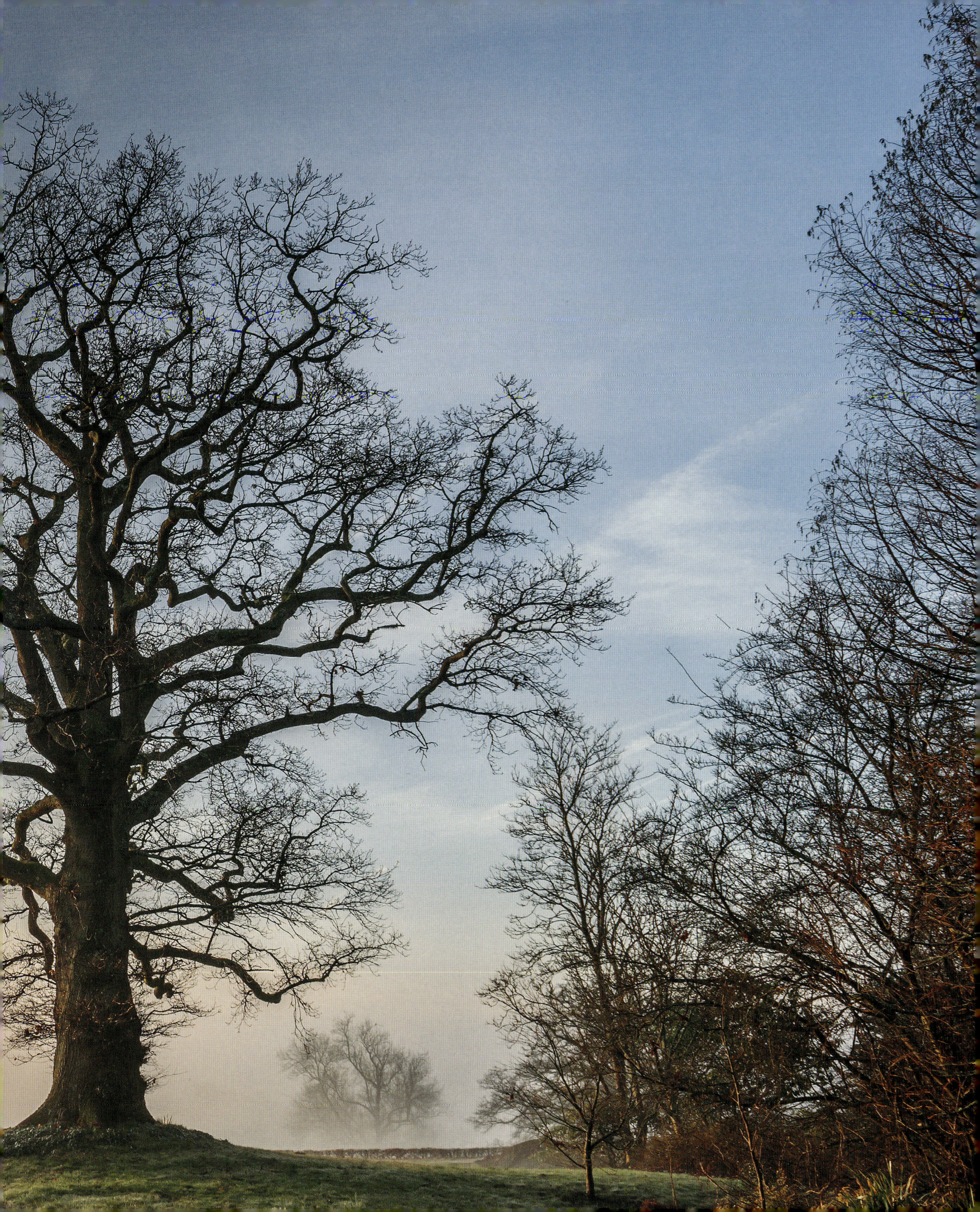

South Lawn and Mid-Summer Border

Shortly after buying Borde Hill, Stephie opened out the view from the back of the house to the south. The 1870 sale catalogue shows a parterre from which the ground slopes upwards to a croquet lawn, with the branches of a fine old oak just visible to one side. Stephie retained this centuries-old oak, along with an equally ancient oak on the far side; both still tower above the lawn. But in 1898 he swept away the parterre, levelled the ground and laid a wide apron of grass with a ha-ha beyond so that his new South Lawn would appear to run seamlessly out into the parkland and wooded hills. This is one of the finest prospects at Borde Hill, matching but different from the view to the north over the Ouse Valley and the railway viaduct.

Visitors always linger on the benches and paths of the South Lawn, for this wide expanse of grass, bordered by rhododendrons, camellias and other rare trees and shrubs, represents so much of what Borde Hill has to offer. The vista

Pages 102–103: In winter the ancient oak at the south-western corner of the South Lawn is outlined against the cold sky.

Left: Helenium 'Moerheim Beauty', carpet roses and bright dahlias carry the season on into autumn in the Mid-Summer Border.

Below: Although mostly hot colours are used in this border, agapanthus brings an accent of blue in July and August, and works well with the lime-green leaves of *Catalpa bignonioides* 'Aurea' behind.

THE GARDEN

Far right: Miniature daffodils, including *Narcissus* 'Hawera', and *Tulipa sylvestris* have naturalized beneath the dominant South Lawn oak.

changes constantly. In mid-winter the grass is spangled with frost and the old *Quercus robur* at the south-western corner of the lawn stands like a majestic skeleton against the grey sky. The mellow stonework of the fine old house glows in the cold light, with a dark pine behind and an evergreen *Magnolia grandiflora* 'Goliath' reaching almost to the roof.

Come spring and the ground beneath the oak is carpeted with hundreds of miniature daffodils, *Narcissus* 'Hawera', followed by similar-coloured *Tulipa sylvestris* and blue muscari. Mist rises from the parkland beyond early on hot summer mornings. In autumn, pink and white ivy-leaved cyclamens (*Cyclamen hederifolium*) appear among the roots of the oaks on both sides of the lawn.

In the 1870 picture, there is a suggestion that Victorian shrubberies edged the lawn. These were replaced over several decades in the early twentieth century by Stephie's new rhododendron introductions, at their best in late spring and early summer. Only a selection of small-leaved rhododendrons now remain on the west side, many of those planted by Robert Stephenson Clarke in the 1970s and '80s. These rhododendrons are in pinks, purples and reds, and are mixed with evergreen Kurume azaleas.

Rhododendrons on the east side of the lawn include *Rhododendron* 'Bonfire', *R.* 'Romany Chai' and *R.* 'Wilgen's Ruby', in shades of red. *R.* 'Pink Pearl' grows next to what is probably a parent,

Right: Narcissus 'Hawera'.

BORDE HILL GARDEN
106

SOUTH LAWN AND MID-SUMMER BORDER

Daylilies, echinops and floribunda roses make a bright display against the soft-purple plumes of the smoke bush, *Cotinus coggygria* 'Royal Purple'.

the white-flowered *R.* 'George Hardy'. Standing above other rhododendron hybrids, camellias and azaleas is a splendid Chinese bean tree, *Catalpa bungei* Duclouxii Group (*Catalpa fargesii* f. *duclouxii*), collected in western China around 1900 and with striking pink-freckled white flowers in May and June.

The South Lawn is at its most colourful in late winter and spring, with many camellias flowering amid the banks of dark-green foliage. A wonderful white camellia, *Camellia* × *williamsii* 'Francis Hanger', flowers by the lawn in February and March, followed closely by rosy-pink *C. japonica* 'Akashigata'. Deep-red *C.j.* 'Adolphe Audusson' features on both sides of the lawn.

After their radiant display in May, the rhododendrons become a gleaming-green backdrop to other richly flamboyant and newer planting by Andrewjohn and Eleni. At the south-eastern corner of the lawn, for instance, is the Mid-Summer Border, a teardrop-shaped bed of fiery-coloured perennials, grasses and shrubs. It was designed in 2011 by Dr Tony Lord, a former gardens adviser to the National Trust and a holder of the RHS Victoria Medal of Honour. His starting point was to mix herbaceous perennials with the Gold Standard roses donated to Borde Hill by the British Association of Rose Breeders. The roses here include four floribundas – crimson Red Finesse, tangerine Easy Does It, golden-yellow Nurse Tracey Davies and blush-ivory Champagne Moment – and the bushy purple-red shrub rose Wild Thing.

Pale *Hydrangea paniculata* 'Limelight' acts as a contrast, set against darker *Cotinus coggygria* 'Royal Purple', *Physocarpus opulifolius* Diable D'Or and *Berberis* × *ottawensis* f. *purpurea* 'Superba'. *Verbena bonariensis*, *Hakonechloa macra* 'Alboaurea' and taller *Calamagrostis brachytricha* and *Miscanthus sinensis* 'Gracillimus' flow gracefully through the lower perennials. The grasses turn golden towards autumn, and in winter their seed heads look sensational when edged with frost, as do those of *Phlomis fruticosa*. The rest of the planting is in hot shades, with drifts of *Helenium*

Opposite, top: Grasses, heleniums, dark sedums, roses and phygelius are used in bold blocks in this border.

Opposite, bottom, from left to right: *Helenium* 'Moerheim Beauty'; *Crocosmia* × *crocosmiiflora* 'Carmin Brillant'; *Geum* 'Totally Tangerine'.

SOUTH LAWN AND MID-SUMMER BORDER

'Moerheim Beauty', *Crocosmia* × *crocosmiiflora* 'Carmin Brillant' and various phygelius from the Somerford Funfair range in orange, coral and yellow. There are fleshy, dark-leaved burgundy-red sedums (*Hylotelephium* 'Marchants Best Red' and 'Matrona') and pink-flowered, green-leaved *Heuchera* 'Paris', with *Geranium* 'Brookside' for a touch of violet blue against the hotter colours.

The Autumn Border, across the path, is a gorgeous spread of reds, plums, oranges and purples. It was designed in 1993 by Jack Vass, who lived on the estate and continued to be involved in the garden after his retirement as head gardener in 1979. There are echoes of the Mid-Summer Border, with the reappearance of such shrubs as *Cotinus coggygria* 'Royal Purple' as well as the fierier *Cotinus* 'Grace'. Other planting includes hot-coloured dahlias, heleniums, *Rosa* Hot Chocolate, more *Verbena bonariensis*, *Crocosmia* × *crocosmiiflora* 'Carmin Brillant', *Rosa glauca*, asters, purple corylus, rudbeckia and blue *Salvia uliginosa*. The last is pruned in May (the so-called Chelsea chop) to stop it sprawling in autumn. The herbaceous planting is backed by miscanthus, *Crataegus persimilis* 'Prunifolia', *Hydrangea quercifolia*, podocarpus, yellow pyracantha, purple-berried *Callicarpa japonica* and crab apples *Malus* × *zumi* 'Golden Hornet' and *M.* × *robusta* 'Yellow Siberian'.

Among the rhododendrons, autumn colour comes from the Japanese sumac (*Toxicodendron trichocarpum*), *Liquidambar styraciflua*, *Acer pseudoplatanus* and a Kingdon Ward introduction (KW20856), *A. pectinatum* subsp. *taronense*. Another Kingdon Ward discovery (KW21009) is *Sorbus harrowiana*, with bright-red berries in autumn. In winter *Garrya elliptica* displays grey-green tassels that look like Harrods doormen.

Along the railings above the ha-ha is a line of rambling roses, including Rambling Rosie, and also Gold Standard roses, planted in about 2010. A footpath runs parallel to the ha-ha across the south side of the lawn, past another immemorial oak, towards Paradise Walk. But before we turn our steps there, we shall pause to look at the West Bank.

Above and right: Catalpa fargesii f. *duclouxii* (now known as *Catalpa bungei* Duclouxii Group) was collected in western China in about 1900 and is listed in the 1935 *Catalogue of the Trees and Shrubs at Borde Hill, Sussex*.

Opposite: The edges of the South Lawn are spangled with bluebells beside the evergreen *Rhododendron* 'Hinode-giri', which is a wonderful shade of cerise in May.

Pages 112–13: Robertsmere, a lake created in the South Park in the early 1990s in memory of Robert Stephenson Clarke.

BORDE HILL GARDEN

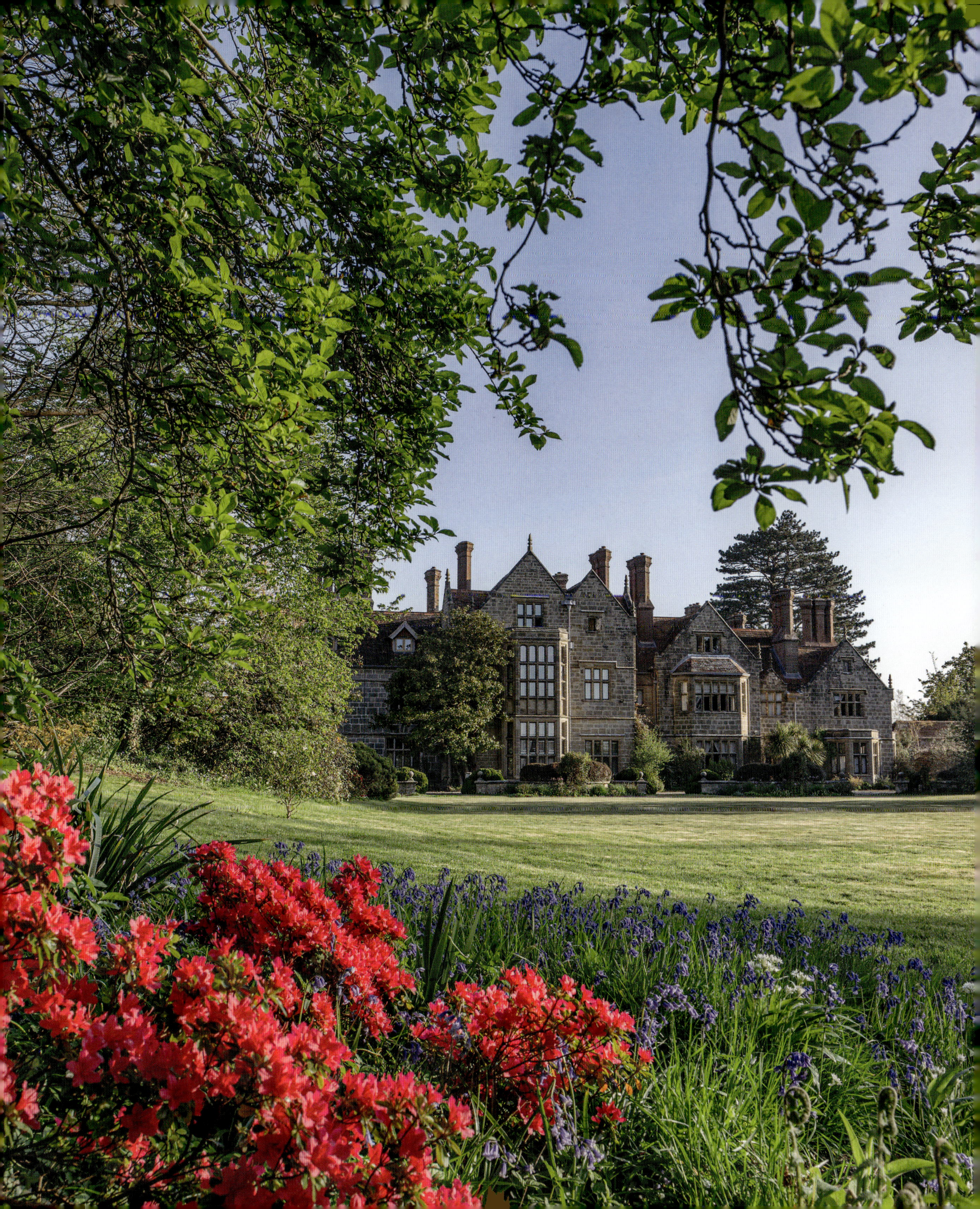

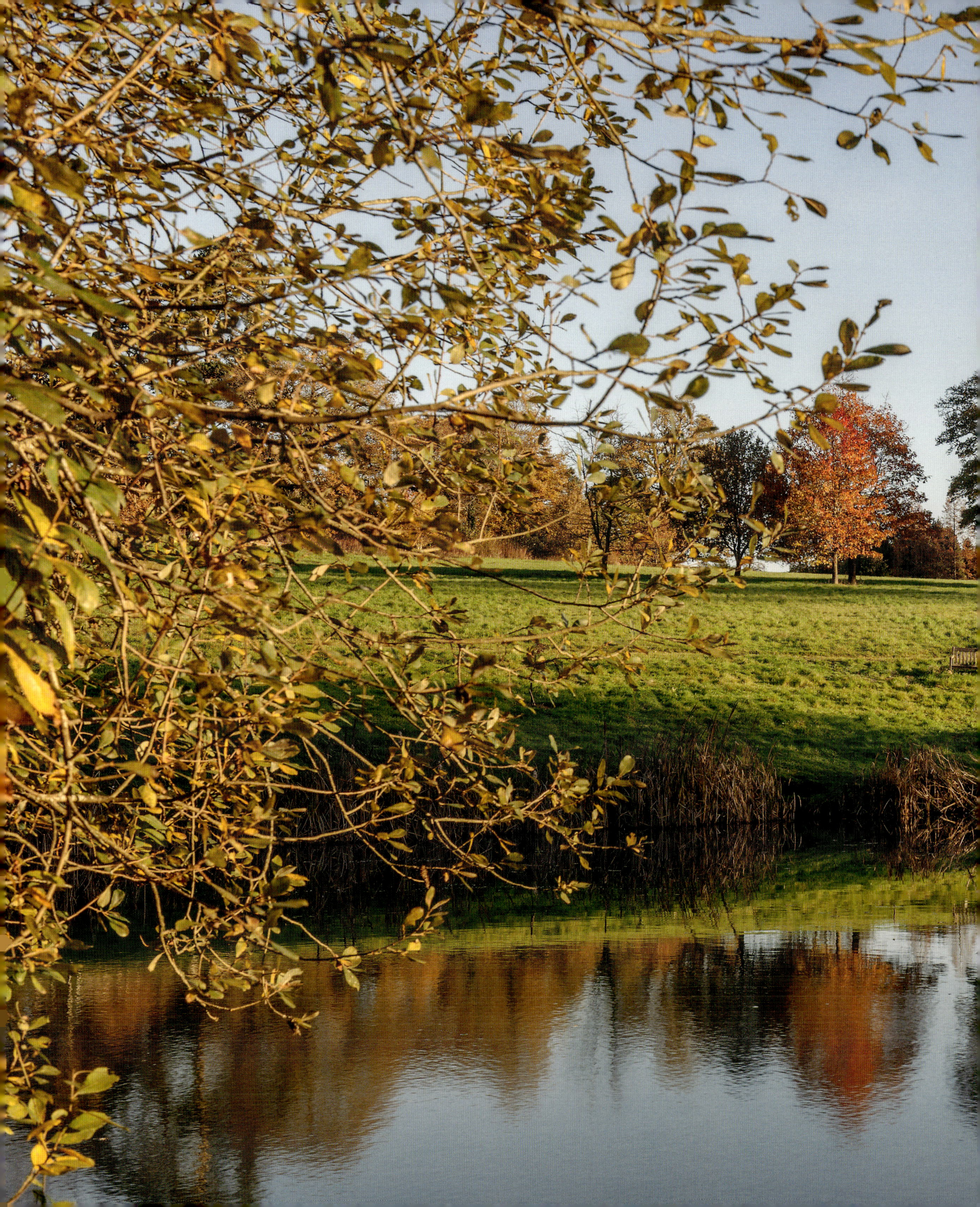

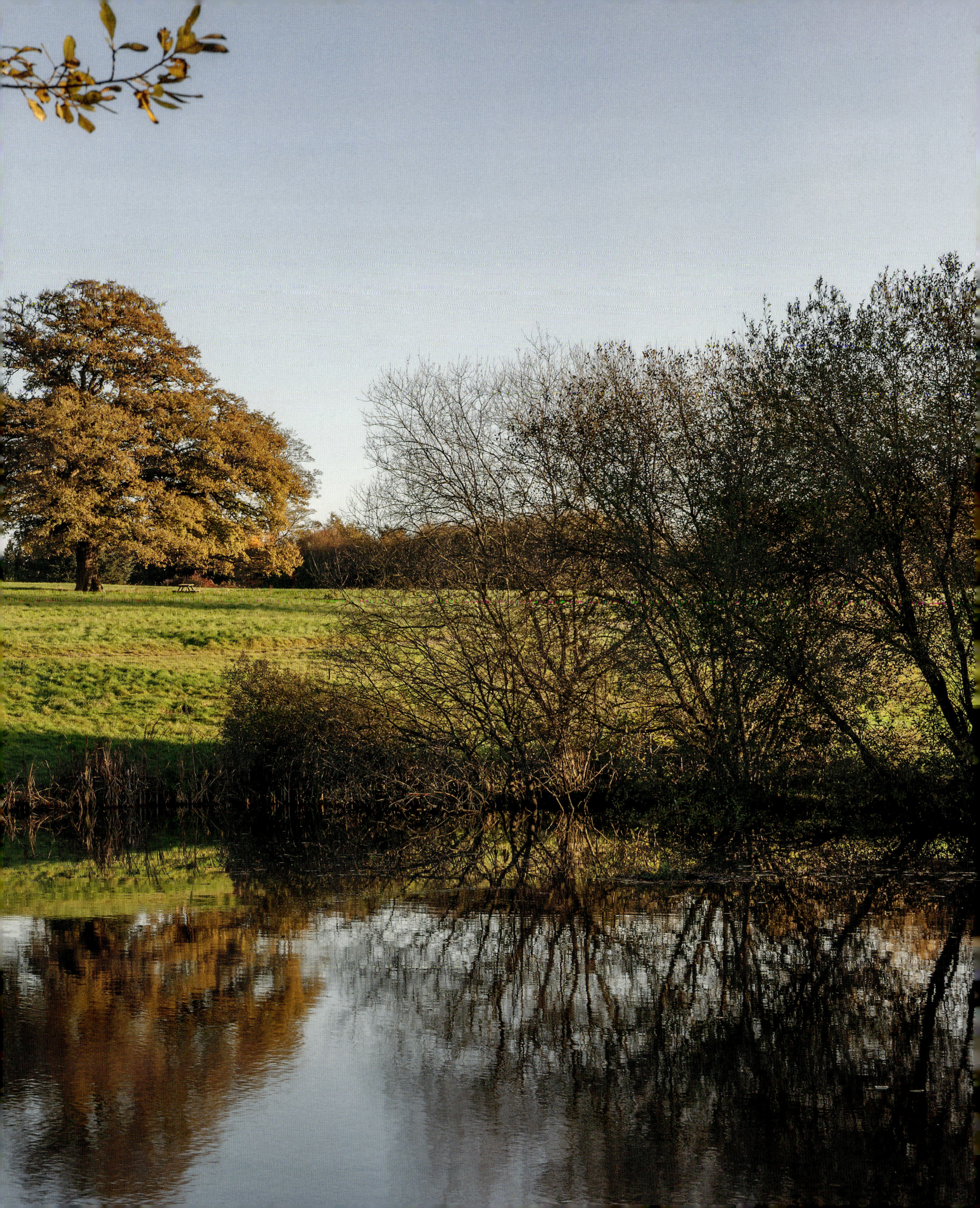

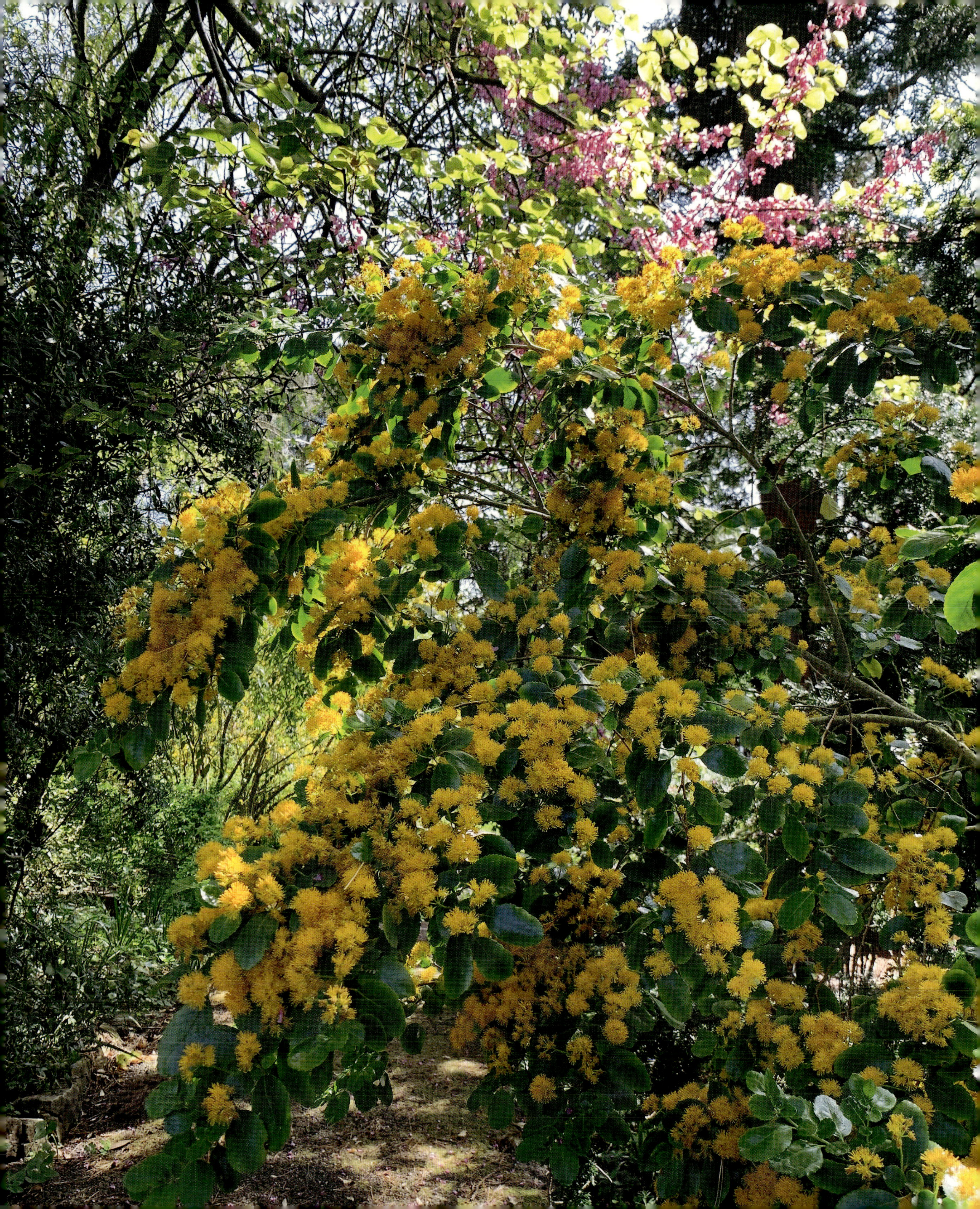

West Bank

Opposite: Azara serrata and pink-flowered *Cercis siliquastrum* beside the path between the West Bank and the West Garden.

'The ground to the west of the lawn contains a small terrace garden with low walls, and a small rock garden', wrote Stephie in the May 1938 issue of the *Journal of the Royal Horticultural Society*. These walls were originally planted with rock plants, and the William Robinson-style planting was admired by the writer himself. Disappointingly, according to Stephie, 'mice formed runs between the "courses" of the stones behind the plants', disrupting his planting of alpines. So, over the years, the planting has gradually changed on the West Bank, which is divided from the South Lawn by a chain of rhododendrons and camellias and by a group of swamp cypresses, *Taxodium distichum*. Also here is a *Crataegus orientalis* (native to the eastern Mediterranean), with a smoky appearance owing to its woolly grey leaves and with chalky-white flowers in May and June.

In the mid-twentieth century a flight of wooden steps in the middle of the bank led from the South Lawn to the tennis court. Robert removed these steps in the early 1980s when he replaced the tennis court with the Bride's Pool (now the site of the Italian Garden) and thereby increased the planting opportunities on the east-facing slope.

Below: There is colour throughout the year on the West Bank, with great golden clusters of *Rudbeckia* 'Goldsturm' in late summer.

THE GARDEN

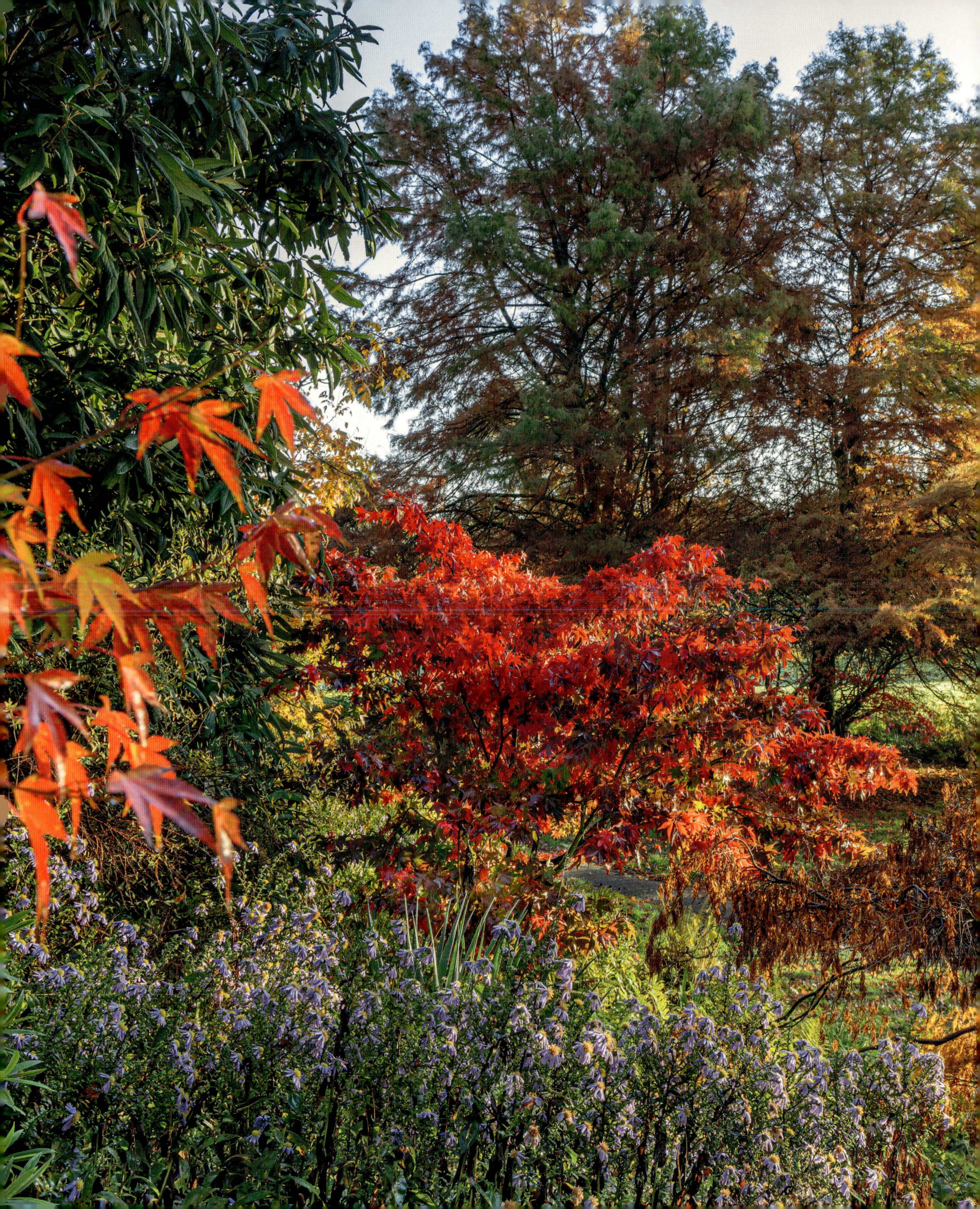

Opposite: Fiery-coloured varieties of *Acer palmatum* are an autumn feature of the West Bank.

In early spring the path curling round to the West Bank from the top of the South Lawn is lined with hellebores, leucojums and primulas. By May, ferns unfurl their shiny green fronds, followed by agapanthus and various hardy geraniums and nepeta. Later still, brilliant purple-red *Acer palmatum* 'Dissectum' and scarlet *A.p.* 'Osakazuki' come into their own, together with *Rudbeckia* 'Goldsturm', asters, fuchsias, *Euphorbia griffithii* 'Fireglow' and dark *Ophiopogon planiscapus* 'Kokuryu' (formerly *O.p.* 'Nigrescens'). In winter the stems of *Cornus sanguinea* 'Midwinter Fire' are a blaze of orange. This area is the ideal spot for the introduction of new acers and other interesting small trees.

At the top of the bank are survivors of the 1987 storm. There are large pines and a *Cryptomeria japonica*, grown from seed collected by one of Stephie's brothers in Japan in 1890. Running through the pines towards the Italian Garden is a short walkway, fringed by camellias and an *Acer palmatum* 'Elegans'. The acer's jagged mid green leaves turn a beautiful orange red in early autumn. Nearby, another flight of steps connecting the West Bank with the Italian Garden was unearthed and repaired by Andrewjohn and Eleni. To the south of the West Bank is a major artery of the garden, linking the South Lawn, Italian Garden, Round Dell and Old Potting Sheds. This is Paradise Walk.

Through the acers at the bottom of the West Bank can be seen *Cyclamen hederifolium*, harbingers of winter, among the roots of the principal South Lawn oak.

WEST BANK

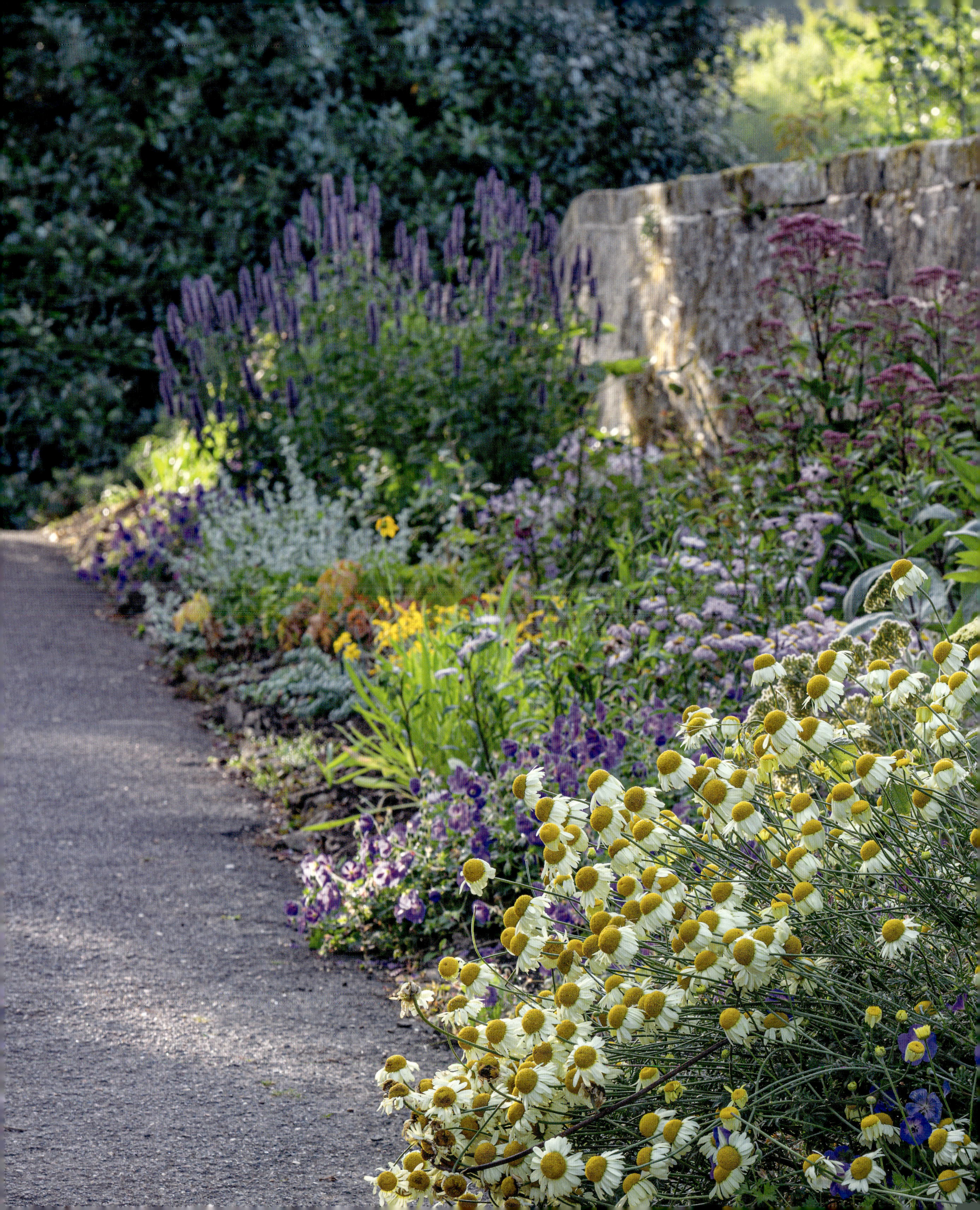

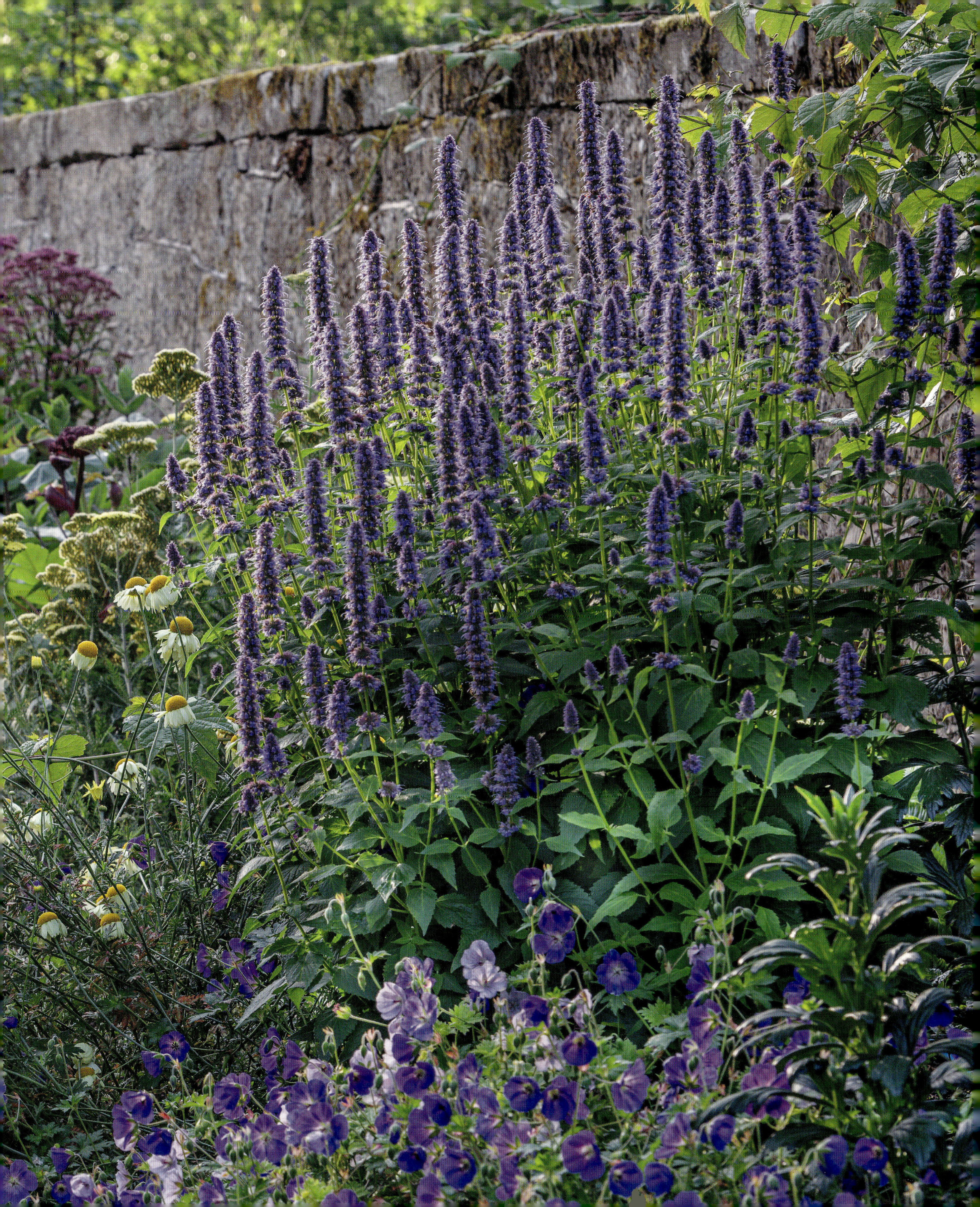

Paradise Walk

Pages 118–19: Bold bands of colour run through the wall-backed border, with pale-yellow *Anthemis tinctoria* 'E.C. Buxton', *Achillea* 'Credo', *Geranium* Rozanne, eutrochium and spires of *Agastache* 'Blackadder'.

Below: Campanula lactiflora, C. latifolia, Geranium palmatum and *Anthemis tinctoria* 'E.C. Buxton' along Paradise Walk.

The path from the South Lawn slopes up to Paradise Walk, past a massive oak on the right. After the open expanse of the lawn, there is more sense of enclosure here as the land falls away sharply behind a wall to your left. You are aware, nevertheless, of the South Park below because its parkland trees form a wonderful backcloth to the wall-backed border.

The Paradise Walk borders have undergone several incarnations since 2000, for this is a challenging area to plant. The wider border, to the left, is north-facing, with clay soil that bakes dry in summer, while the south-facing, narrower borders opposite are set against the retaining walls of the Italian Garden, with thinner soil most suitable for drought-tolerant Mediterranean plants. In 2020 the wider border was redesigned by Chris Beardshaw, winner of thirteen gold medals for his RHS Chelsea Flower Show gardens. He selected seventy different perennials for colour and scent to last from spring to late autumn, including such bee attractors as origanum and angelica. His palette is mostly soft blues, lilacs, creams and pale yellows, with darker spikes of colour along the 263-foot-long (80 m) border.

The view eastwards along Paradise Walk, through wrought-iron gates.

From left to right: Paeonia delavayi; *Kniphofia* 'Tawny King'; *Agapanthus* 'Midnight Star'.

From left to right: Geranium Rozanne; *G. palmatum; Angelica gigas.*

From left to right: Gladiolus 'Ruby'; *Allium ursinum; Paeonia* 'Anne Rosse'.

BORDE HILL GARDEN

Achillea 'Credo', *Anthemis tinctoria* 'E.C. Buxton', *Geranium* Rozanne, *G. palmatum* and *Campanula latifolia* with the daylily *Hemerocallis lilioasphodelus*.

Dark *Salvia* 'Blue Spire' (formerly known as *Perovskia* 'Blue Spire'), kniphofias, *Geranium* Rozanne and *Epilobium canum* (formerly *Zauschneria californica*) by the steps to the Italian Garden.

The plants are set not in clumps, but in bands at forty-five degrees to the path to give an impression of depth to the relatively narrow border. The first display of the year is a carpet of 3000 *Muscari armeniacum* 'Peppermint', followed in mid-summer by creamy *Anthemis tinctoria* 'E.C. Buxton' and the tight umbels of *Achillea* 'Credo' along the front of the border. These are interspersed with grey-green foliage plants, such as aromatic evergreen *Ballota pseudodictamnus*, and the ground-covering *Eriophyllum lanatum*, with yellow daisy flowers in late spring and early summer. Other plants at this lower level are soft-pink and long-flowering *Astrantia* 'Roma', mauvy-blue *Geranium* Rozanne, and *Gillenia trifoliata*, with dainty star-shaped white flowers from June to September. In tiers behind are deep-blue *Agapanthus* 'Marchants Cobalt Cracker', along with stands of sapphire *Aconitum carmichaelii* 'Arendsii' and *Agastache* 'Blackadder' for late summer and autumn. Joe Pye weed (*Eutrochium maculatum* (Atropurpureum Group) 'Purple Bush'), the umbelliferous *Asclepias incarnata* and *Betonica macrantha* (with scalloped leaves) inject shades of mauve, while the evergreen *Lepechinia hastata* has salvia-like magenta flowers in summer. Beardshaw also planted tall *Actaea simplex*

Clockwise from top left: Asplenium scolopendrium; Erigeron karvinskianus; the foliage of Euphorbia characias subsp. *wulfenii; E. cyparissias.*

PARADISE WALK

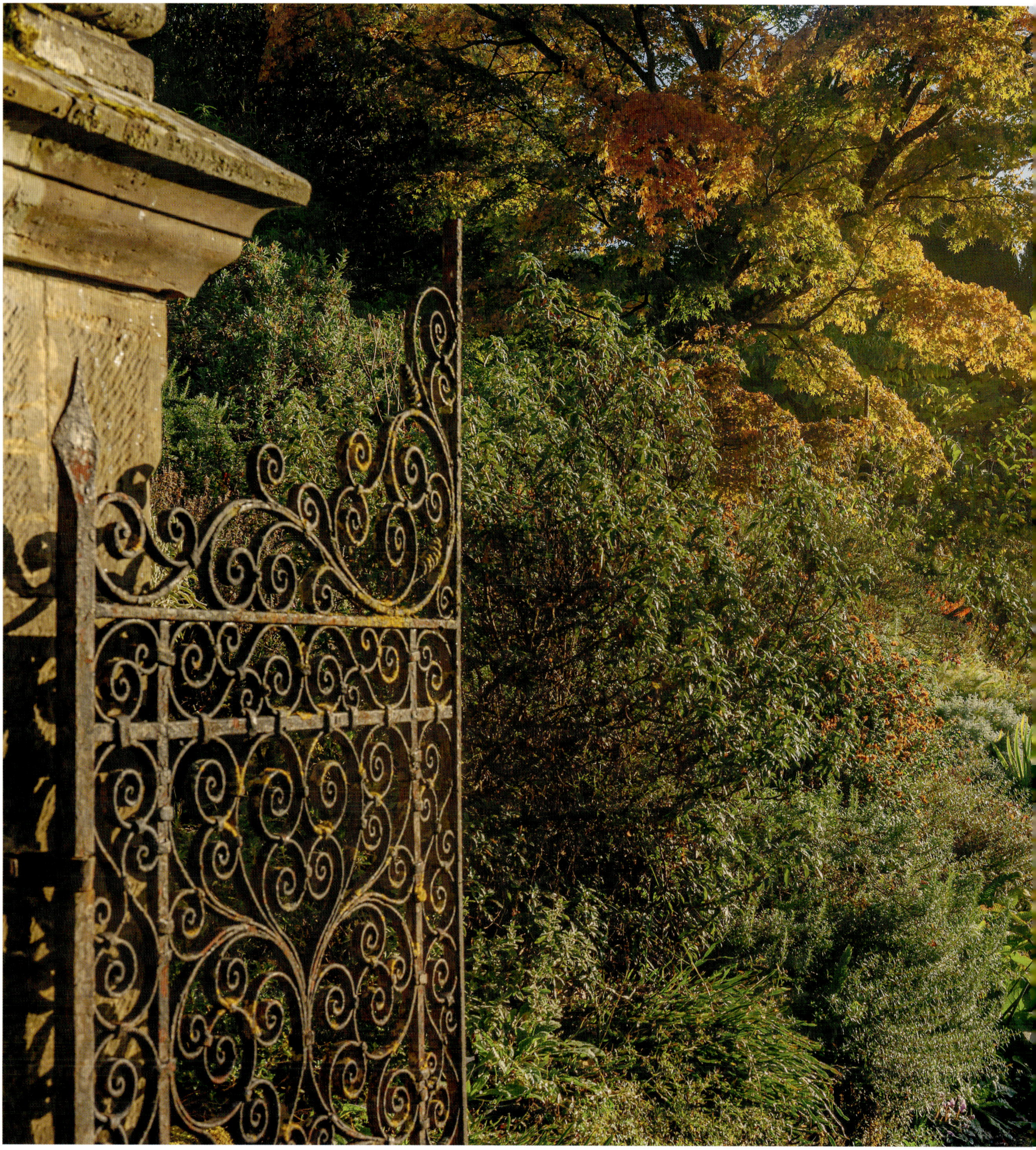

(Atropurpurea Group) 'Hillside Black Beauty', with bronze stems and foliage and fragrant small white flowers in early autumn; honey-scented *Euphorbia × pasteurii* 'John Phillips', with yellow-green foliage that reddens in autumn and winter; and dramatic *Angelica archangelica*, which has crimson stems and good seed pods through spring and summer. Wine-dark *Hemerocallis* 'American Revolution' and repeat-flowering rich-crimson *Rosa* Falstaff recur through the border and stand out from the softer shades.

A few of the same plants appear in both the border and the wall beds opposite. *Geranium* Rozanne flowers in the south-facing beds from June through to late autumn, and is planted with the dark-centred magenta *G.* 'Ann Folkard', more euphorbia, high-summer deep-blue *Agapanthus* 'Midnight Star' and *Amaryllis belladonna*. Other key plants through these raised wall beds are dark-blue perovskias, red-hot pokers (including *Kniphofia* 'Tawny King') and *Gladiolus* 'Ruby' for late summer, and nerines for autumn. Ferns, such as *Asplenium scolopendrium*, thrive in the slightly shadier areas against the walls. A splendid sight in summer and autumn are the crinkly shocking-pink flowers of the Chinese crape myrtle (*Lagerstroemia indica*), a historic shrub that has flourished in this border for several decades (and also grows in the Old Potting Sheds). Below, the miniature pink-and-white daisy *Erigeron karvinskianus* spreads happily through the gravel and up the steps leading to the Italian Garden.

Left: Textural contrasts of foliage play an important part in the autumn scene, with trees including an acer, a catalpa and *Lagerstroemia indica*.

Below: The early flowers of *Euphorbia characias* subsp. *wulfenii* bring colour to Paradise Walk in late winter.

PARADISE WALK

Italian Garden

The formality of the south-facing Italian Garden above Paradise Walk is markedly different in style from the looser, more relaxed planting elsewhere on the west side of the house. Whether you approach this grand garden from the upper terrace or from Paradise Walk below, the impact is dramatic: the impression is that you have strayed from Sussex into the Mediterranean – despite views of English oak and beech in the South Park below the ha-ha. The large rectangular pool, the sound of water, the terracing, topiary and the encircling pines and eucalyptus mirrored in the pool together evoke hillside gardens around Florence and Rome. This echo is all the more potent on a hot summer's day, when the pool shimmers in strong sunlight and visitors seek out shady seats.

The design is symmetrical and enclosed, with a bench placed facing the pool in each quadrant. The influence of early Persian paradise gardens can be seen, transmuted through the gardens of Italy and Spain. The characteristic feeling of enclosure is created by packed middle-level planting of cherry, cupressus and elaeagnus, all of which would have grown in Persian gardens. A rill bisects steps connecting upper and lower terraces, and runs into the pool.

Left: Tall pines and eucalyptus surrounding the Italian Garden evoke the Mediterranean in this part of the garden.

Below: The different colours of the interlaced box hedging are highlighted in this aerial view.

THE GARDEN

The pool terrace was originally the family's tennis court, but in 1982 Robert and his wife, Maria, created what they called the Bride's Pool, after a mid-nineteenth-century marble statue by Antonio Tantardini that once stood here. Since then, the Italian Garden has gradually evolved. A first redesign was carried out in 1997 by Robin Williams, who filled the upper terrace with roses and planted box hedging (*Buxus sempervirens*) around the pool terrace. He designed the rill that runs down to the pool from the statue of a naked female, arms outspread. This statue, *Welcoming the New Year*, is a marble resin copy of an original by the local artist Ev Meynell. Williams also introduced the twelve swagged Whichford terracotta pots that flank the pool.

More detail was added in 2010, inspired by Andrewjohn and Eleni's travels in Italy. Helped by Williams's son, Robin Templar Williams, they gave the garden even greater formality. Parterre beds on the upper terrace were framed by myrtle (*Myrtus communis* subsp. *tarentina*). Each bed was planted with a single standard *Magnolia grandiflora* 'Kay Parris', a summer-flowering creamy-white cultivar with waxy lanceolate leaves smaller than those of the *M.g.* 'Goliath' on the south front of the house. More box hedging was added around the pool terrace, framing parterre beds of annual and perennial planting, and with indentations for benches. These indentations are marked by pyramids of yew, with a line of larger *Pittosporum tenuifolium* pyramids at the intersections of the box beds and a spire of golden yew behind each bench.

This firm structure means that the Italian Garden is as attractive in winter as in summer. Reflections in the black-dyed water of the pool are a feature of every season, from spectral oatmeal-coloured grasses in winter to the rich colours of the summer planting. From the upper terrace in mid-winter, the view is framed by evergreen eucalyptus leaves and by the leafless and twisting branches of *Discaria chacaye* (*D. discolor*), one of Borde Hill's many champion trees, originally from Patagonia. This gnarled tree grows out at forty-five degrees to the bank, and in summer its small spiny leaves evoke the Mediterranean. In early summer, side beds facing the discaria are filled with *Alstroemeria* 'Walter Fleming'.

Planting changes across the seasons and from year to year. Colour comes to the fore in late April/early May with the tulip display in the terracotta pots by the pool. In the past, the colour theme was shades of pink and red, but more recently in the beds yellows and oranges have been favoured for spring bulbs, such as *Fritillaria imperialis* 'Rubra'. The colours chosen for tulips in the pots continue to vary each year. In June drifts of large-headed *Allium* 'Globemaster' and smaller *A. hollandicum* 'Purple Sensation' appear in the triangular beds of yellow *Buxus sempervirens* 'Latifolia Maculata' behind the greener box hedging.

When the tulips have gone over, the pots are planted alternately with deep-blue agapanthus and red or pink oak-leaved pelargoniums.

White cherry blossom arches over a side entrance to the Italian Garden.

A kinetic water sculpture, *Aquapoise* by Angela Conner, creates both movement and sound in the Italian Garden.

Fritillaria imperialis 'Rubra' are used en masse for a spectacular May show in the parterre beds.

ITALIAN GARDEN

Allium 'Globemaster' and *A. hollandicum* 'Purple Sensation' are planted within triangles of golden box (*Buxus sempervirens* 'Latifolia Maculata').

Right: Changes are rung in the pots around the pool terrace from season to season and year to year. Here, agapanthus and pale-pink pelargoniums are alternated.

Opposite: Standing in her bed of myrtle and erigeron, *Welcoming the New Year*, a statue by the local artist Ev Meynell, appears to be preparing to dive into the pool. On the right is one of Borde Hill's champion trees, *Discaria chacaye* (*D. discolor*), with a eucalyptus on the left.

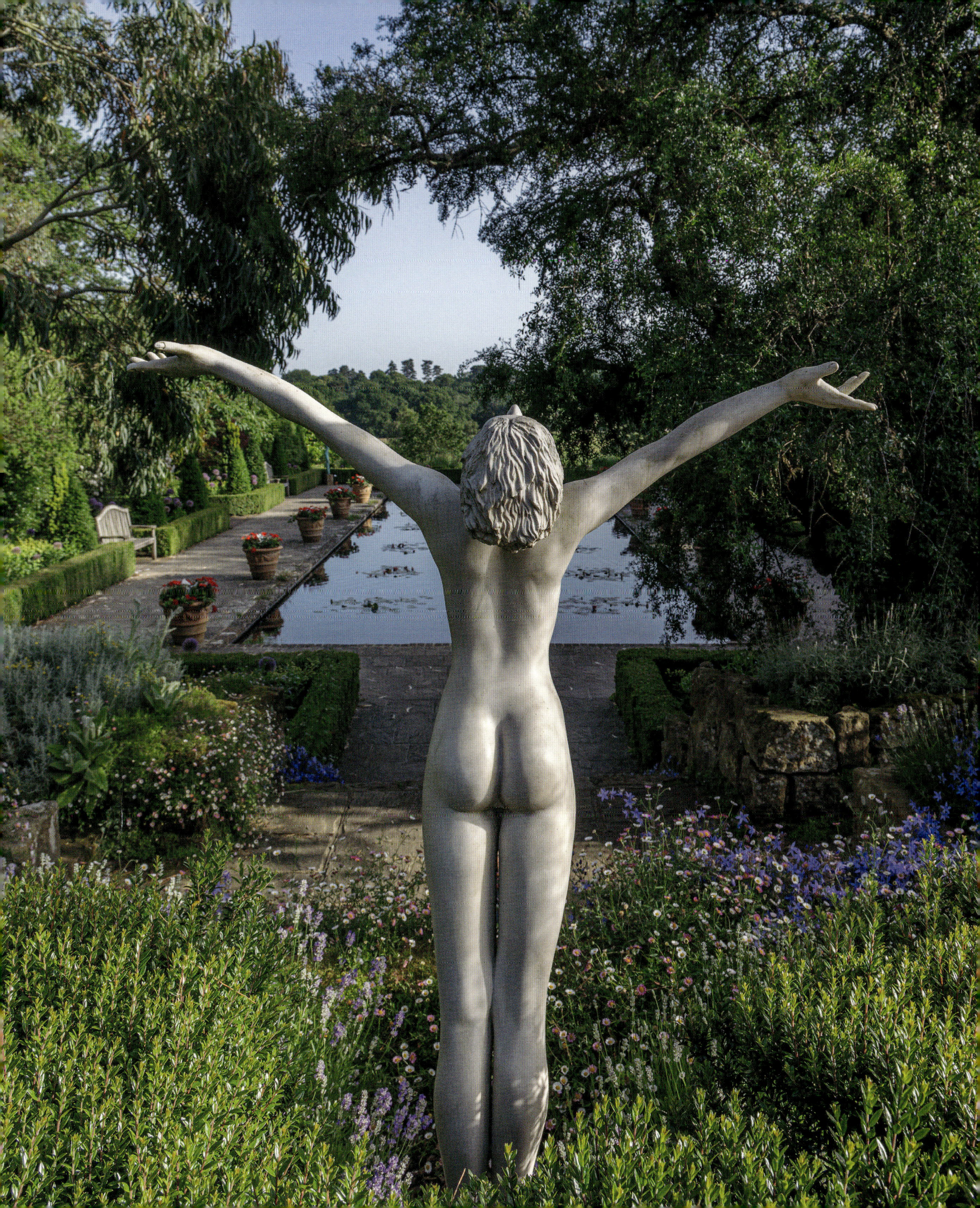

Right: Fritillaria imperialis 'Rubra'.

Far right: The beautiful white flowers of *Magnolia grandiflora* 'Kay Parris' bloom in August on the terrace above the Italian Garden.

Right: One of the garden's signature plants, *Alstroemeria* 'Walter Fleming', bred by Stephie's head gardener.

Far right: In high summer *Lilium lancifolium* 'Splendens' takes over from the spring-flowering *Fritillaria imperialis* to maintain the colour scheme in the parterre beds.

Reflections are interrupted by red, pink and white water lilies (*Nymphaea*), which increasingly cover the surface of the pool in summer.

In 2020 Chris Beardshaw redesigned the planting in the Italian Garden as well as in Paradise Walk, putting greater emphasis on perennials. He mixed subtle background plants, such as stachys (*Betonica officinalis* 'Hummelo'), perovskia (*Salvia* 'Little Spire'), *Salvia* Mystic Spires Blue and pale-yellow *Santolina pinnata* subsp. *neapolitana*, with bolder *Dietes grandiflora* (a lily-like white South African flower with a purple-and-yellow centre), the long-flowering perennial wallflower *Erysimum* 'Bowles's Mauve' and *Agapanthus* Silver Moon. A signature plant of the Italian Garden has remained: the orangey-red *Lilium lancifolium* 'Splendens', a good contrast to the strong blues.

There are layers of texture and colour throughout the garden, with a middle tier of planting behind the box beds and around the steps to the upper terrace. The flowering season begins with several hybrid camellias, including the rose-pink *Camellia* 'Leonard Messel', a

BORDE HILL GARDEN

cross between *C. reticulata* and *C. williamsii*, and named after Stephie's gardening friend at nearby Nymans. In a similar shade is another *williamsii* cross, *C. × w.* 'Water Lily', along with pinky-apricot *C. japonica* 'Tinker Bell' and, by contrast, scarlet *C.j.* 'Red Dandy'. Other spring showstoppers are the bridal-white blossom of *Prunus* 'Tai-haku' and the big rose-pink flowers of *Magnolia sargentiana* var. *robusta*. Euphorbia, *Elaeagnus* 'Quicksilver' and tender ginger lilies (hedychiums), along with spiky *Trachycarpus fortunei*, add to the hot, southern feel of this garden.

In recent years, a biennial sculpture exhibition has been held throughout the summer at Borde Hill. Although most pieces appear only during the exhibition, several commissioned sculptures have become major features of the garden. The kinetic water sculpture *Aquapoise* was specially made for the centre of the Italian Garden pool by Angela Conner and was installed here in 2015. Water runs down the surface of its leaves as they tip from side to side, creating movement and a refreshing sound on a hot summer's day.

Above: Pink pelargoniums start the summer season off on the pool terrace before the agapanthus come into flower.

Overleaf: Its firm structure ensures that the Italian Garden looks as spectacular in winter as it does in high summer.

ITALIAN GARDEN

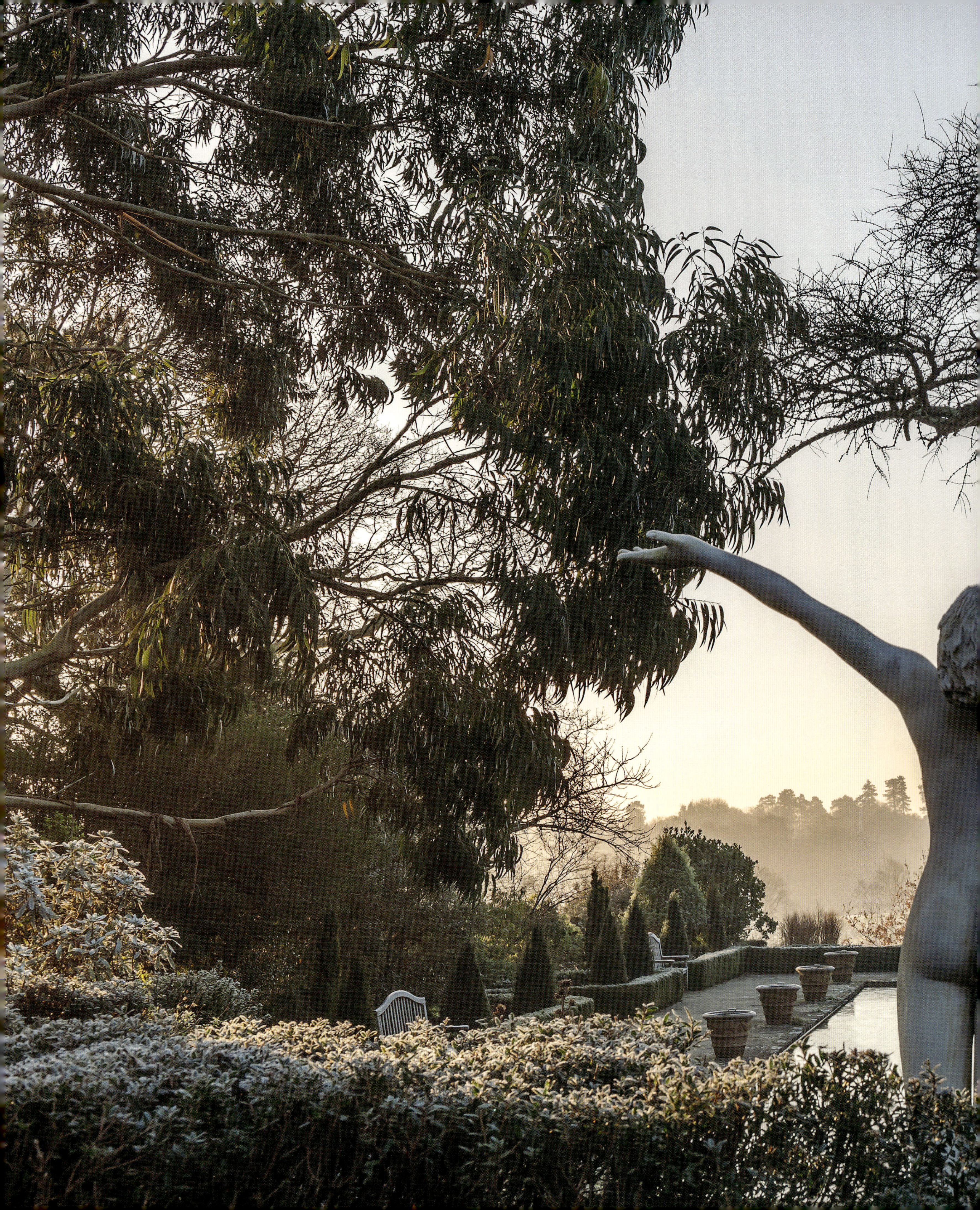

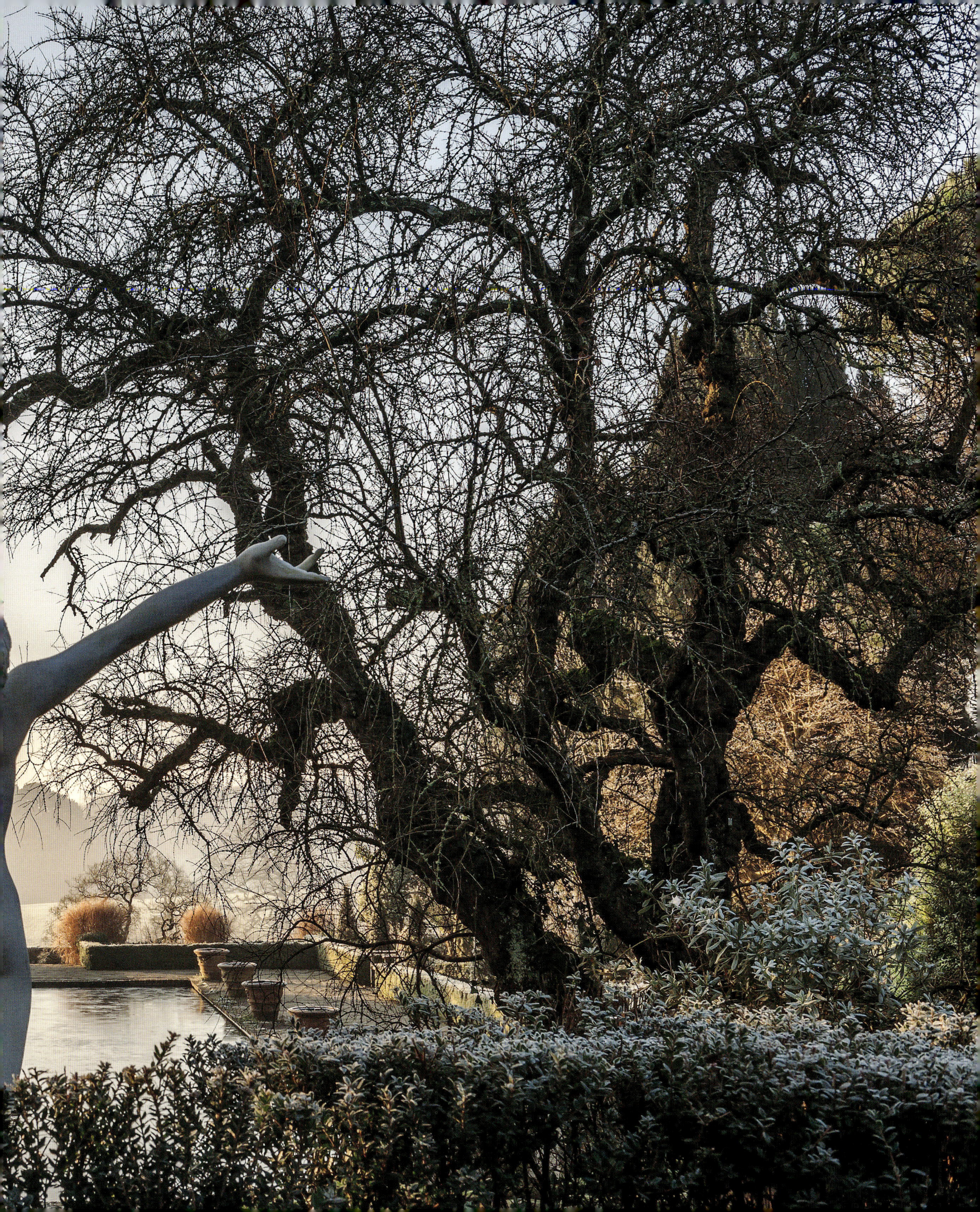

Round Dell

At Borde Hill there is a pleasurable sense of shifting scenes as you move from area to area through the loose structure of banks of trees and shrubs, many originally planted by Stephie but renewed or augmented by subsequent generations of the family. This is very different from many twentieth-century English gardens, where discrete 'rooms' are divided one from another by clipped hedging or walls; by contrast, the Borde Hill approach gives greater permeability and naturalism to the garden. Nowhere is this more distinctive than between the gardens linked by Paradise Walk. The transition is marked, for instance, in the raised beds to the west of the Italian Garden, where hot, colourful summer planting gives way via grey Mediterranean rock plants to the subtropical green opulence of the Round Dell. Agaves and pines (dwarf *Picea glauca* var. *albertiana* 'Conica' and *Pinus mugo*) are planted with pinky-white *Salvia sclarea* var. *turkestaniana* and waxy-leaved *Pittosporum tobira*.

The Round Dell, a south-facing former quarry, sheltered and with water at its heart, has been filled with subtropical planting since Stephie's time. This rainforest lushness has been retained in a redesign by Sophie Walker, one of the youngest winners of an RHS show-garden medal. Previously, one entered the dell almost by stealth, slipping in through the thick foliage and taking one of the paths around the central pond. In 2017 Walker created a bold new architectural entrance that draws visitors in to explore the dell's green heart. The arrow-shaped concrete path plunges into the dell like the prow of a ship and leads to a pool of water fed by a waterfall fountain overhead.

The chief impression is of jungle-like foliage, so the dell comes into its own from June onwards, when these key plants leaf up. Existing plants retained when the hard landscaping was redesigned include the Japanese angelica tree (*Aralia elata*), Japanese banana (*Musa basjoo*), bamboo, gunnera, *Trachycarpus fortunei*, *Fatsia*

The flowers of *Aralia cachemirica* turn into clusters of black fruit in late summer.

Lysimachia paridiformis.

Left, top and bottom: An arrow-shaped concrete path drives through lush vegetation towards a waterfall fountain.

Overleaf: The Round Dell is almost entirely green, with effects created through contrasting leaf shapes and stem structure. Planting here includes different types of fern, *Tetrapanax papyrifer*, *Eucomis bicolor* and *Melanoselinum decipiens*, with its remarkable stripy trunk.

THE GARDEN

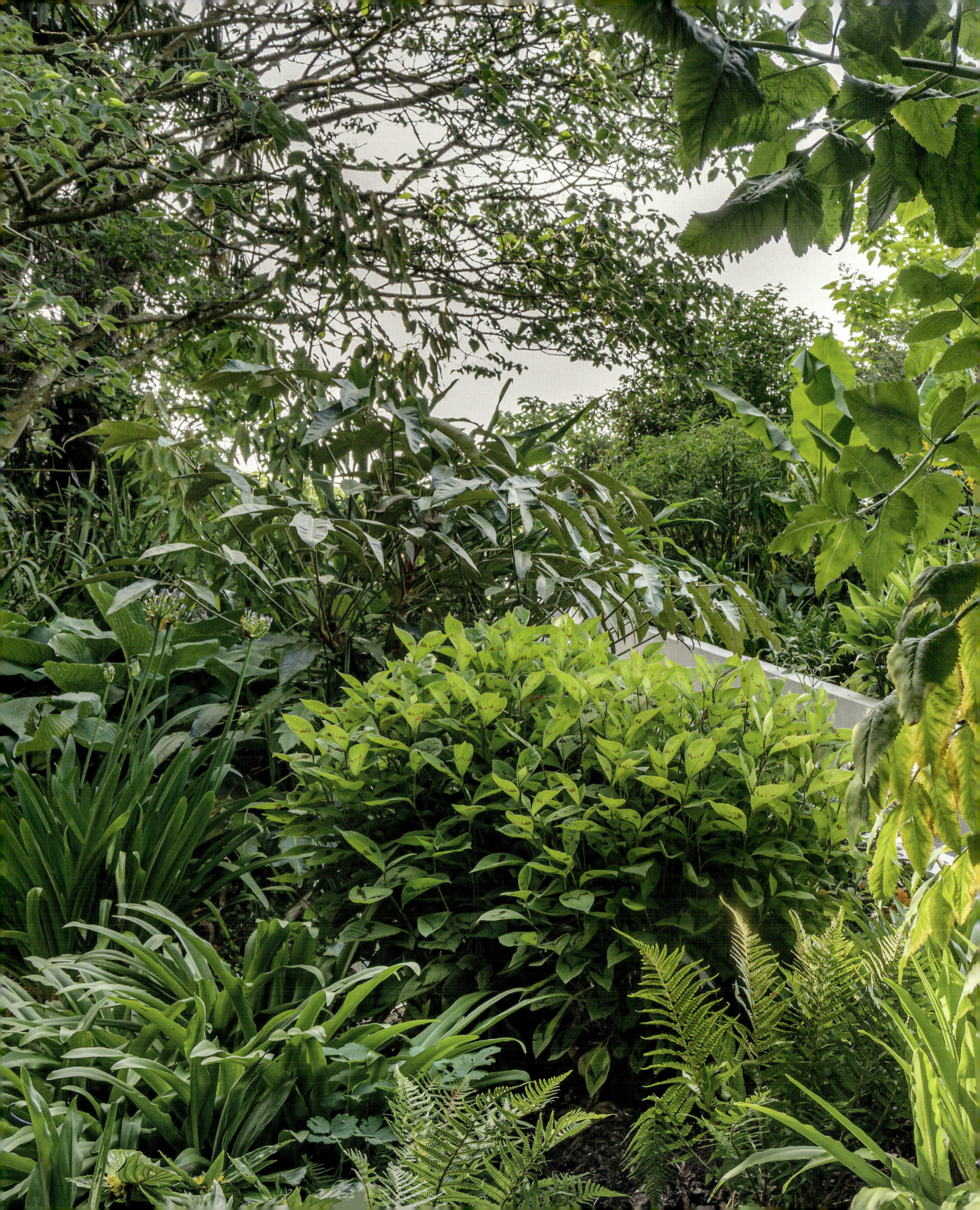

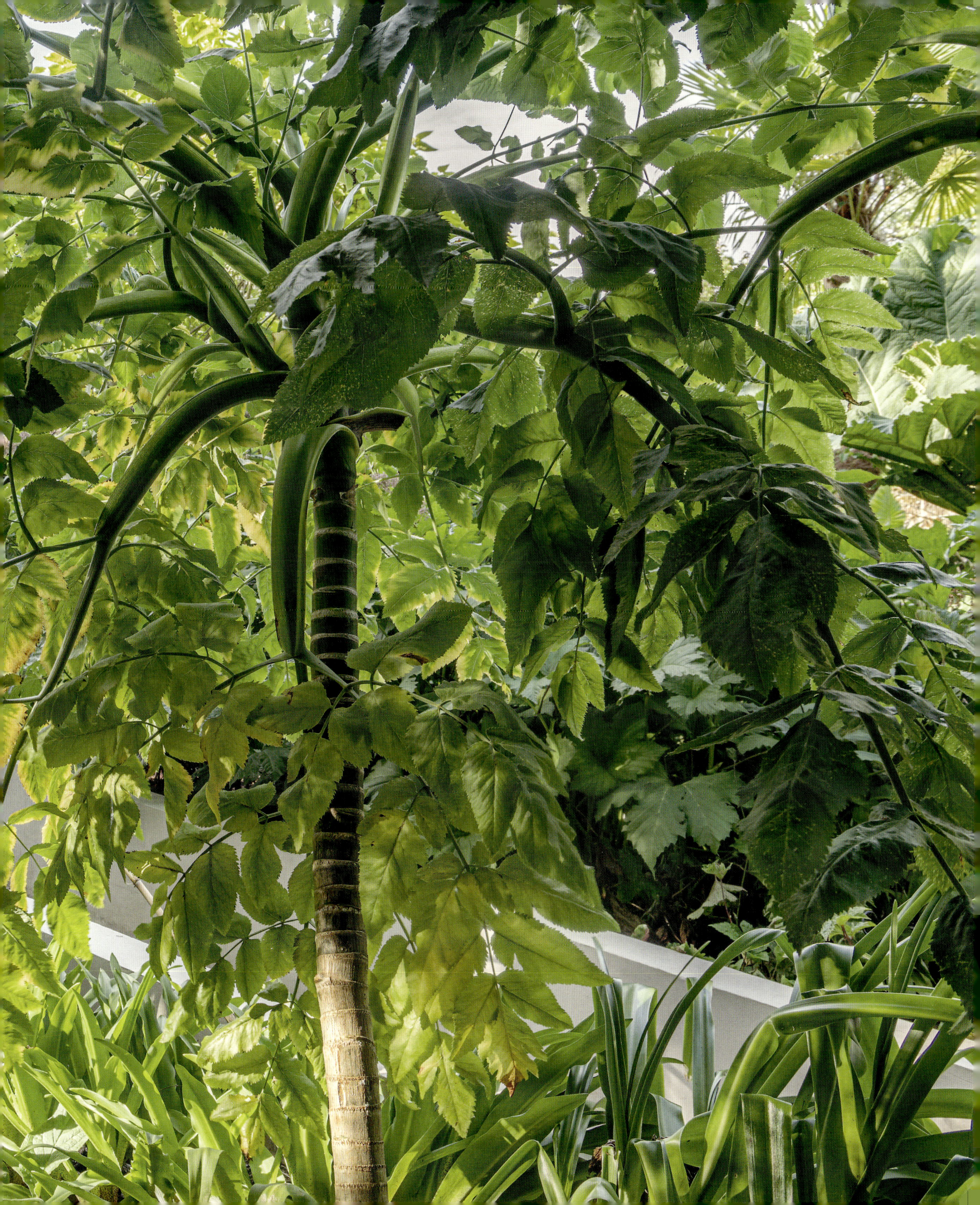

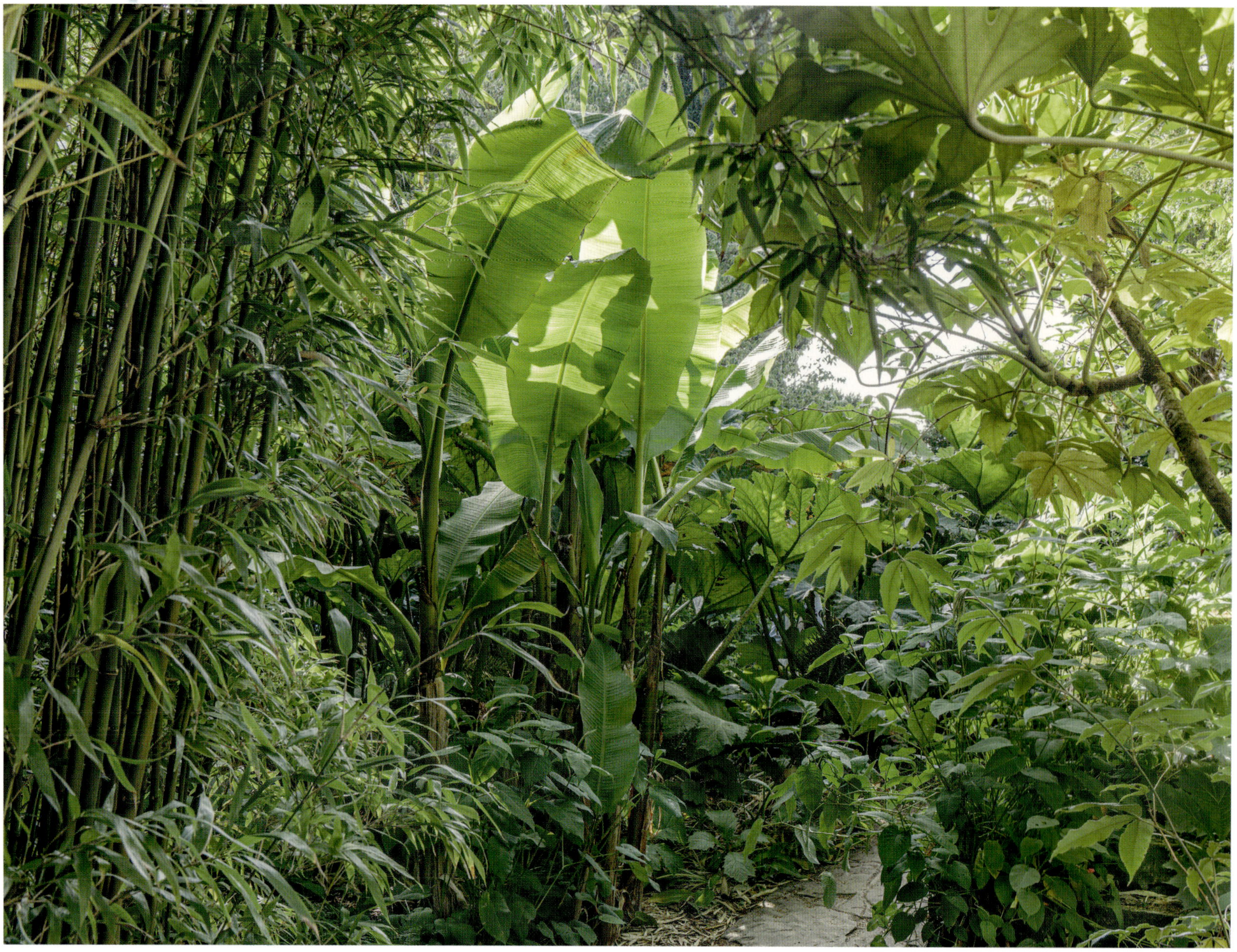

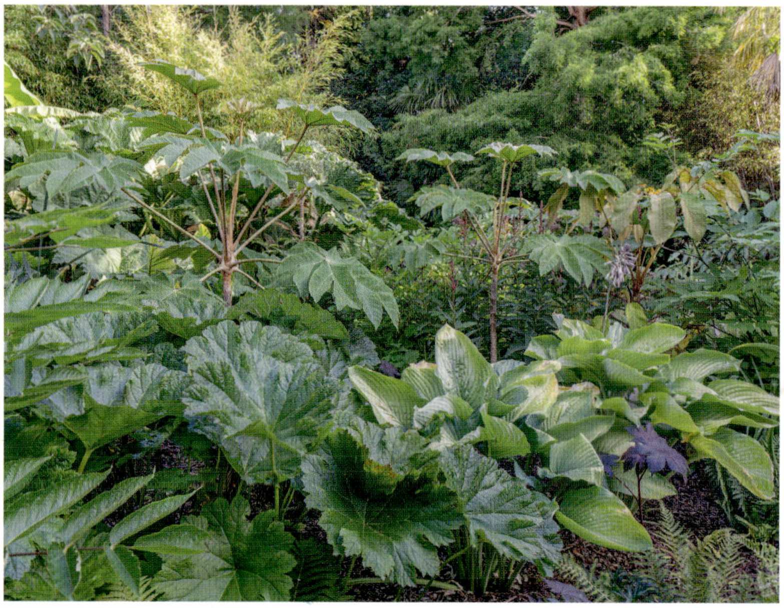

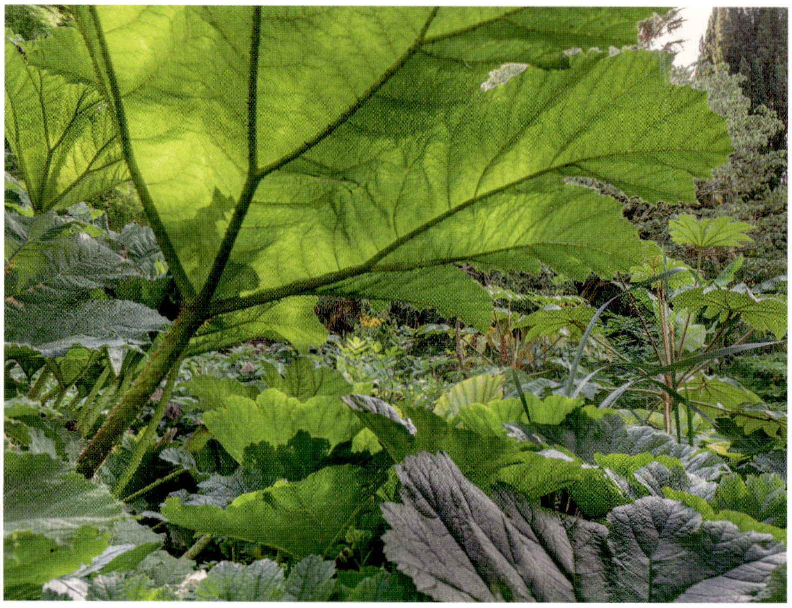

japonica, the veined *Veratrum nigrum* and several large-leaved *Tetrapanax papyrifer*. A swamp cypress, *Taxodium distichum*, probably planted by Robert in the 1970s, rises over the back of the garden, fringed by *Populus lasiocarpa* (the Chinese necklace poplar), which has spreading, magnolia-like leaves, and *Magnolia macrophylla*. The last is coppiced in spring to ensure large foliage. Shade-lovers include the multi-stemmed paper mulberry, *Broussonetia papyrifera*, with mottled stems and pale-green flowers followed by marble-sized round seeds, and evergreen, yellow-flowered *Lysimachia paridiformis*.

There were new introductions, including Australasian palms from Big Plant Nursery in West Sussex. Walker also worked with modern-day plant hunters Bleddyn and Sue Wynn-Jones of Crûg Farm Plants in North Wales, her plant choices informed by Borde Hill's history and the plant hunters' legacy. The first phase of the planting is complete and features rare specimens from Crûg Farm such as water marginals *Ligularia japonica* 'Rising Sun' and *Rodgersia podophylla* 'Crûg Colossus'. Other Crûg exotics planted in the dell include *Aconitum arcuatum*, a dark-purple monkshood from South Korea; *Aralia apioides*, with upright black stems and good autumn colour; *Farfugium japonicum*, with big, round dinner-plate leaves; hedychiums; schefflera; and the prehistoric-looking *Zingiber mioga* 'Crûg's Zing', with yellowish stems and narrow leaves.

Opposite, clockwise from top: Japanese banana (*Musa basjoo*), bamboo and *Tetrapanax papyrifer*; *Gunnera manicata*; *Darmera peltata*.

Left, from top: Paths strike out through the Round Dell on either side of the arrow path; bamboo and gunnera; many different types of fern thrive in the damp conditions.

ROUND DELL

143

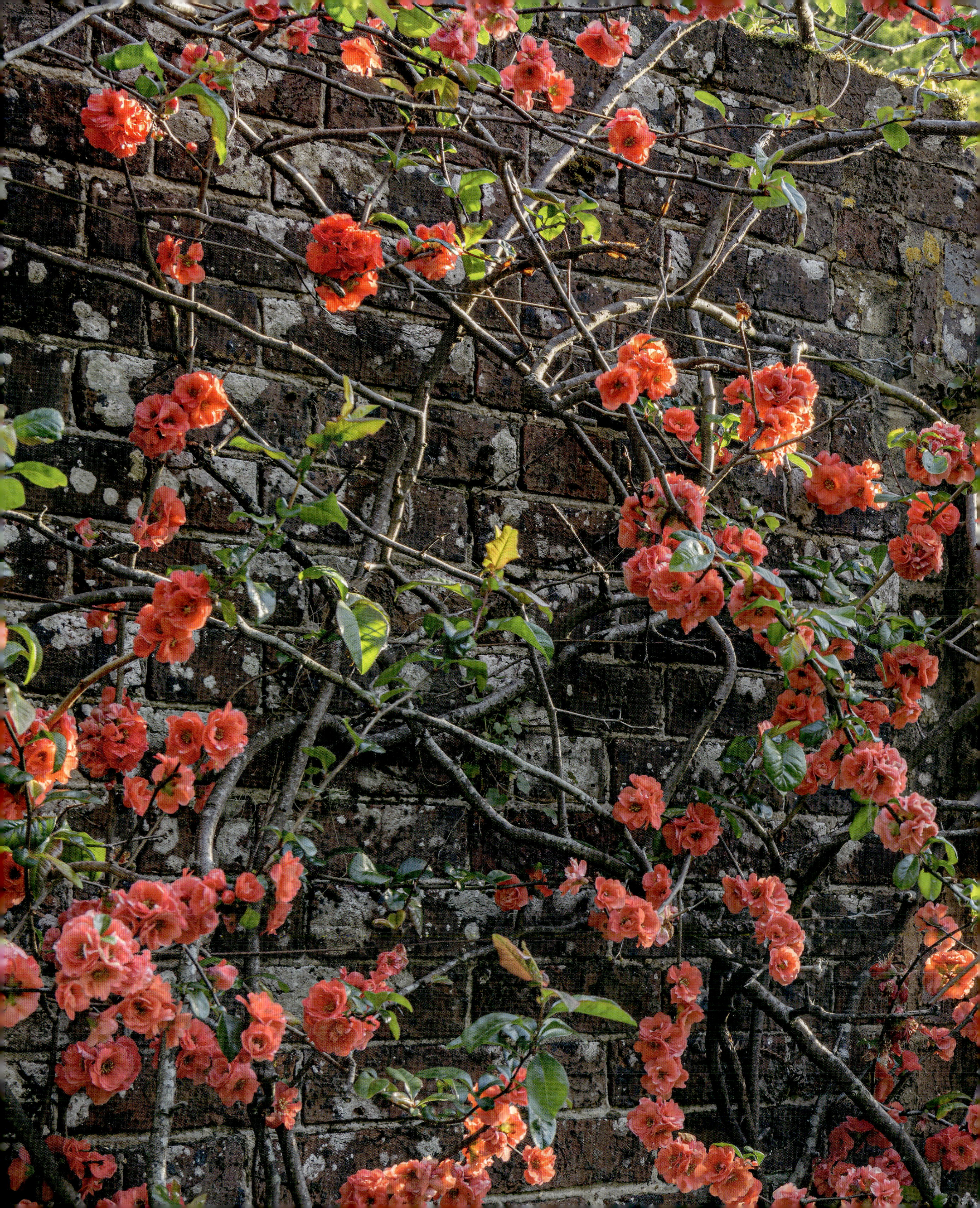

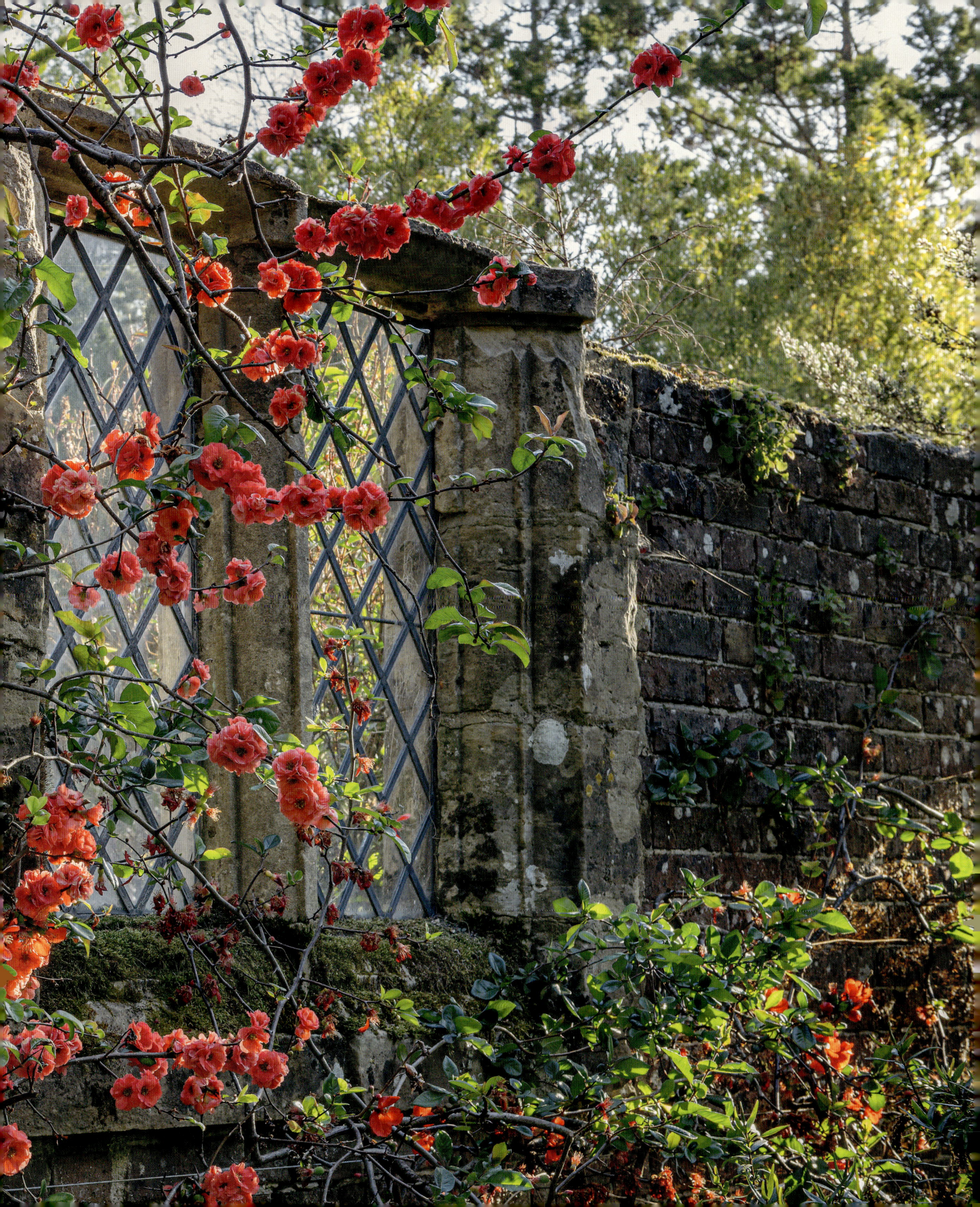

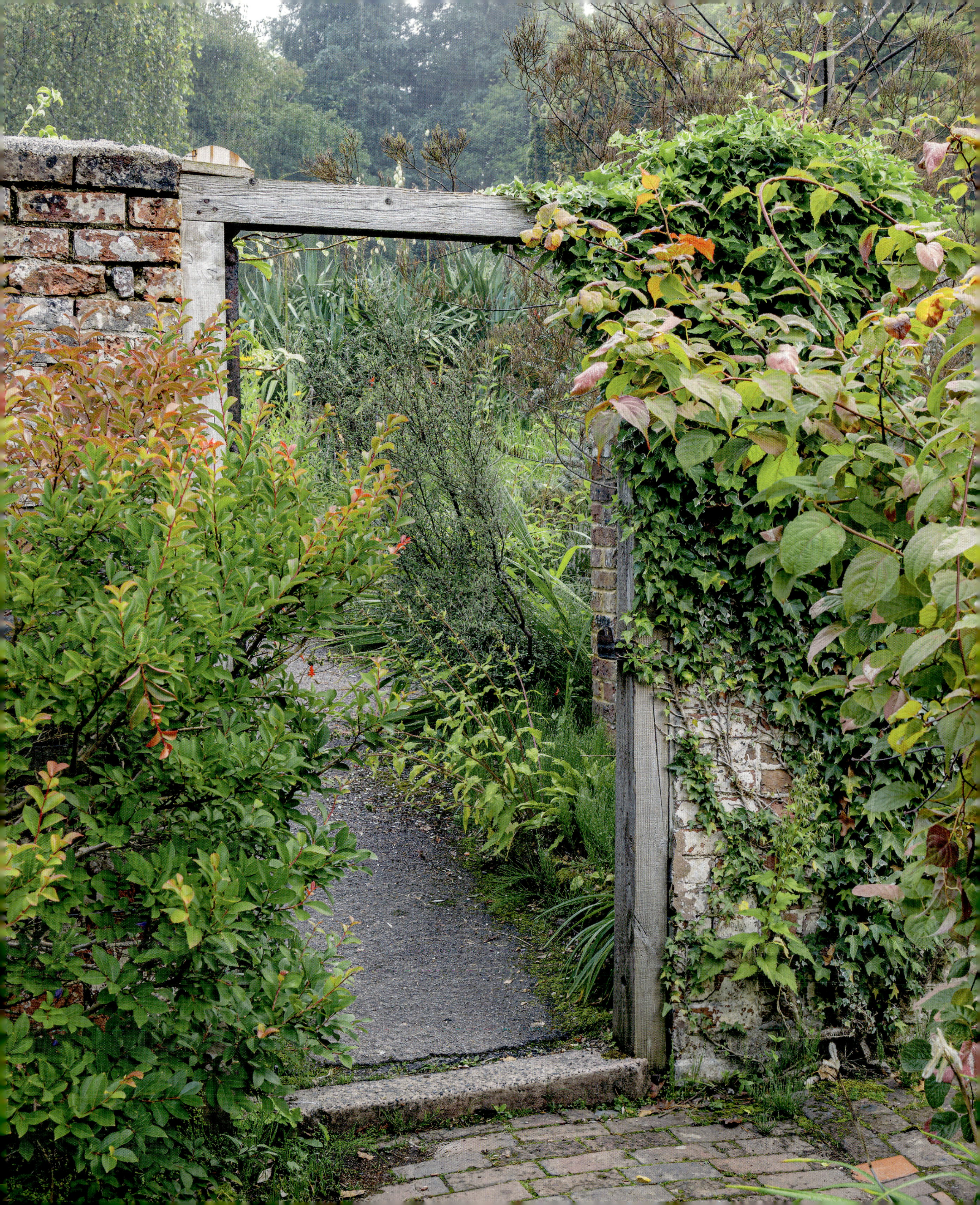

Old Potting Sheds

When Stephie bought Borde Hill House in 1893, he also acquired the bailiff's house, West Garden Lodge, which became the estate office. The lodge had a smallholding with a pigsty, cowshed and chicken sheds, latterly used as potting sheds by the Stephenson Clarkes' gardeners. Along with the greenhouses on the other side of the garden, these were a centre of propagating activities, where plants were hardened off before being planted out in the garden. But as the gardening team shrank, the sheds gradually fell into disrepair, and the roof finally collapsed in the 1970s. The ruined building was used as a herb garden until 1990, when it was decided to plant semi-hardy southern hemisphere species in this enclosed, south-facing site. Other planting was introduced here, too, including a double rosy-red chaenomeles that looks romantic in late winter running up a ruined wall and around one of the still-intact leaded windows.

The ruined walls proved something of a frost pocket, however, so only hardier climbers and shrubs have survived. But the evergreen Chilean shrub *Azara serrata* has flourished, scenting the air with its mimosa-like flowers in summer. This is one of the original plants, along with the pink-flowered *Indigofera amblyantha* and the crape myrtle, *Lagerstroemia indica*. Against another wall is *Actinidia kolomikta*, a climbing shrub from the temperate mixed forests of the Russian Far East, Korea, Japan and China. With leaves that appear to have been dipped into pinky-white paint, it is an excellent foil to lower perennial planting such as the iris-like *Moraea huttonii*, a South African perennial with sword-shaped leaves. Semi-hardy *Abutilon megapotamicum*, a Brazilian shrub, has trailing stems of yellow-tipped red flowers throughout summer.

Also around the walls are the New Zealander *Dacrycarpus dacrydioides*, a coniferous tree planted by Harvey Stephens; a narrow-leaved laurel, *Laurus nobilis* f. *angustifolia*; various fuchsias; a bottlebrush tree (*Callistemon*); a rampant woody vine, *Celastrus orbiculatus*; and the yellow-flowered willow-leaved jessamine, *Cestrum parqui*, from Chile. On the back wall of the second room is *Sophora* Sun King, a tall, broad evergreen shrub with drooping yellow flowers in late winter and early spring.

The thin soil of the Old Potting Sheds suits a range of hardy perennials, among them varieties of salvia, grouped in a wall-backed

Pages 144–45: Chaenomeles flowers in late winter over a ruined wall in the Old Potting Sheds.

Opposite: A roofless doorway is outlined by *Lagerstroemia indica* and *Actinidia kolomikta*.

Below, from left to right: Paeonia ludlowii; Azara serrata; Actinidia kolomikta; a double-flowering chaenomeles.

There are a number of quiet places to sit. Here, *Actinidia kolomikta* is in the foreground and *Solanum crispum* 'Glasnevin' beside the bench.

Top: The bright-pink flowers of the crape myrtle, *Lagerstroemia indica*.

Above, left: Abutilon megapotamicum flowers unchecked all summer long.

Above, right: The late-summer display of *Salvia involucrata* 'Bethellii'.

OLD POTTING SHEDS

BORDE HILL GARDEN

Opposite: Belichened stone, wood and old ironwork contribute to the established character of Borde Hill.

Right: The ruined walls of the Old Potting Sheds create a charmingly intimate atmosphere.

Below: Clumps of *Rudbeckia* 'Goldsturm' line the path leading from the Old Potting Sheds to the Long Dell and the West Garden.

bed – pure-blue *Salvia patens* and darker *S. nemorosa* 'Caradonna' for mid-summer, with cerise *S. involucrata* 'Bethellii' for the late season. Elsewhere are planted *Euphorbia characias*, *Echinacea purpurea* 'Magnus', echiums, phlomis, santolina, prostrate rosemary and self-seeded tree peonies, among them bright-yellow *Paeonia ludlowii*. In the clean air of Borde Hill Garden, the epiphytic Mediterranean lichen *Ramalina farinacea* has attached itself to some of the shrub branches.

The path leading from the Old Potting Sheds round to the top of the Long Dell is flanked by a bed of grasses and by large clumps of late-summer *Rudbeckia* 'Goldsturm', the latter recalling similar planting on the West Bank.

Long Dell

Walking up the slight incline from the Old Potting Sheds, you approach Josephine's Way, named after a granddaughter of Stephie. A bank here has been designed by Noel Kingsbury, with grasses giving colour, movement and texture as they fill out in late summer. They include the fountain grass *Pennisetum alopecuroides* 'Hameln'; *Panicum virgatum* 'Heavy Metal', with soft-grey leaves and stems; whispering *Stipa tenuissima*; the patterned *Miscanthus sinensis* 'Zebrinus'; and a golden edging of *Hakonechloa macra* 'Alboaurea'. For contrast, there are golden rudbeckias ('Goldsturm'), fiery *Crocosmia* 'Lucifer' and blue *Libertia sessiliflora* 'Caerulescens'. The path opens up beyond a grove of holm oaks, and is lined with elaeagnus, pale-pink fuchsias, bergenias, cotoneaster and hypericum. This is the rim of the Long Dell, and below is a canopy of trees, shrubs and herbaceous plants from the Sino-Himalayan region, among them the glossy-leaved *Magnolia delavayi*, which has impressive creamy flowers in summer. As you look down, over the crowns of *Trachycarpus fortunei*, *Metasequoia glyptostroboides*, *Paulownia tomentosa* and *Toona sinensis*, it is as though you are on a Chinese mountainside rather than in West Sussex.

This obsolete Victorian quarry was where many plant hunters' introductions were planted in the 1920s and '30s, as Stephie described in 1938 in his article for the *Journal of the Royal Horticultural Society*: 'Some large-leaved Rhododendrons in the pit are doing well, among them two varieties of *R. sinograande*, the form first introduced, and var. *septentrionale*. Both seem hardy, but whereas the first form holds its leaves in their natural position during a frost, *septentrionale* under such conditions droops its leaves until they hang parallel with the stem.' As ever when reading anything Stephie wrote, you are conscious of his detailed knowledge of every plant in his garden.

As Stephie's words suggest, the Long Dell proved only partly suitable for rhododendrons: the north side can catch the frost; the soil of the former quarry is poor; and the dell fills with water in a wet winter. The rhododendrons that Stephie mentioned have now vanished, and the hurricane of 1987 caused further damage to other original plantings. Yet the storm was not an unmitigated disaster for the dell, as the felling of dominant forest trees opened up areas of light and allowed

Right: Rhododendron hunnewellianum, a native of Sichuan in China, flowers in early March.

Far right: The tiny creamy-yellow flowers of *Stachyurus praecox* are a welcome sight in winter.

shorter plants to flourish. Plant exchanges and gifts, so crucial when Stephie was building up the garden's collections, proved invaluable again. Donations of Himalayan plants came via Charles Erskine, then head of the arboretum at Kew, and also from Howick Hall in Alnwick, Northumberland. Lord Howick is an avid plant hunter who since 1980 has collected trees and shrubs on expeditions to China, Korea and Japan.

Rhododendrons now tend to be planted on the warmer, southern side of the dell. Among them are a young *Rhododendron griffithianum*, as well as *R. glanduliferum* and *R. argyrophyllum* subsp. *hypoglaucum*. In late March, early pale-purple flowers appear on *R. hunnewellianum*, a native of Sichuan. There are several camellias, too, including red *Camellia japonica* 'Imbricata', *C.j.* 'Mathotiana Alba', *C.j.* 'Mathotiana Rosea' and white *C. forrestii*. Also planted along the floor of the dell and up its banks are bamboos, acers, berberis, abelia and *Cornus controversa*.

New Asian introductions include deciduous flowering shrubs. Making a splash in winter are the bell-shaped creamy-yellow flowers on the bare branches of *Stachyurus praecox* from Japan. In summer the paper mulberry, *Broussonetia papyrifera*, has pale-green flowers followed by edible orange fruit, while *Philadelphus delavayi* is covered in fragrant white flowers in June. Also from the Far East is a fast-growing member of the elm family, *Zelkova schneideriana*.

In the centre of the dell is *Infinity Box*, an installation with a particular appeal for children. This huge galvanized-metal cube was brought here from the African Vision Malawi Garden, designed for the 2015 RHS Hampton Court Flower Show. Originally planted with African food crops, it now features clipped *Pittosporum tenuifolium* 'Tom Thumb' and hardy palms, visible through the portholes in its sides. The mirrored walls reflect one another so it seems as if the planting within the box stretches on endlessly.

The rim of the Long Dell is outlined by a dramatic range of trees introduced from the Sino-Himalayan region.

THE GARDEN
153

West Garden

This secluded, wooded area is tucked away between the Italian Garden, the Long Dell and the West Bank. In its midst is West Garden Lodge, the estate office until it was wrecked by falling trees in the 1987 hurricane, with the loss of some of the family correspondence and archives. The roof and internal walls were subsequently rebuilt, and the house is now let out to tenants.

Paths snake through a dense and colourful grove of magnolias, rhododendrons and camellias planted up by Stephie from 1900 onwards, with other shrubs and perennials subsequently added to the mix. Although some trees were lost in the storm, many of Stephie's introductions remain, as well as centuries-old oaks that provide a lofty canopy. Ivy (*Hedera helix*) grows up one, while another is covered with wisteria, at its best in May. The season in the West Garden is well into its stride by then, having started in March with the pendulous white flowers of *Oemleria cerasiformis* and the early magnolias. Plantings by Stephie include the pinky-white *Magnolia* × *veitchii*, bred by Peter Veitch in 1907 at the Veitchs' nursery in Exeter, and *M. campbellii* subsp. *mollicomata*, with mid-pink flowers like large teacups. A contrasting splash of red can be spotted in one corner: these are the flowers of *Camellia japonica* 'Donckelaeri' (now *C.j.* 'Masayoshi'), one of the parents of Borde Hill's award-winning *C.* × *williamsii* 'Donation'.

Beneath magnolias and mahonia flower leucojums (or summer snowflakes) and hellebores in shades of white, pink and purple, including a very pretty double picotee introduced by Eleni. In late April small creamy-green flowers appear on *Magnolia* 'Gold Star' and yellow ones on *M.* 'Lois'. These are followed in May by cream, pink, pale-purple and coral-red rhododendrons, in places arching over the woodland path. Among them are the pink-frilled blooms of *Rhododendron* 'Loderi King George' and *R.* 'Nicola Newman', a particular favourite with pollinating insects and a cross bred by Robert Stephenson Clarke.

Other May delights include carpets of pinky-purple *Primula pulverulenta*, and, in contrast to the strong colours of the rhododendrons, creamy *Cornus controversa* 'Variegata', with variegated foliage, and the big-headed profusion of *Viburnum macrocephalum*.

There is a wonderfully rich mix of colour, texture and fragrance throughout the year in the West Garden, where later ground cover includes hostas and ferns. In August sprays of *Verbena bonariensis* line the path and *Hoheria angustifolia* × *sexstylosa* is a mighty cascade of delicately scented white flowers.

Pools of Primula pulverulenta are a feature of the West Garden in May.

Camellia japonica 'Donckelaeri' (now C.j. 'Masayoshi') is one of the parents of Borde Hill's award-winning 'Donation' camellia.

Opposite, left: Two rhododendrons planted by Stephie form an arch over the entrance to the West Garden.

Opposite, top right: Native to mainland China, *Viburnum macrocephalum* produces huge white balls of flowers in late spring.

Opposite, centre and bottom right: Two unnamed examples of Stephie's extensive rhododendron collection.

BORDE HILL GARDEN

THE GARDEN

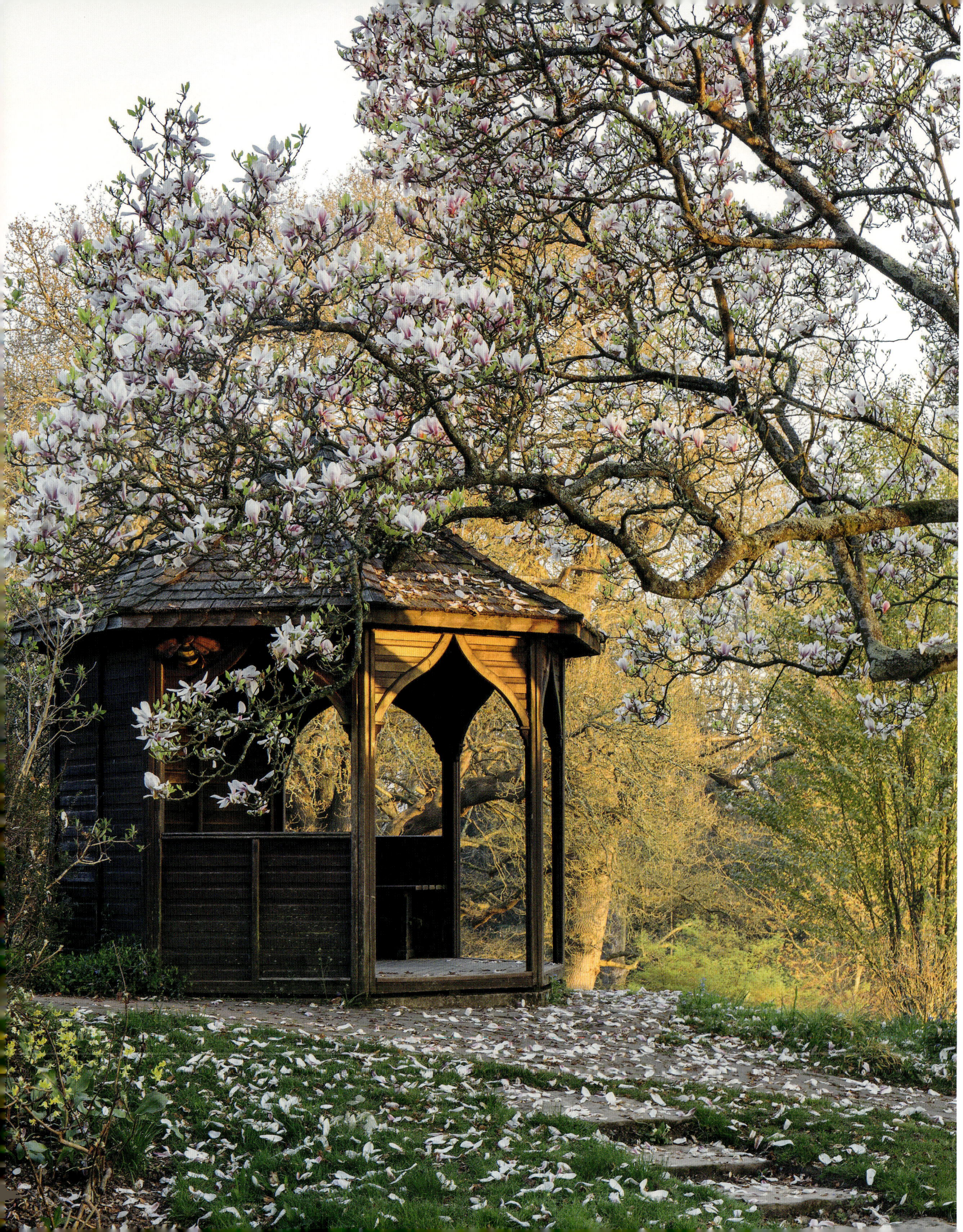

Garden of Allah

The Garden of Allah was created by Stephie in 1925 and later given its name by his son Ralph, who said the glade was so peaceful and secret that 'one might have met Allah's spirit' here. It is perhaps the most abundantly planted area of the garden, with an impressive range of rare trees, shrubs and perennials enhanced over four generations. This semi-woodland has always been special to the Stephenson Clarke family partly because of its proximity to the house. Steps lead up through banks of camellias to the private turning circle by the north front, giving the Garden of Allah its intimacy even though it is open to the public.

Stephie reclaimed the land from the North Park, its sandy soil suitable for special introductions from George Forrest's and Frank Kingdon Ward's expeditions in China and Burma. He described the conditions in the *Journal of the Royal Horticultural Society* in 1938: 'The soil is excellent and no carting is required when making new beds; there is a pit, probably also an old quarry, at the west end; the side of it facing north has proved valuable for Lilies and Nomocharis ... Two rare Magnolias planted here are *M. Fraseri* and *M. officinalis*.'

The two trees mentioned by Stephie flower in late April or early May. They form part of a commanding group of magnolias known as the 'Three Sisters' or the 'Holy Trinity', all champion trees by girth. The huge *Magnolia obovata*, planted in 1935, is a large-leaved Japanese tree with fragrant milky-white, red-stemmed flowers. Planted in 1933, the rare 'fishtail' *M. fraseri*, native to the southern Appalachians, has showy creamy flowers, while the third sister is probably a seedling of the *M. officinalis* collected in China by Ernest Wilson. It was 'a much-appreciated present' to Stephie from his fellow collector Colonel Leonard Messel of Nymans and was planted here also in 1933 at 6 feet (1.8 m) high.

An even earlier flowerer is *Magnolia campbellii* subsp. *mollicomata*, with mid-pink flowers in March. Also here are pinky-white *M.* × *soulangeana* and *M.* × *veitchii* and the rich-purple and unusual *M.* Black Tulip. Another gem is the late-May-flowering

Opposite: A magnificent *Magnolia* × *soulangeana* flowers on bare wood beside Becky's Bower, which was built in memory of Andrewjohn's grandmother.

Left: The splendid dark-purple flowers of *Magnolia* Black Tulip.

THE GARDEN

Magnolia × *veitchii*, a hybrid, was bred in 1907 by the Exeter nurseryman Peter Veitch to combine the large pink flowers of *M. campbellii* with the upright tepals and almost pure-white flowers of *M. denudata*.

Far left and left: The mid-pink flowers of *Magnolia campbellii* subsp. *mollicomata* in the Garden of Allah.

Growing between the Garden of Allah and Warren Wood, the rare *Magnolia campbellii* subsp. *mollicomata* 'Borde Hill' was reintroduced to Borde Hill in the early 2000s and has deep-pink, almost purple flowers.

Above and right: Collected in China by Ernest Wilson, *Magnolia officinalis* was a gift to Stephie from fellow plant collector Colonel Lionel Messel of Nymans.

Above and left: Another of the so-called Three Sisters, *Magnolia fraseri* is native to the southern Appalachians.

Above and left: The Japanese *Magnolia obovata*, with a view of the North Park beyond. All three magnolias are champion trees by girth.

GARDEN OF ALLAH

From the house in March, you can look towards the Victorian Ouse Valley Viaduct over the pink blooms of *Camellia* × *williamsii* 'Donation' and the paler flowers of *Rhododendron rubiginosum*.

Chinese tulip tree, *Liriodendron chinense*, now more than 60 feet (18 m) high. Raised from seed collected in central China by Wilson in the early 1900s, a sapling was bought by Stephie from Veitch in Chelsea in 1913. It flowered for the first time in the summer of 1927, when Stephie sent a flowering shoot to W.J. Bean, curator of the Royal Botanic Gardens, Kew, and author of the authoritative *Trees and Shrubs Hardy in the British Isles*. (First published in 1914, the book went into numerous editions, and in 1988 was updated by Desmond Clarke, a Stephenson Clarke cousin and sometime member of the Borde Hill Garden Council.) Bean told Stephie: 'As far as I know you are the first to flower this tree in Europe ... I might write a note about it for "Country Life".' Wilson also sent his congratulations from America.

Hellebores multiply promiscuously across the Garden of Allah.

BORDE HILL GARDEN

Right: Pale-purple *Rhododendron rubiginosum*.

Below: Stone paths wind between banks of rhododendrons, including 'J.G. Millais', *R. rubiginosum* and *R. annae*, in the Garden of Allah.

GARDEN OF ALLAH
163

The wall-backed bed in the Garden of Allah, below the north front of the house, is packed with woodland planting, including ferns, hellebores, various camellias, cardiocrinums, *Kirengeshoma palmata* and hydrangeas, the last two extending the season into summer.

Other trees through this enclosed garden include varieties of oak (*Quercus palustris* and *Q. robur*), birches, *Prunus* 'Tai-haku' and some smaller specimen trees, such as *Sorbus pseudohupehensis* and *Liquidambar acalycina* 'Spinners'. The many decorative shrubs include *Cornus kousa* 'John Slocock', with carmine-splashed white petals, and, for spring colour, *Corylopsis sinensis* var. *sinensis* 'Spring Purple' and various pieris; later hydrangeas carry the interest into late summer and early autumn. Around the pond in the lower part of the garden grow *Gunnera manicata*, *Primula pulverulenta*, osmunda ferns, various hostas and *Cardiocrinum giganteum* var. *yunnanense*. Glimpses of the rolling North Park beyond can be seen through occasional breaks in the planting.

Few remain of Forrest's and Kingdon Ward's rhododendrons originally planted by Stephie, but newer hybrids encircle the lawn in an open glade. Banks of camellias through the Garden of Allah and around Becky's Bower feature another *Camellia* × *williamsii* 'Francis Hanger', *C.* 'Salutation' and one of its parents, *C. saluenensis*, and varieties of *C. japonica*, not all of them identified. Substitutions and new planting continue: a *Toxicodendron vernicifluum* is a replacement for a taller sumac lost in the 1987 hurricane. New is *Edgeworthia chrysantha*, bringing the early colour and scent that are also supplied by creamy wintersweet flowers (*Chimonanthus praecox*) and glowing witch hazels (*Hamamelis* × *intermedia* 'Frederic', 'Jelena' and 'Angelly'). The Stephenson Clarkes are still adding plants to the wall-backed border below the steps; for instance, in 2018, for late winter and early spring, Eleni introduced cream hellebores speckled with purple, from the Evolution Group of Ashwood Garden Hybrids. Along the path, and in full, radiant rose-pink flower in March, is one of Borde Hill's major contributions to the gardening world: *Camellia* × *williamsii* 'Donation'.

A path lined in winter and spring with hellebores, and later with wild garlic, snakes through the garden towards Becky's Bower, an eastern-style summer house built in memory of Ralph's wife, Becky, who died in 1985.

The flower of *Liriodendron chinense*, which appeared for the first time in Europe on this tree in 1927.

BORDE HILL GARDEN

Liriodendron chinense, bought by Stephie from the Veitch nursery in Chelsea in 1913, now towers above Becky's Bower in the Garden of Allah.

Azalea Ring

A path from the Garden of Allah skirts round below the house, skimming the top of the North Park. At any time of year, this is a splendid outlook, and it is more open since the 1987 hurricane razed the Pinetum. Out of morning mists emerges the Victorian viaduct, composed of thirty-seven arches and 11 million bricks, and spanning the River Ouse, the northern boundary of the estate. On the slopes are parkland trees: beech, oak, ash and many exotics planted by Stephie, including *Sequoiadendron giganteum*, *Populus* × *berolinensis* 'Petrowskyana', *Carya ovata*, *Quercus pyrenaica*, *Fraxinus pennsylvanica* and *Malus baccata* var. *mandshurica* (the Manchurian Siberian crab apple). Skeletal against the winter sky, these become magnificent spreading specimens in summer. Rising beyond the viaduct is a line of wooded hills, the far western extension of the High Weald.

An *Acer griseum* stands by the path, its peeling golden bark as lovely in spring as in autumn. This tree was damaged at some point, but has

A star attraction of the Azalea Ring is a remarkable *Magnolia campbellii*, one of Borde Hill's champion trees.

A colourful display of Knap Hill and Mollis azaleas in the Azalea Ring, one of Stephie's early planting projects.

Top, from left to right:
Camellia × *williamsii*
'Francis Hanger';
Rhododendron 'Humboldt
Picotee'.

Above, from left to right:
Camellia × *williamsii*
'Donation'; *Anemone*
× *hybrida* 'Honorine
Jobert'.

BORDE HILL GARDEN

Creamy *Rhododendron* 'Delicatissimum', in the foreground, and yellow *R. luteum*, centre, are among the paler-coloured specimens in the Azalea Ring.

Right and far right:
Emmenopterys henryi was planted in 1928 in the Azalea Ring from seed collected by George Forrest in China. It flowered here for the first time in 2011 and has flowered four times since then.

Halesia carolina, originally from the south-eastern United States, has bell-like flowers in late spring.

come back as a sturdy sentinel beside the gate to the private drive. According to the former head gardener Andy Stevens, the slow-growing *Acer griseum* is difficult to propagate despite producing 'bucketfuls' of seed. This tree, like so many others at Borde Hill, has a historic provenance: it was almost certainly grown from an Ernest Wilson introduction.

From the gate, the wide lawn that spreads out was a paddock for children's ponies in the early 1900s. Stephie planted a line of conifers (mostly silver firs raised from seed sent from Japan by one of his brothers in 1890) to obscure the Balcombe–Haywards Heath road beyond and as a shelter belt for the Azalea Ring. This horseshoe of formal semicircular beds fringes the lawn and was planted by Stephie with Ghent and Knap Hill azaleas, as well as the species *Rhododendron molle* and Mollis hybrids.

Stephie described the layout in detail in the *Journal of the Royal Horticultural Society* in May 1938, and evoked one of his long-standing gardening friendships: 'The Ghent Azaleas, now over forty years old, are twelve feet high, and make a brave show after the Knap Hill hybrids are past their best; the last were nearly all bought in bloom in company with the late Mr Anthony Waterer, to whose Nursery [Knap Hill Nursery, Woking] I paid an annual visit for many years. They are planted on either side of a walk in front of the Ghents and range through white, lemon, buff and orange, to rich crimson, and there are also a few good pinks, but perhaps of all the colours, pure white is least common among them. On the outside of their beds are some *Rhododendron molle* and "Mollis hybrids"; these open the Azalea season by blooming before the Knap Hill Azaleas … although I am a great admirer of the Mollis I undoubtedly prefer the Knap Hill strain.'

BORDE HILL GARDEN

These hybrids were bred in the mid-nineteenth century when the widespread interest in rhododendrons and azaleas was triggered by Joseph Dalton Hooker's and Robert Fortune's introductions. The Ghents, the oldest hybrid deciduous azaleas, were propagated by crossing north-eastern American species with the European *Rhododendron luteum*. The Knap Hill strain was cultivated in the 1850s by the father of Stephie's friend, also Anthony Waterer, and his partner, Robert Godfrey, who enhanced the Ghents by crossing them with the Chinese azalea, *R. molle*. Their work was praised in *The Gardeners' Chronicle and Agricultural Gazette* in 1861: 'Some fine seedlings have been obtained, with blooms of large size and possessing great richness and variety of colour. They have also the good property of being late bloomers.'

Those assets endeared the azaleas to Stephie, and their display is as dazzling today as it was almost a century ago when he was writing. Stephie's relationship and plant exchanges continued with both Waterer's (in Bagshot) and Knap Hill nurseries until the late 1930s. In October 1938 the assistant managing director of John Waterer Sons & Crisp wrote to Stephie to say that 'in return for the Camellia grafts you so kindly sent us in August last, we have much pleasure in enclosing herewith gratis invoice for a Rhododendron Loderi Venus, which was sent to you on the 1st October'. Every corner of Borde Hill has a snatch of personal history behind it.

Before the azaleas flare up, the show begins in early March with the flowering of rose-pink *Camellia* × *williamsii* 'Donation'. *C.* × *w.* 'Francis Hanger' stars here, too, another appearance of the lovely white camellia that also grows on the South Lawn and in the Garden of Allah. This repetition of signature plants in different areas gives depth and coherence to the planting across the garden. Within the Azalea Ring, white and pink camellias flower along with several magnolias. One graceful, tall magnolia with arching branches has pink-throated white flowers and at its foot clumps of colchicums. Another

Cornus kousa in full May flower on the lawn by the Azalea Ring.

AZALEA RING

Right: Stewartia pseudocamellia (left) and *Cornus kousa* (right) introduce fiery autumn colour to the Azalea Ring.

has buds like white candles. Nearby is a *Magnolia × soulangeana* 'Brozzonii', planted in 1908. This opens in April, with long-lasting goblet-shaped white blooms like a covering of snow.

But head and shoulders above the other magnolias and with a massive girth is the star of stars. This specimen of *Magnolia campbellii*, introduced to cultivation in the 1920s by George Forrest, was planted here by Stephie. The rich-pink buds open to flowers of a paler pink. Another rarity is *Emmenopterys henryi*, planted in 1928 from seed also collected by Forrest in southern China, and a slow developer: it did not open its delicate creamy blooms until 2011, since when it has flowered four times. A scene-stealer is *Cornus kousa*, covered with virginal bridal bracts in May and a fiery red in autumn. *Halesia carolina*, originally from the south-eastern United States, has bunches of bell-like pure-white flowers that emerge from apple-blossom-pink buds. On the bark of one tree in the Azalea Ring grows a very rare form of rag lichen, *Cetrelia cetrarioides*.

As you leave the Azalea Ring and head for the visitor centre, you will see a charming small magnolia, the head-high *Magnolia* 'Premier Cru', with strong purple-pink flowers on bare branches in March. This was selected by plantsman Maurice Foster, whose White House Farm, near Sevenoaks in Kent, is home to more than 200 different types of magnolia. 'Premier Cru', a new introduction by Eleni, is further proof that Borde Hill is a garden that never stands still.

Below: Cornus kousa is a rich red in early autumn before its leaves turn to gold.

BORDE HILL GARDEN

AZALEA RING

Warren Wood

A grassy track leads down from beside Becky's Bower in the Garden of Allah into Warren Wood, and, beyond it, to Stephanie's Glade (named after another granddaughter of Stephie). These woods are enjoyable year-round and are full of historical associations, for this is where Stephie planted many of his early acquisitions. In winter, shafts of light illumine the bare trees like the columns of a Gothic cathedral. Old pheasant's-eye daffodils (*Narcissus poeticus* var. *recurvus*) drift down through the grass from Becky's Bower to meet the woodland in late April. In autumn, leaves and acorns are crunchy underfoot, the tree canopy is a tapestry of yellow, red, brown and gold, and the near-silence is broken by the barking cries of pheasants. But the peak season is late spring, when the tree-sized rhododendrons are in full bloom, their white, pink and red flowers a perfect foil for the woodland carpet of bluebells, wood anemones and wild garlic.

Pathways through the woods are lined with rhododendrons in May and early June.

BORDE HILL GARDEN

Bluebells beneath a Loderi Group rhododendron.

Overleaf: Bluebells flower abundantly throughout Warren Wood in May.

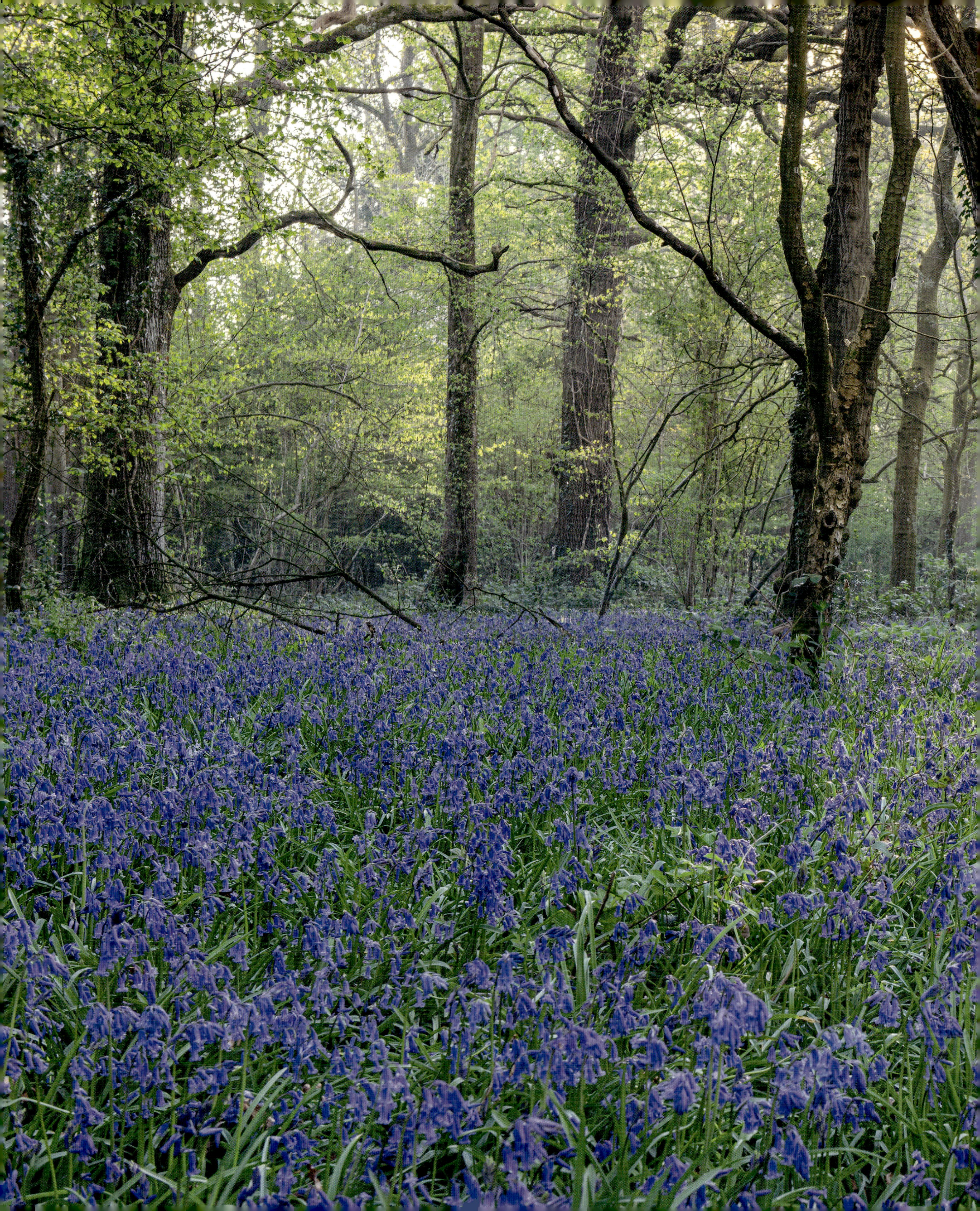

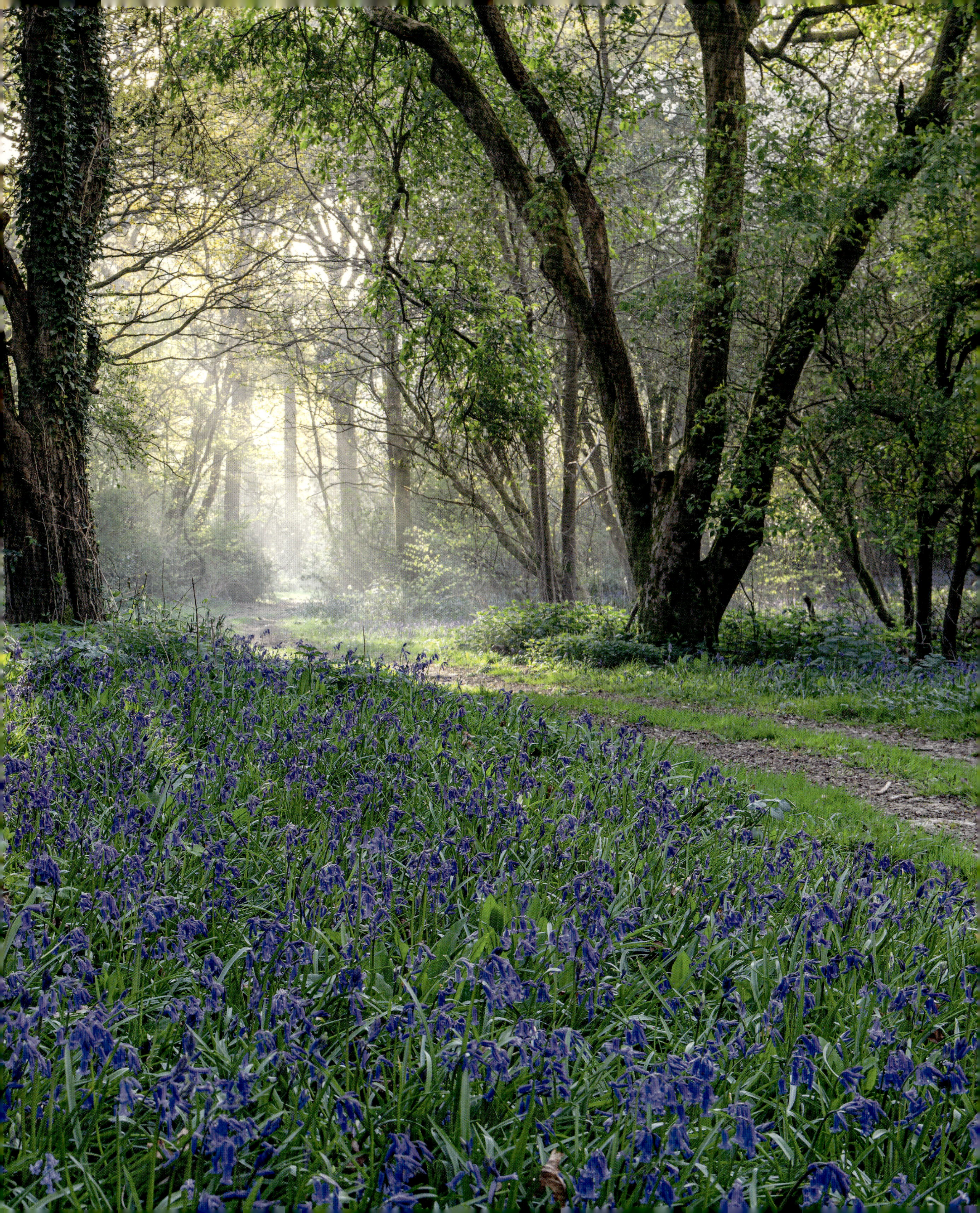

Stephie's opening comments in the 1935 *Catalogue of the Trees and Shrubs at Borde Hill, Sussex* suggest that his first intention on buying the estate in 1893 was to improve the landscape and the outlook from the house. But by 1905, urged on by his friend Henry Elwes, Stephie was becoming a serious collector: he was clearing excess oak, ash, hazel and beech in Warren Wood and planting new introductions in the shelter of the remaining trees. Planting started five years later in what became Stephanie's Glade. The conditions in the wood are mixed, as Stephie described in the *Catalogue*: 'The Warren Wood on the north slope of the Central Ridge possesses a band of rich loam along the east and centre of its southern edge; unfortunately, at the west end of the wood this deteriorates into an extremely poor shaley clay, in which Pines, Spruces and Brooms alone seem to be happy; its north-eastern part has a distinctly better soil than the west end, though it is of similar appearance, but here vegetation suffers severely from spring frosts.'

Stephie recognized the challenges, but he successfully established a range of species through Warren Wood and Stephanie's Glade, planting according to the right conditions for individual trees or shrubs rather than according to a predetermined design scheme. More than 200 exotic rhododendron species were listed in the woods in 1968, and, despite losses in the 1987 hurricane, many of Borde Hill's champion trees and mature rhododendrons from Stephie's original plantings remain. Indeed, rhododendrons in Warren Wood grew often to three times the size of those struggling with the heavy clay of the Old Rhododendron Garden.

Just below the Garden of Allah stands a majestic *Platanus orientalis* var. *insularis*, the seeds for which were collected by Ralph on the Greek island of Lemnos during the First World War. Opposite are fragrant hybrids of *Rhododendron fortunei*, and behind those a path leads to the handkerchief tree, the May-flowering *Davidia involucrata*. Felled by the storm of 1987, it has regrown from its stump. Also striking in May, with its creamy panicles, is the deciduous tree *Meliosma beaniana* (now *M. alba*), an Ernest Wilson introduction and one of only three in the UK. Nearby are a fine *Chamaecyparis formosensis*, collected by Elwes in Taiwan in 1912, and an impressive evergreen conifer, *Podocarpus salignus*, which – with its glossy narrow, willow-like leaves – Eleni describes as looking as 'soft as a teddy bear'.

A dainty English bluebell, *Hyacinthoides non-scripta*, among the moss-covered roots of a beech tree in Stephanie's Glade.

The handkerchief tree (*Davidia involucrata*) is so called because of the distinctive shape of its May flowers.

BORDE HILL GARDEN

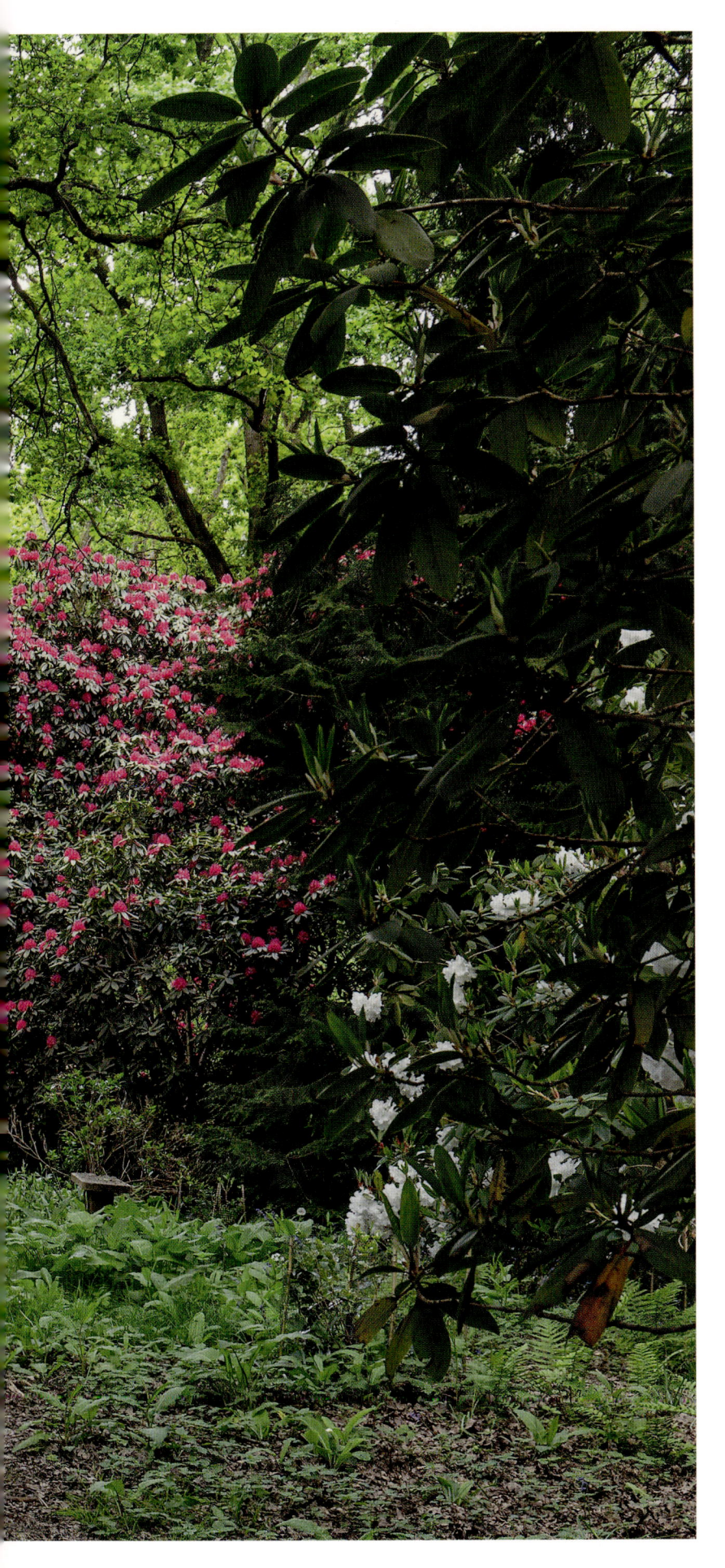

One of the most imposing trees in the wood is *Magnolia campbellii*, with an enormous trifurcated trunk and branches like a candelabrum. It flowers in early April, seemingly unsusceptible to frost.

Planting of new rhododendrons is beginning in a glade that was opened up in 2019 by the loss of an old abies planted by Stephie. Some of the rhododendrons have been propagated from existing species and hybrids at Borde Hill, while others will come from specialist rhododendron nurseries owned by the descendants of Stephie's gardening contacts: Kenneth Cox at Glendoick near Perth and David Millais at Farnham in Surrey. Other new work includes the installation of steps near a bridge over the stream that runs through the wood, and the channelling of the stream above the Victorian sandstone dam to reinstate the waterfall.

Among a group of pines and junipers planted by Stephie is the tall and graceful *Juniperus rigida*, with soft needles hanging in bunches. It is a sacred tree in Japan, where it is often planted near temples. Although it is hardy, its foliage tends to turn brown in winter. This species was introduced to the UK in 1861 by the collector John Gould Veitch, and has coped with the poorer shaly clay in this part of the garden.

On the other side of the path is the rare Spanish juniper, *Juniperus thurifera*, planted where

Left: A path through the wood cuts between a *Pieris japonica* and *Rhododendron* 'Cynthia'.

Below, left: Rhododendron *arboreum*, native to the Himalayas.

WARREN WOOD

it avoids the worst of the winter frosts. A more recent introduction to the woodland is a dawn redwood or fossil tree, *Metasequoia glyptostroboides*, thought at one time to be extinct. It was rediscovered in 1941 in Hubei and north-eastern Sichuan, and Stephie subsequently acquired two plants from Harold Hillier. In summer the tree has feathery light-green foliage that turns warm, rusty brown in autumn. Other redwoods through this part of the wood have been planted by Andrewjohn.

The Chile pine or monkey puzzle tree, *Araucaria araucana*, is a species that has survived since the Jurassic period, and grows along the mountain ranges of Chile and Argentina. It was introduced to Britain in the late eighteenth century and became a great favourite with Victorian gardeners for its strange, spiky shape. Its cones, the size of coconuts, are carried high up in the canopy of the tree.

Picea likiangensis, the Lijiang spruce, was discovered in 1884 by the French Jesuit missionary Père Delavay (who gave his name to *Magnolia delavayi*, among other plants) in the Lichiang (Lijiang) range of Yunnan. It was introduced to Britain by Wilson in 1904, and has brilliant-red cones in April and May. There is also *Abies procera* 'Glauca', a cultivar of the noble fir species discovered by the intrepid Scotsman David Douglas in Oregon in 1825. Very hardy, it grows up die-straight, with shimmering blue-grey needles.

Continuing through a clearing into Stephanie's Glade, the path passes the shagbark hickory, *Carya ovata*, one of several American hickories planted here between 1911 and 1913. It is a conical deciduous tree, with peeling grey-brown bark, golden-yellow leaves in autumn and thick-shelled nuts. The path beyond is lined with bamboo, behind which a *Picea smithiana* emerges, a spruce from the western Himalayas, introduced to Scotland in 1818. *Fagus engleriana*, the rare Engler beech with unusual sea-green foliage, was found by Wilson in central China and introduced first to the United States and then to the UK in the early 1900s. Also in the glade is a variant of the Siberian crab apple, the lofty *Malus baccata* 'Jackii', originally introduced from Korea to western cultivation at the Arnold Arboretum in Boston, Massachusetts, in 1905. It is covered in white blossom in spring and has small purple crab apples in autumn.

To the north are slopes planted by Stephie with specimen trees, under which bluebells have seeded themselves, a fitting frame to these celebrated woodlands.

Left, top and bottom: Meliosma alba (previously *M. beaniana*), an Ernest Wilson introduction, has creamy panicles in May.

Opposite: The seeds of *Platanus orientalis* var. *insularis*, planted between Becky's Bower and Warren Wood, were collected by Ralph in Greece during the First World War.

Pages 184–85: In Warren Wood, the damaged branch of a parkland tree forms an impressive right angle. The woods are particularly lovely when the leaves begin to turn colour.

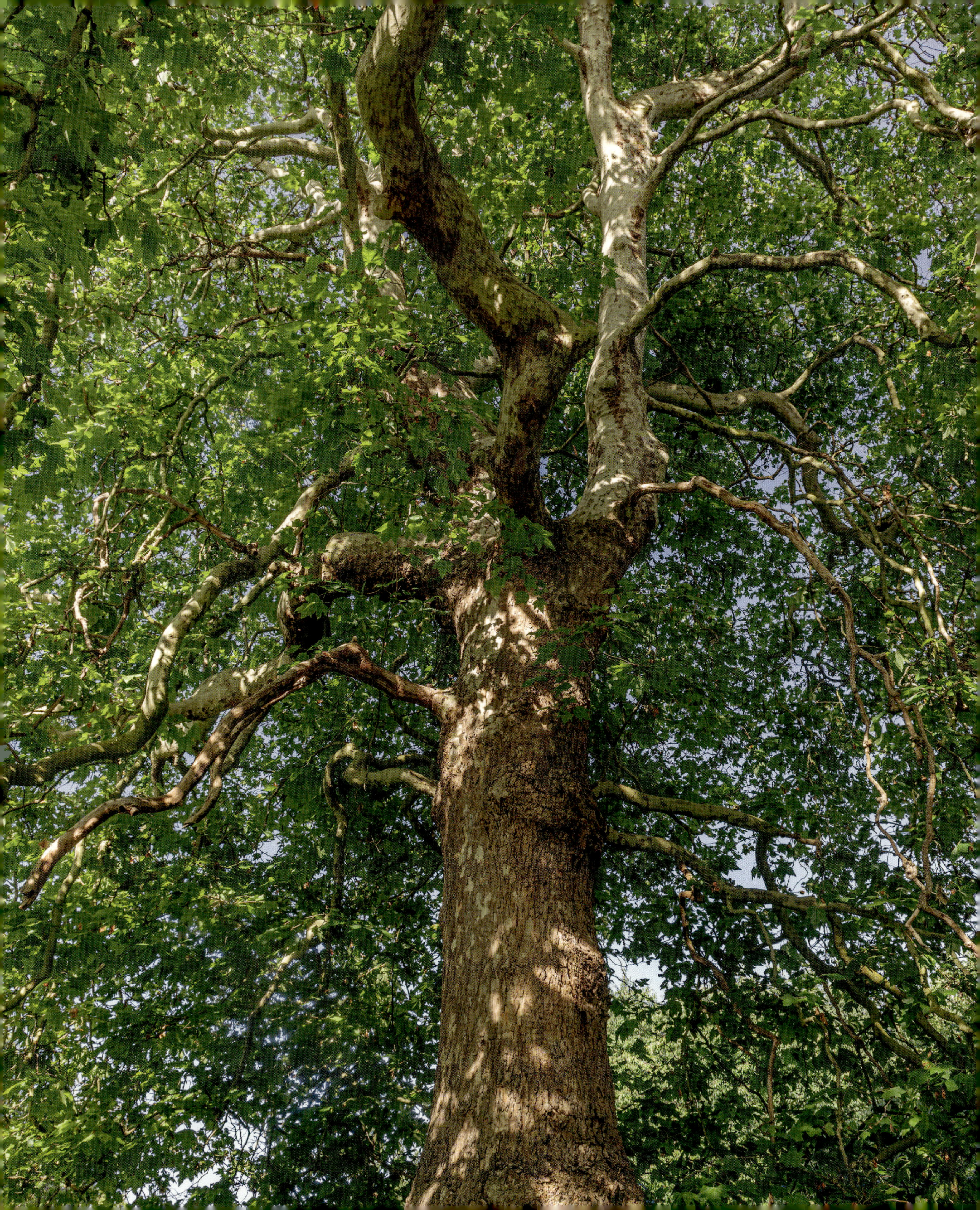

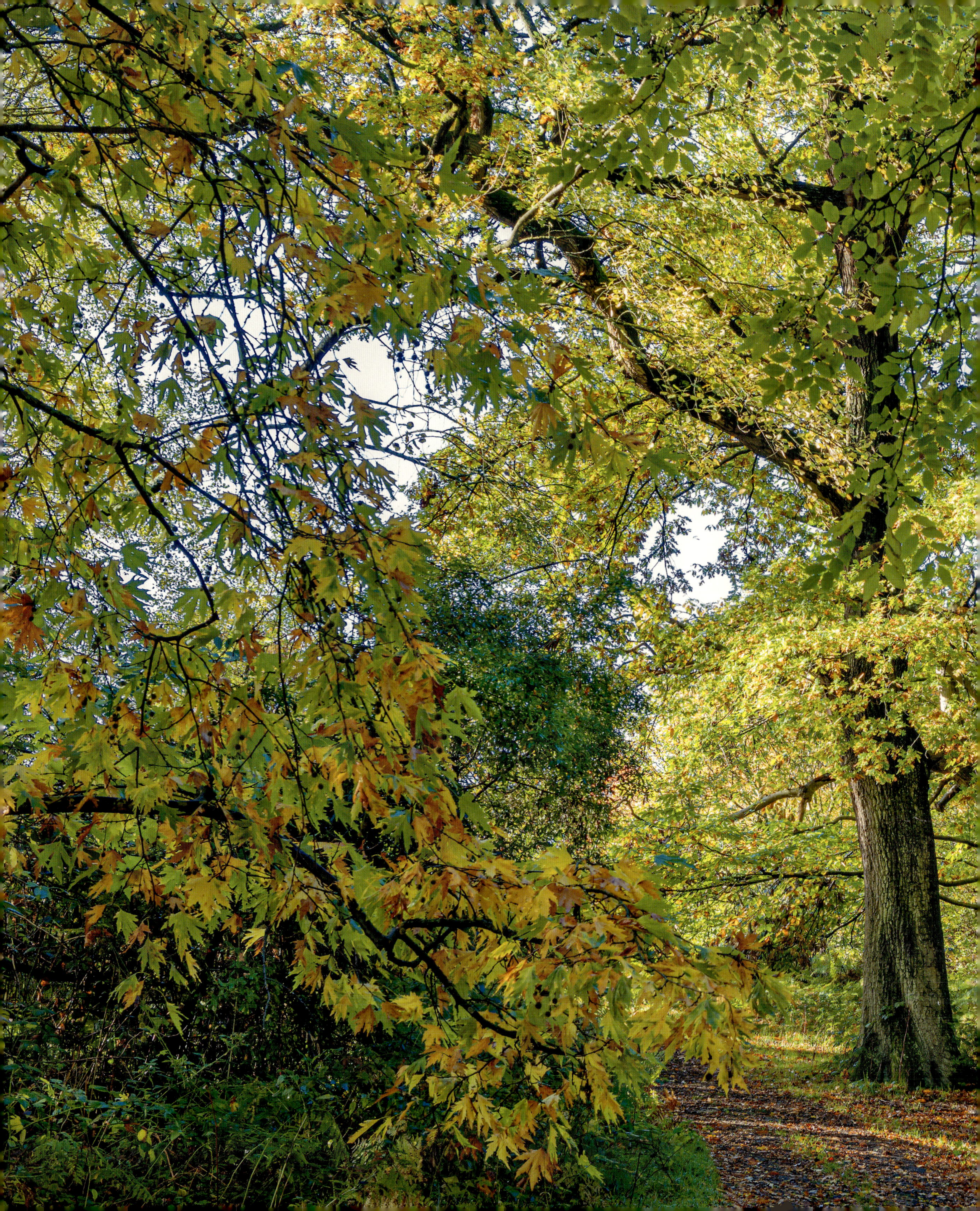

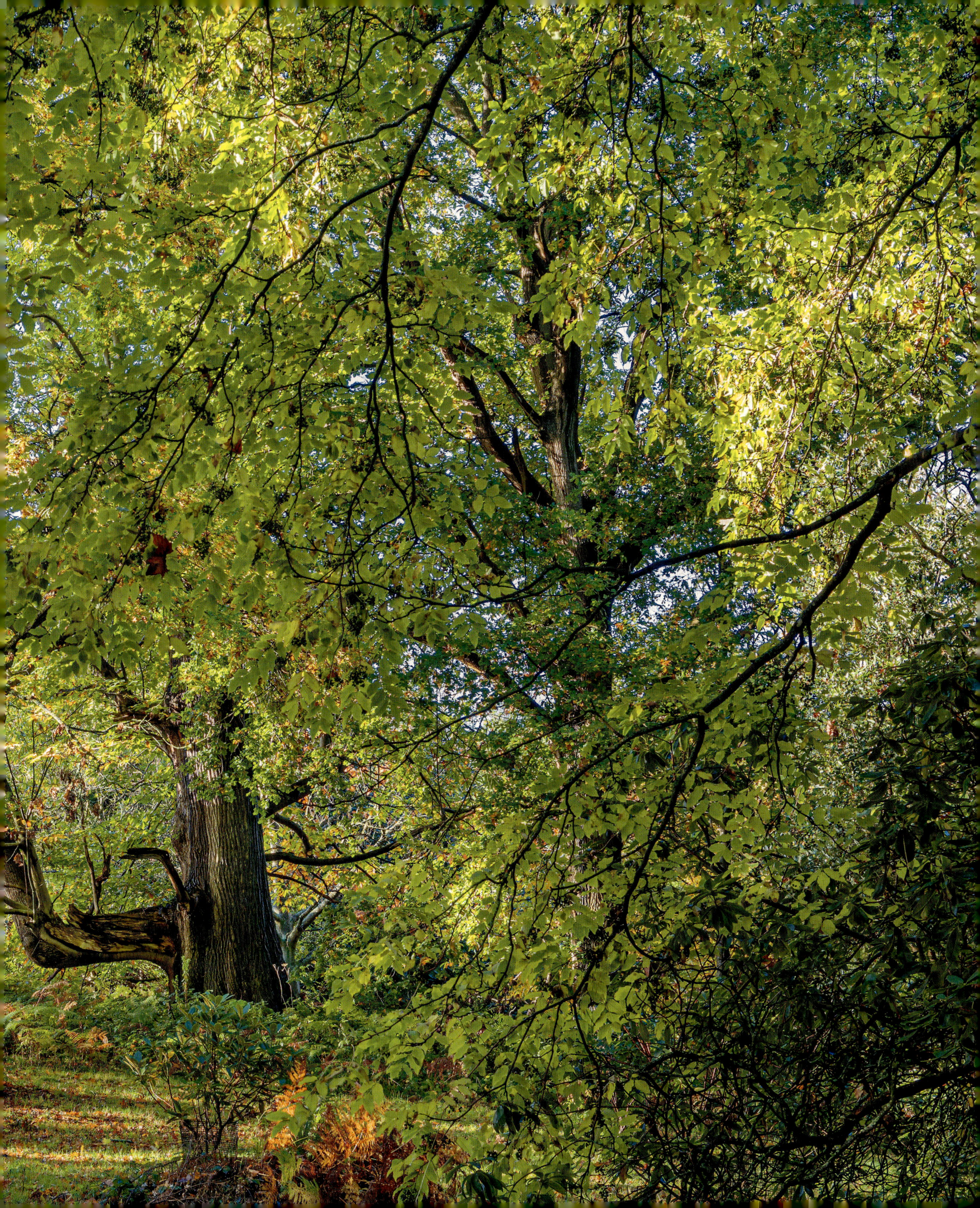

HISTORIC BORDE HILL PLANTS

Alstroemeria 'Walter Fleming'

Although Stephie devoted much of his time to collecting trees and shrubs, he also loved flowers, and in particular nerines and alstroemerias. He shared this interest with his daughter-in-law Becky, and they both corresponded and swapped plant material with other enthusiasts. In 1945 Stephie exchanged nerine bulbs for seeds of *Alstroemeria violacea* (now *A. paupercula*) with E.O. Orpet, a horticulturalist in Santa Barbara, while an E.B. Anderson from West Porlock wrote to Becky in 1960, saying, 'I should very much like a plant of A. 'Walter Fleming',' and offered her *A. haemantha* seeds as a trade. The new cultivar to which Fleming, Stephie's head gardener, gave his name was the result of crossing *A. violacea* with *A. aurantiaca* (now *A. aurea*). It grows to a height of 3 feet (0.9 m), has lance-shaped dark-green leaves and purple-marked cream flowers with yellow-and-orange striping. In June 1948 Stephie exhibited his new alstroemeria at an RHS show, where it won an Award of Merit.

Camellia 'Salutation'

One of Walter Fleming's great successes was *Camellia* 'Salutation', bred by him some years before *C.* 'Donation' (see opposite), as it is listed in the *Catalogue of the Trees and Shrubs at Borde Hill, Sussex*, published in 1935. There, Albert Bruce Jackson says that *C. saluenensis* was crossed with the wild *C. reticulata* to create 'Salutation': 'The resulting hybrid bears a double flower of a very pleasing light pink.' Like 'Donation', this hybrid was also deemed to be hardy, withstanding 'several degrees of frost without perceptible damage'. There was later some controversy about the hybrid's parentage, but Francis Hanger, curator of RHS Garden Wisley, satisfied himself on a visit to Borde Hill in 1956. With a colleague, he 'studied the foliage of the original *C.* 'Donation' and *C.* 'Salutation' very closely and came to the conclusion that the former possessed a glossy leaf confirming its parentage as *C. saluenensis* and *C. japonica* 'Donckelaeri' and the latter *C.* 'Salutation' possessed a more dull matt leaf showing distinct resemblance to *reticulata*.' Even eight years after his death, Stephie and his plants continued to remain under discussion in the horticultural world. The silvery-pink flowers of 'Salutation' can be seen in early spring in the Garden of Allah and above the wall of the White Garden.

Camellia × williamsii 'Donation'

Walter Fleming was a skilled hybridizer and propagator, but perhaps his greatest achievement was to raise Camellia × williamsii 'Donation', over the winter of 1937–38. Fleming crossed red *C. japonica* 'Donckelaeri' (now *C.j.* 'Masayoshi') with pale-pink *C. saluenensis* (the latter a gift from J.C. Williams of Caerhays) to breed the semi-double 'Donation'. 'I do not think it possible for any lover of camellias to visualize its outstanding beauty unless he or she has been favoured with the opportunity of seeing the plant in full bloom', wrote Francis Hanger in the 1957 *Rhododendron and Camellia Year Book*. The camellia was also much admired by George Johnstone of Trewithen in Cornwall, a friend to whom Stephie gave a plant in 1941. It was, Johnstone wrote, 'the greatest contribution that any single plant has made to this garden'. This beautiful, hardy camellia became a worldwide bestseller; it won an RHS Award of Merit in 1941 and an Award of Garden Merit in 1993. The original *C.* × *williamsii* 'Donation' is now in the private garden, to which it was removed from the old rose garden by the then head gardener, Brian Doe, 'to protect it from merciless pilfering when it was all the rage during the sixties'.

Emmenopterys henryi

The Irish plant hunter Augustine Henry first discovered this tree in central China in 1887, although it was not until 1907 that it was introduced into western cultivation, by Ernest Wilson; he described it as 'one of the most strikingly beautiful trees of the Chinese forests'. The tree took its time to demonstrate its arresting beauty at Borde Hill: it was only in 2011 that the larger of the two *Emmenopterys henryi* in the Azalea Ring flowered for the first time, eighty-three years after it was planted in 1928. This particular specimen was collected by George Forrest and has flowered four times since 2011, most recently in 2021. Now endangered in the wild, in spring the rare tree has orange-tinged leaves, which later become a glossy green. When it flowers, it does so in August, producing clusters of creamy blooms surrounded by large soft-white bracts. It is a jewel indeed.

Hoheria 'Borde Hill'

Hoheria 'Borde Hill' came originally from New Zealand, and was bought by Stephie from Hillier. This evergreen cultivar was identified as having slightly narrower leaves than the species. With bell-like pure-white flowers in late summer, it is also rather smaller, growing to a height of no more than 16 feet (4.9 m). Its relatively compact size has probably led to its widespread popularity as a garden shrub and its listing on many different websites, including Burncoose Nurseries in Cornwall and Botanica Plant Nursery in Suffolk. *H.* 'Borde Hill' is perfectly hardy in our now much milder winters, but, needing some protection from fierce winds, thrives on Jack Vass Walk in the sheltered Old Rhododendron Garden at Borde Hill.

Magnolia campbellii subsp. *mollicomata* 'Borde Hill'

Magnolia campbellii subsp. *mollicomata* (F25655) was collected by George Forrest in 1924 during his sixth expedition to China (1924–26). Forrest originally came across this subspecies in Yunnan in 1904: 'I shall always remember my first sight of a group of these magnificent Magnolias in full flower! I got within a mile of them from which distance the masses of pink blossoms showed up distinctly.' The magnolia listed as F25655 is mentioned in Jackson's 1935 *Catalogue*. Originally, J.C. Williams's son raised F25655 at Werrington Park in Cornwall, where it first flowered in 1943. Another was planted by J.C.'s cousin P.D. Williams at Lanarth, also in Cornwall. A third plant came to Borde Hill and, according to George Johnstone of Trewithen, was planted 'in an exposed position, so was somewhat stunted with a straggling top'; it died in 1953. Johnstone was given scions that he successfully propagated at Trewithen, and from which he handed grafting material to Hillier. *M.c.* subsp. *mollicomata* 'Borde Hill' returned to Borde Hill in the early 2000s and, now 20 feet (6 m) tall, grows on the edge of Warren Wood and has rich cyclamen-purple flowers. Larger *M.c.* subsp. *mollicomata*, with lavish displays of mid-pink flowers, grow in the West Garden and the Garden of Allah.

Magnolia sprengeri var. *diva*

The 'Goddess Magnolia' is the visitor's introduction to Borde Hill, arching as it does over the entrance to the Old Rhododendron Garden. When Ernest Wilson travelled to China in the early 1900s to find *Davidia involucrata* for Harry Veitch, he also collected seed of this magnolia species from various locations under W688. *Magnolia sprengeri* were subsequently grown on at Veitch's Coombe Wood nursery at Kingston upon Thames in Surrey. When the nursery closed in 1914, J.C. Williams at Caerhays bought young magnolia plants that had yet to flower, as did Lord Aberconway at Bodnant, North Wales, and the Royal Botanic Gardens, Kew. When the Caerhays magnolia flowered, it did so with rich-pink flowers and was subsequently named *M.s.* var. *diva* 'Diva'; the others flowered white (*M.s.* var. *sprengeri*). Jim Gardiner believes that the splendid *diva* at Borde Hill was grown by Stephie from a first-generation seedling from Caerhays.

Meliosma alba

The May-flowering *Meliosma beaniana* (now *M. alba*) was planted on the south side of Warren Wood by Stephie in 1932, and was already a big plant, at '23ft. high and 1ft. 8in in girth', according to the 1935 *Catalogue* record. The tree was bought from the Aldenham estate in Hertfordshire when it was auctioned off after the death of Vicary Gibbs, a financier who had amassed a larger collection of Chinese flora than that owned by Kew. 'It was brought here by road,' wrote Stephie, 'and the ball of earth around its roots weighing considerably over a ton, occupied a whole lorry.' Meliosma were first cultivated in Europe in 1901, and the *beaniana* is believed to have been raised from seed collected by Ernest Wilson in western Hubei (Hupeh) in 1907; the meliosma flowered at Borde Hill in May 1933, the first time in the UK. The *Catalogue* quotes Wilson as saying, 'It is one of the handsomest and most striking of Chinese trees when in full flower. As a native tree it is scattered through western Hupeh and Szechuan at altitudes between 3,000ft and 6,000ft.' Handwritten notes were added later to the printed *Catalogue*. By 1945 Stephie noted that the tree had attained a height of 25 feet (7.6 m), while Ralph recorded its reaching 28 feet (8.5 m) in May 1957. In May 1971, in Robert's time, 'flowered specimens [were] sent to Kew and Wisley Gardens for their herbarium'. Plant exchanges between Borde Hill and botanical gardens continued into the third generation and beyond. This tree now flowers regularly.

RHS AWARDS OF MERIT FOR PLANTS CULTIVATED OR BRED AT BORDE HILL

This list uses the plant name as given on the Award of Merit certificate; names in parentheses are those accepted by the RHS today, where these differ. Plants marked in **bold** are ones mentioned elsewhere in the book.

COLONEL STEPHENSON ROBERT CLARKE

Sorbus munda f. *subarachnoidea* (*Sorbus munda*)..................1923
Magnolia denudata 'Purple Eye'..................1926
Rhododendron fargesii (*Rhododendron oreodoxa* var. *fargesii*)..................1926 [& 1969]
Hippeastrum reticulatum..................1928
Hydrangea quercifolia..................1928
Alstroemeria violacea (*Alstroemeria paupercula*)..................1930 [& 1965]
Illicium religiosum..................1930
Magnolia wilsonii..................1930
Rhododendron 'Luna'..................1930
Styrax hemsleyanus..................1930
Cypripedium japonicum..................1931
Petrocosmea nervosa..................1931
Rhododendron 'Thomasine'..................1931
Rhododendron 'Chalice'..................1932
Rhododendron 'Cock of the Rock'..................1932
Rhododendron 'Damask'..................1932
Rhododendron verruculosum (*Rhododendron* × *verruculosum*)..................1932
Rhododendron zaleucum..................1932
Stewartia serrata..................1932
Rhododendron mallotum..................1933
Camellia 'Salutation'..................1936
Olearia chathamica..................1938
Asteranthera ovata..................1939
Camellia × williamsii 'Donation'..................1941
Protea cynaroides..................1942
Rhododendron 'Panoply'..................1942
Richea scoparia..................1942
Scutellaria ovalifolia..................1944
Alstroemeria 'Walter Fleming'..................1948
Halesia diptera..................1948
Magnolia fraseri..................1948

SIR RALPH AND LADY STEPHENSON CLARKE

Nerine filifolia (*Nerine masoniorum*)..................1949
Nerine 'Nena'..................1949
Nerine 'Stephanie'..................1949
Nerine 'Arthur Turner'..................1959
Nerine 'Angela Limerick'..................1960
Platanus orientalis..................1966
Carya glabra..................1967
Hoheria angustifolia..................1967

ROBERT NUNN STEPHENSON CLARKE

Rhododendron metternichii
    (*Rhododendron degronianum* subsp. *heptamerum*)..........1976
Rhododendron vellereum (*Rhododendron principis* Vellereum Group).....1976
Rhododendron phaeochrysum...1977
Cupressus guadalupensis...1978
Fitzroya cupressoides...1978
Picea abies 'Virgata'..1978
Rhododendron bergii 'Papillon'
    (*Rhododendron augustinii* subsp. *rubrum* 'Papillon')...................1978
Rhododendron eclecteum 'Kingdom Come'
    (*Rhododendron eclecteum* var. *eclecteum* 'Kingdom Come').........1978
Rhododendron iodes (*Rhododendron alutaceum* var. *iodes*)..............1978
Rhododendron smithii 'Fleurie' (*Rhododendron argipeplum* 'Fleurie').....1978
Rhododendron sutchuenense 'Seventh Heaven'..........................1978
Pinus wallichiana..1979
Rhododendron coryanum..1979
Rhododendron 'Duchess of Cornwall' × *R. calophytum*....................1979
Rhododendron jucundum (*Rhododendron selense* subsp. *jucundum*)..........1979
Rhododendron laxiflorum (*Rhododendron annae* Laxiflorum Group).....1979
Cunninghamia konishii..1980
Liriodendron chinense..1980
Paeonia lutea 'Jack Vass'...1980
Rhododendron sanguineum × *R. williamsianum*..............................1980
Rhododendron sinogrande × *R. lacteum*......................................1980
Camellia saluenensis..1981
Cotoneaster 'Rothschildianus'..1981
Nerine 'Janet'...1981
Picea asperata..1981
Nerine 'Hertha Berg'..1982
Berberis glaucocarpa..1983
Lonicera syringantha...1984
Rhododendron sperabile var. *weihsiense*....................................1985

ANDREWJOHN STEPHENSON CLARKE

Pyrus ussuriensis var. *hondoensis*..1990
Mahonia rotundifolia (*Mahonia repens* 'Rotundifolia')...................1991
Skimmia × *confusa* 'Kew Green'..1991
Rhododendron 'Nicola Newman'..1990s

BORDE HILL'S CHAMPION TREES

The number of champion trees fluctuates from year to year, but these seventy trees were listed on the Tree Register in 2020 as being the largest by girth and/or height in the British Isles. In those instances where a species appears twice, the list refers to two different trees at Borde Hill.

Abies sachalinensis var. *nemorensis* .... girth and height
Acer erianthum .... height
Acer × *rotundilobum* .... girth and height
Acer trautvetteri .... girth
Alnus × *spaethii* .... height
Betula papyrifera .... girth
Buxus wallichiana .... girth and height
Carpinus laxiflora .... girth and height
Carya laciniosa .... girth
Celtis tetrandra .... girth
Chamaecyparis lawsoniana 'Hillieri' .... height
Chamaecyparis obtusa var. *formosana* .... girth and height
Crataegus scabrifolia .... girth and height
Cupressus lusitanica .... height
Cyclocarya paliurus .... girth and height
Discaria chacaye .... girth
Escallonia rosea .... girth and height
Fagus engleriana .... girth
Fagus sylvatica 'Prince George of Crete' .... girth
Fraxinus excelsior 'Aurea' .... girth and height
Fraxinus pennsylvanica .... height
Ilex integra .... girth
Ilex pedunculosa .... girth and height
Illicium henryi .... girth and height
Juniperus virginiana 'Glauca' .... height
Larix gmelinii var. *principis-rupprechtii* .... girth
Larix griffithii .... girth and height
Lindera megaphylla .... girth
Maackia amurensis .... girth
Magnolia campbellii .... remarkable
Magnolia campbellii .... girth
Magnolia delavayi .... girth
Magnolia fraseri .... girth
Magnolia obovata .... girth
Magnolia officinalis .... girth
Magnolia officinalis .... height
Magnolia × *soulangeana* 'Verbanica' .... girth and height
Magnolia sprengeri var. *sprengeri* .... height
Malus baccata 'Jackii' .... girth and height
Malus prattii .... girth
Picea alcoquiana var. *acicularis* .... height
Picea alcoquiana var. *reflexa* .... height

Picea pungens	height
Pinus sibirica	girth and height
Pyrus cossonii	girth and height
Pyrus pyrifolia 'Chojuro'	girth and height
Pyrus ussuriensis var. *hondoensis*	girth
Pyrus ussuriensis var. *hondoensis*	height
Quercus acuta	height
Quercus × *auzendei*	girth and height
Quercus coccifera	girth and height
Quercus dolicholepis	girth and height
Quercus glauca	height
Quercus ilicifolia	height
Quercus kelloggii	girth and height
Quercus × *ludoviciana*	height
Quercus × *morehus*	girth and height
Quercus petraea 'Acutiloba'	girth and height
Quercus semecarpifolia	height
Quercus variabilis	height
Quercus velutina	height
Rhododendron rubiginosum Desquamatum Group	girth and height
Robinia × *slavinii*	height
Robinia viscosa var. *hartwigii*	girth and height
Sorbus esserteauana	girth and height
Sorbus × *kewensis*	height
Sycopsis sinensis	height
Tilia japonica	girth and height
Tilia mandshurica	girth and height
Viburnum cinnamomifolium	girth and height

TIMELINE
HISTORY OF BORDE HILL AND THE CLARKE FAMILY

BORDE HILL ESTATE PRE-CLARKES

1598
Borde Hill House is built by Stephen Borde.

1603
Stephen Borde is knighted by King James I.

1705
The Borde family move to their larger property, Paxhill Park. Borde Hill is sold to Walter Gatland, of Nymans, who extends the house.

1720
Direct descendants of Stephen Borde die out in Sussex.

1803–70
Borde Hill House passes through several hands, during which time the house is further extended.

1870
Borde Hill House is sold again. A watercolour from the sale catalogue shows the railway viaduct in the background.

1893
A Mrs Cunliffe Lister sells the Borde Hill estate to Stephenson Robert Clarke (Stephie).

THE CLARKES AND BORDE HILL

1898
The ha-ha is built below the South Lawn.

1900–22
Stephie begins to collect systematically and sponsors Ernest Henry Wilson's plant-hunting expeditions to China.

1902
A *Country Life* article describes Stephie's formal flower garden.

1905 onwards
Exotic species are added to the existing oak, ash, hazel and beech in Warren Wood.

1906
Stables and a walled kitchen garden are built to the south-east, near Borde Hill Lane.

1910 onwards
Stephanie's Glade is planted.

1912
Stephie further extends the house.

1916
On the Greek island of Lemnos, Ralph Stephenson Clarke collects seeds of *Platanus orientalis* var. *insularis*, which is sown and still grows south-east of Warren Wood.

1917–20
Stephie sponsors George Forrest's fourth expedition to China and Burma (now Myanmar).

1918–48
Stephie's correspondence with plant hunters, botanical gardens, nurserymen and garden owners indicates his position at the heart of the horticultural world.

1919–20
Stephie sponsors Reginald Farrer's expedition to Upper Burma.

1921–23/1924–26
Stephie sponsors Forrest's fifth and sixth expeditions.

1925
Creation of the Garden of Allah by extending the garden into the North Park for plant introductions from the Far East.

1925–27
Stephie sponsors Harold Comber's expeditions to Argentina and the Andes.

1927
Borde Hill is one of the first gardens to open for the National Garden Scheme. W.J. Bean, curator of the Royal Botanic Gardens, Kew, and Ernest Wilson, its original collector, congratulate Stephie on flowering *Liriodendron chinense*.

1928–54
Walter Fleming is head gardener.

1930–32
Stephie sponsors Forrest's seventh and final expedition.

1930–36
Stephie sponsors expeditions by Frank Kingdon Ward to Assam, Burma and Tibet.

1934 onwards
Gore's Wood is planted.

1935
Publication of *Catalogue of the Trees and Shrubs at Borde Hill, Sussex*, compiled by Albert Bruce Jackson.

1936
Stephie is awarded the RHS Victoria Medal of Honour (VMH).

1937–38
Camellia × williamsii 'Donation' is raised by Fleming and becomes a worldwide bestseller.

1940–45
Borde Hill House and estate are requisitioned by the British and Canadian armies.

1941
Camellia 'Donation' receives an RHS Award of Merit.

1944
Stephie is awarded the RHS Veitch Memorial Medal.

1948
Stephie wins an RHS Award of Merit for *Alstroemeria* 'Walter Fleming' in June. He dies in November. Ralph inherits Borde Hill and begins restoring the garden and woodlands devastated by war. Becky follows in Stephie's footsteps by hybridizing nerines and alstroemerias.

1953
Ralph and Becky move to Borde Hill from Brook House when Stephie's widow, Gwennie, leaves.

1958
The woods, including Warren Wood, are recatalogued by the dendrologist Hatton Gardner.

1965
Sir Ralph sets up Borde Hill Garden as a charity and begins opening regularly to the public.

1968–79
Jack Vass, formerly head gardener at Sissinghurst Castle, is head gardener. On his retirement, John Humphris (VMH, 2009) becomes head gardener (until 1983). Both Vass and Humphris win the RHS A.J. Waley Medal for their work on cultivating rhododendrons.

1970
Robert inherits Borde Hill and becomes a top expert on growing and hybridizing rhododendrons. Carries out detailed labelling and checking of the collection.

1976
Stephie is described by Harold Hillier as 'the greatest amateur all-rounder in the gardening world of the twentieth century'. Robert wins an RHS Award of Merit for *Rhododendron metternichii*, one of many such awards.

1980
Paeonia lutea 'Jack Vass' wins an RHS Award of Merit.

1982
A hard tennis court is converted into the 'Bride's Pool'.

1987
A hurricane in October devastates woodland planting at Borde Hill. When Robert dies in November at the early age of sixty-two, Andrewjohn inherits. With the help of his wife, Eleni, he sets about putting the garden and estate on a more commercial footing.

1990–92
Robertsmere, a large lake, is created in the South Park in memory of Robert, for fishing and watering the garden in dry summers. Harry's Lake, named after his grandson, is created nearby.

1995
Jack Vass dies in his cottage at Borde Hill.

1996
Planting of Jay Robin's Rose Garden, designed by Chelsea gold medallist Robin Williams senior.

1997
Redesign of the Bride's Pool as the Italian Garden by Robin Williams senior.

1997–99
Restoration of two Victorian greenhouses from a Heritage Lottery Fund grant.

2008–21
Andy Stevens is head gardener.

2011
Planting of the Mid-Summer Border, designed by Tony Lord (VMH, 2005). *Emmenopterys henryi*, a Forrest introduction, flowers in the Azalea Ring for the first time, eighty-three years after it was planted. Also flowers in 2012, 2016, 2018 and 2021.

2017
Reimagining of the Round Dell by Sophie Walker, an RHS medal-winning garden designer.

2018
Gardiner Grove (named after long-term council member Jim Gardiner) of magnolias is planted to celebrate the 125th anniversary of Borde Hill Garden.

2020
Redesign of the planting in the Italian Garden and Paradise Walk by Chelsea gold medallist Chris Beardshaw.

2021
In November, Harry Baldwin becomes head of horticulture.

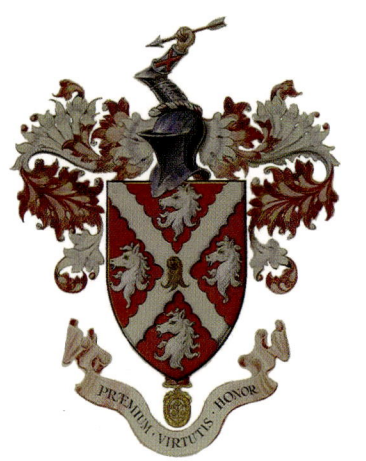

CLARKE FAMILY TREE

Of necessity, not all family members are included. Names in **bold** indicate those who have played a significant role in the garden's development.

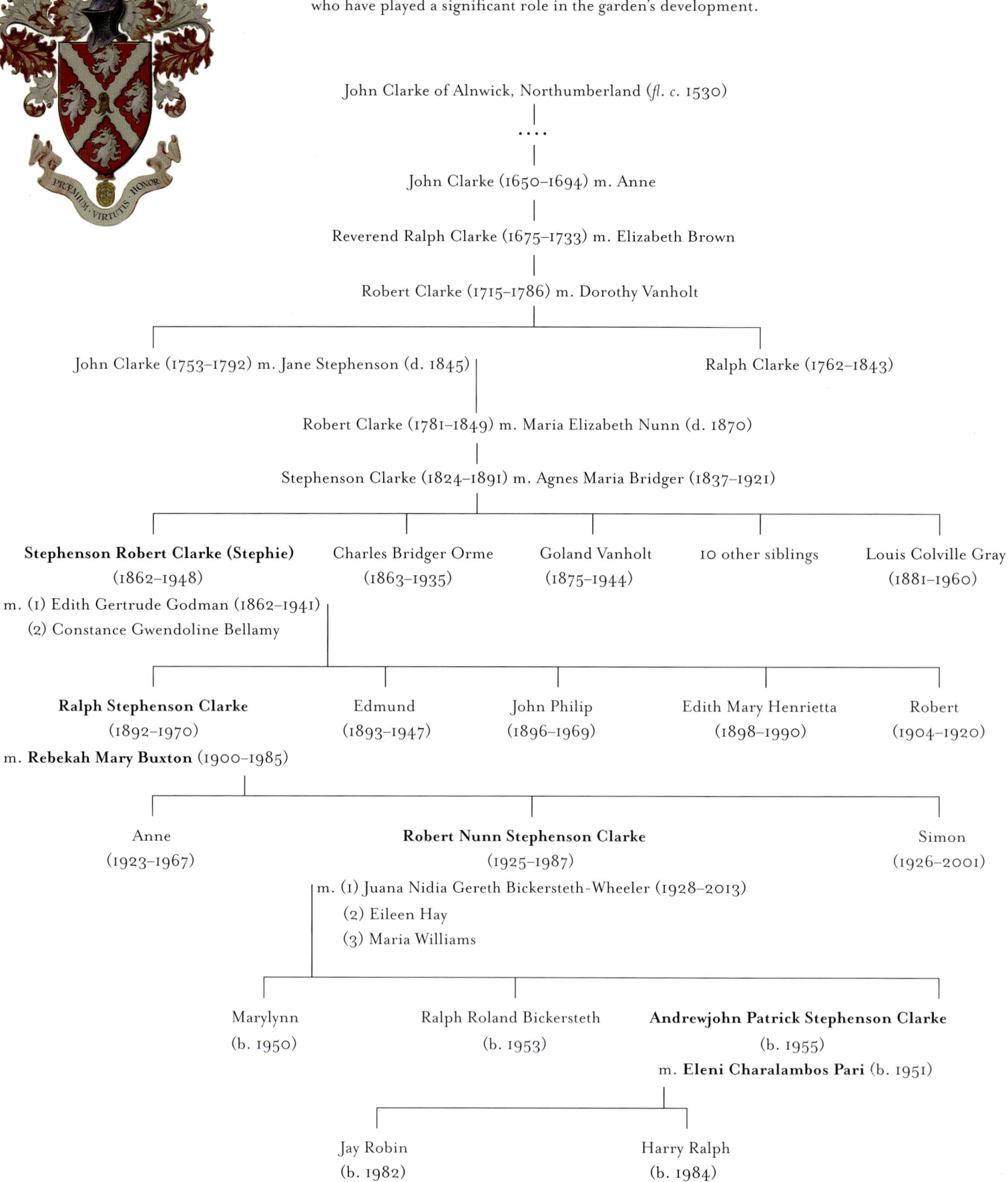

John Clarke of Alnwick, Northumberland (*fl. c.* 1530)

....

John Clarke (1650–1694) m. Anne

Reverend Ralph Clarke (1675–1733) m. Elizabeth Brown

Robert Clarke (1715–1786) m. Dorothy Vanholt

- John Clarke (1753–1792) m. Jane Stephenson (d. 1845)
- Ralph Clarke (1762–1843)

Robert Clarke (1781–1849) m. Maria Elizabeth Nunn (d. 1870)

Stephenson Clarke (1824–1891) m. Agnes Maria Bridger (1837–1921)

- **Stephenson Robert Clarke (Stephie)** (1862–1948)
  m. (1) Edith Gertrude Godman (1862–1941)
  (2) Constance Gwendoline Bellamy
- Charles Bridger Orme (1863–1935)
- Goland Vanholt (1875–1944)
- 10 other siblings
- Louis Colville Gray (1881–1960)

Children of Stephenson Robert Clarke:
- **Ralph Stephenson Clarke** (1892–1970) m. **Rebekah Mary Buxton** (1900–1985)
- Edmund (1893–1947)
- John Philip (1896–1969)
- Edith Mary Henrietta (1898–1990)
- Robert (1904–1920)

Children of Ralph Stephenson Clarke:
- Anne (1923–1967)
- **Robert Nunn Stephenson Clarke** (1925–1987)
  m. (1) Juana Nidia Gereth Bickersteth-Wheeler (1928–2013)
  (2) Eileen Hay
  (3) Maria Williams
- Simon (1926–2001)

Children of Robert Nunn Stephenson Clarke:
- Marylynn (b. 1950)
- Ralph Roland Bickersteth (b. 1953)
- **Andrewjohn Patrick Stephenson Clarke** (b. 1955) m. **Eleni Charalambos Pari** (b. 1951)

Children of Andrewjohn:
- Jay Robin (b. 1982)
- Harry Ralph (b. 1984)

BORDE HILL GARDEN

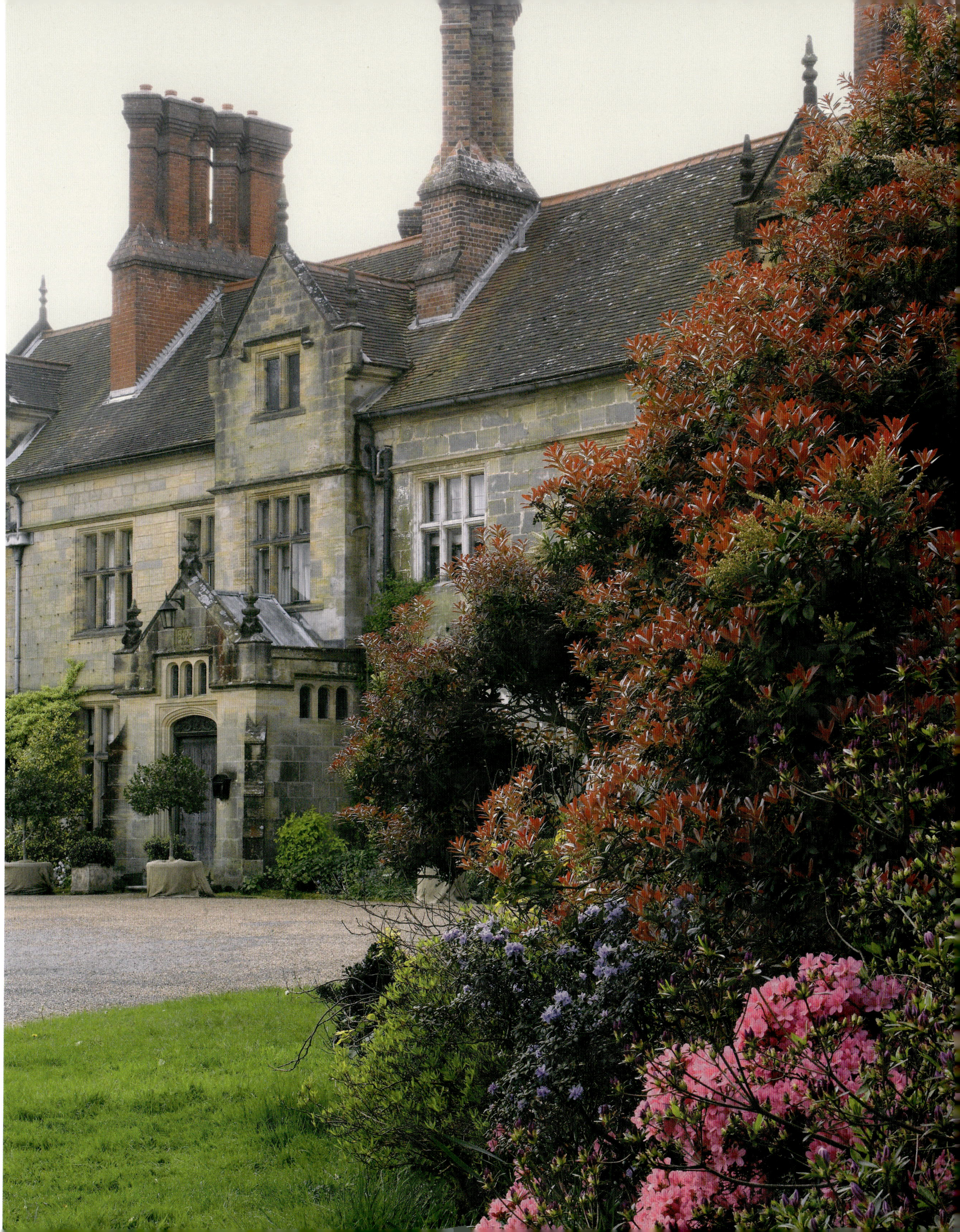

SELECT BIBLIOGRAPHY

MANUSCRIPT SOURCES

Haywards Heath, West Sussex, Borde Hill Garden, Borde Hill Archive

London, The Rothschild Archive
rothschildarchive.org
XI/15/65/4

PRINTED SOURCES

Berridge, Vanessa, *Great British Gardeners: From Early Plantsmen to Chelsea Medal Winners*, Stroud, Gloucestershire (Amberley) 2018

'Borde Hill, Sussex, the Seat of Mr Stephenson Clarke', *Country Life*, vol. 12, no. 312, 27 December 1902, pp. 840–45

Carter, Craig J.M., 'The Stephenson Clarke Fleet Story', *Sea Breezes*, January and February 1958

Clarke, Stephenson R., 'The Garden at Borde Hill', *Journal of the Royal Horticultural Society*, vol. 63, no. 6, May 1938, pp. 258–64

Cooper, Wilbraham Villiers, *A History of the Parish of Cuckfield*, Haywards Heath (C. Clarke) 1912

Edwards, Ambra, *The Story of the English Garden*, London (National Trust) 2018

Gardiner, Jim, *Magnolias: A Gardener's Guide*, Portland, Ore. (Timber Press) 2000

Hadfield, Miles, *Pioneers in Gardening* [1955], London (Bloomsbury) 1998

Hellyer, A.G.L., 'Landscape for Trees and Shrubs: The Gardens of Borde Hill, Sussex', *Country Life*, vol. 165, no. 4262, 15 March 1979, pp. 702–704

Hillier, Jean, *Hillier: The Plants, the People, the Passion*, Winchester, Hampshire (Hillier Nurseries) 2014

Jackson, Albert Bruce, *Catalogue of the Trees and Shrubs (excluding Rhododendrons) at Borde Hill, Sussex, in December 1932*, with a foreword and notes by Col. Stephenson Robert Clarke, Oxford (Oxford University Press) 1935

Jekyll, Gertrude, *Wood and Garden: Notes and Thoughts, Practical and Critical, of a Working Amateur*, London (Longmans, Green) 1899

Lacey, Stephen, *Gardens of the National Trust*, rev. edn, London (National Trust) 2016

McLean, Brenda, *George Forrest: Plant Hunter*, Woodbridge, Suffolk (Antique Collectors' Club in association with the Royal Botanic Garden Edinburgh) 2004

Primrose, Sandy, *Modern Plant Hunters: Adventures in Pursuit of Extraordinary Plants*, London (Pimpernel Press) 2019

Robinson, William, *Alpine Flowers for English Gardens*, rev. edn, London (John Murray) 1875

Shulman, Nicola, *A Rage for Rock Gardening: The Story of Reginald Farrer, Gardener, Writer and Plant Collector*, London (Short Books) 2002

Stroud, Dorothy, *Capability Brown*, rev. edn, London (Faber & Faber) 1975

Whitsey, Fred, 'Into the Second Century', *Country Life*, vol. 188, no. 24, 16 June 1994, pp. 68–71

Wilson, E.H., *A Naturalist in Western China* [1913], London (Cadogan Books) 1986

ONLINE SOURCES

Jaffé, A.M., 'Clarke, Louis Colville Gray (1881–1960)', *Oxford Dictionary of National Biography*, Oxford (Oxford University Press) 2004, https://doi.org/10.1093/ref:odnb/32430 (subscription only; accessed January 2021)

ACKNOWLEDGEMENTS AND PICTURE CREDITS

My first and greatest debt of thanks goes to Eleni and Andrewjohn Stephenson Clarke. After visiting Borde Hill for more than twenty years, I was delighted to be entrusted by them to tell the history of the Clarke family and of their extraordinary garden. I worked in a sunlit room overlooking the South Lawn with unlimited and privileged access to their family archive, including correspondence from such towering figures as George Forrest. It was wonderfully numinous to handle Forrest's letters and imagine the adverse conditions in which many were written. The archive itself has been curated by Julia Foster, helped by Maggie Hill from Sussex Gardens Trust and supported by the Culture Recovery Fund. Andrewjohn and Eleni generously hosted me on many occasions at Borde Hill, while, at the depth of the pandemic, their children, Jay Robin and Harry, spent several hours talking to me by Zoom.

The commitment of the Borde Hill Garden Council has been crucial, in particular that of Jim Gardiner, former chairman and the longest-standing member, who helped me to understand better the garden and its history. Jim steered me through the intricacies of magnolia nomenclature, while Philip Holmes played an invaluable role in identifying the rhododendrons. John Humphris (gardener and then head gardener at Borde Hill between 1968 and 1983) conjured up a colourful picture of his predecessors, Brian Doe and Jack Vass, and of Robert Stephenson Clarke and his mother, Becky. Andy Stevens (head gardener from 2008 to 2021) led me on long, informative tours of the garden. Both he and his successor, Harry Baldwin, read my chapters on the garden and gave valuable guidance. Thanks also go to the gardening team: Dori Watmore, Heidi Jenkins, Lucie Villedieu, Koula Prevett and Robin Izzard.

Other major contributors have been John Glover, who took most of the photographs that evoke the garden so beautifully in this book, and Neil Gower, who drew the handsome map. Supplementary picture research was carried out by Nick Wheldon.

The team at Merrell Publishers have once again been a tower of strength: Hugh Merrell backed me to write the book, and Nicola Bailey showed her customary skill and patience in laying it out. I am again thankful for Claire Chandler's meticulous editing and sharp eye, and also to the proofreader, Rosanna Fairhead, and the indexer, Hilary Bird, for their expertise.

Without our sponsors, this book would not have been possible, so I would like to thank the Adelphi Group of Companies, Brachers Solicitors, Saffrey Champness Chartered Accountants and Borde Hill Events for their contribution.

My most faithful reader has, as ever, been my husband, Chris Evans. He has read everything I have written for forty years with remarkable good humour and understanding.

All illustrations copyright © 2022 John Glover Photography Ltd, with the exception of the following (key: l = left, r = right, t = top, b = bottom):

ANL/Shutterstock: 41l

The Art Archive/Shutterstock: 38t

Nick Barrie: 14–15, 26–27, 89, 106–107, 129

Roger Bloxham: 65

Borde Hill Garden: 20b, 21l, 21r, 22t, 23, 24b, 25t, 25b, 29, 30t, 30b, 31t, 33, 34t, 35, 37r, 38bl, 38bc, 38br, 39tc, 39tr, 39b, 43, 44tl, 44bl, 44r, 45, 46, 47, 49, 50t, 50bl, 50br, 51l, 51tr, 51br, 52, 53t, 53bl, 53br, 54tl, 54tr, 54bl, 54br, 55, 56, 57, 58t, 58b, 59, 60t, 60b, 61t, 61b, 62t, 62b, 63, 66, 67, 70l, 81, 95bl, 95bc, 95br, 100br, 109t, 114, 122tl, 149t, 162t, 168br, 172

@brightonpictures: 104–105, 105, 108

© The Caerhays Estate: 41r

© Nicky Flint, Sussex Stills: 8, 48, 156, 180–81, 181

© Gravetye Manor: 32t

George W. Hales/Getty Images: 40

© Hillier Nurseries Ltd: 42

Richard Kendal: 70r

Frank Kingdon-Ward/Royal Geographical Society/Getty Images: 39tl

© Millais Nurseries: 69t

© Mark Moore: 88tc, 88tr

RHS Lindley Collections: 32b, 37l

Howard Rice: 171

© The Board of Trustees of the Royal Botanic Gardens, Kew: 31b

© Derek St Romaine: 76–77, 110t, 197

© Umoya Photography: 69b, 71

Verity Wakeham: portrait of Vanessa Berridge on jacket flap

Sarah Wright: 178

The map on pp. 6–7 was drawn by Neil Gower.

Every effort has been made to trace and contact copyright holders of the illustrations reproduced in this book. The publisher will be happy to correct in subsequent editions any errors or omissions that are brought to its attention.

BORDE HILL GARDEN
199

SPONSORS

Est. 1947. Future-proofing sustainable research and manufacturing, Adelphi empowers businesses to reduce waste and increase process efficiency. We are delighted to support community green spaces such as our local Borde Hill Garden.

Saffery Champness LLP is delighted to support Borde Hill Garden, the publication of this new book and the Warren Wood rejuvenation project, and wishes everyone involved much success.

Brachers is an award-winning law firm that has been supporting individuals, businesses and the local community since 1895.

We are delighted to support this notable book, and offer an exciting events programme with music, food, horticulture, children's trails and well-being, to ensure every visit to Borde Hill is memorable.

INDEX

Page numbers in *italic* refer to the illustrations.

A

Abelia 30, 153
Aberconway, Charles Melville McLaren, 3rd Baron 61
Aberconway, Henry McLaren, 2nd Baron 40, *40*, 46
Abies 182; *see also* fir trees
Abutilon 147, *149*
Acer *10–11*, 33, 81, 110, *116–17*, 117, 153, *166–70*
Achillea 101, *118–19*, 123, *124*
Aconitum 125, 143
Actaea 89, 125–27
Actinidia *146*, 147, *147*, *148–49*
Africa 34–35
Africa House 92, *94*, 95
Agapanthus *72–73*, 92, 95, 101, *105*, 117, 122, 125, 127, 130, *132*, 134
Agastache *118–19*, 125
agaves 138
Alexander-Sinclair, James *64*, 68
Allium 83, 122, 130, *132*
Alstroemeria 43, 49, 53
  A. violacea 39, *44*, 45, 190
  A. 'Walter Fleming' 45, 130, *134*, 186, *186*, 190
Amaryllis 127
Andes 40
Anemone 35, *98*, 101, *168*; *see also* wood anemones
Angelica 120, 122, 127
Anthemis *118–20*, 123, *124*
Aralia 138, *138*, 143
Araucaria 182
Argentina 40
Argyrocytisus 92
Arnold Arboretum, Massachusetts 81, 182
Arts and Crafts movement 33
Aruncus 101
Asclepias 125
ash trees 166, 178
Asplenium 125, 127
Asteranthera ovata 42, 190
asters 101, 110, 117

Astilbe 101
Astrantia 125
Austin, David 68, 87, 89
Autumn Border 110
Azalea Ring 12, 43, 69, 74, *166–72*, *166–73*
azaleas 40, 53, 54, 65, 106, 108, *166–67*, *170–71*
Azara 42, 114, 147, *147*

B

Bacon, Miss W.M. 40
Baldwin, Harry 70
Ballota 124
Balls, Edward K. 40
bamboo 138, *142–43*, 153
Banks, Sir Joseph 31
Baxter, Christine 94
Bean, W.J. 59, 162
Beardshaw, Chris 68, *70*, 120, 125–27, 134
Becky's Bower 157, *164*, *165*, 174
bedding plants 13, 31–32
Bee, A. & Co. 31
beech trees 166, 178
Bellamy, Constance Gwendoline *see* Clarke, Constance Gwendoline (Gwennie)
Berberis 33, 108, 153
bergenias 152
Betonica 125, 134
Bickersteth-Wheeler, Lt Col. John 57
Bickersteth-Wheeler, Juana Nidia Gereth *see* Stephenson Clarke, Juana Nidia Gereth
Big Plant Nursery, West Sussex 143
Birch Hall, Essex 50
birch trees 164
Blue Border 89, *96–97*
bluebells *2*, 174, *174–77*, 178, 182
Bodnant, North Wales 40, 61
Boer War, Second (1899–1902) 34
Borde, Andrew 19, 21
Borde, John 19
Borde, Ninian 20
Borde, Stephen 19, 20, 33, 68
Borde, William 20
Borde Hill, West Sussex
  becomes a charitable trust 55
  Borde Hill House 20, *20*, 33, *33*, 85, 197

champion trees 65, 74, 89, 130, *133*, 157, *160–61*, 166, *192–93*
conifer collection 61
flower gardening 67–68
garden developed 29, 32–33
gardeners 44, *54*, 70, 147
history 19–25, 194–95
hurricane (1987) 43, 63, *63*, 65, 67, 92, 117, 152–53, *154*, 166, 178
maps *6–7*, 53
sculpture exhibitions 68, 94, 135
Stephie buys 30, *30*
visitors 45, 53, *53*, 55, 57, 63, 69
Borde Hill Archive 43
Borde Hill Garden Council 40, 41, 55, 59, 61, 63, 67, 162
box hedging 98, *129*, 130, *132*
Bride's Pool 63, 67, 68, 115, 130
Bride's Shelter 89
Bridger, Agnes Maria *see* Clarke, Agnes Maria
British Army 40
British Association of Rose Breeders 95, 108
British East Africa 34–35
British Empire 13
British Ornithologists' Union 29, 30
Brook House, Ardingly, West Sussex 23, *24*, 29, 30, 34, 50, 58, 59, 66
broom 178
Broussonetia 143, 153
Brown, Elizabeth 21
Brown, Lancelot 'Capability' 13
Brunnera 81–83
Bulley, Arthur K. 31
Burma (Myanmar) 13, 31, 35, 37, 38, 157
Burrell, Sir Charles 20
Burrell family 20
Buxton, Rebekah Mary *see* Stephenson Clarke, Rebekah Mary (Becky)
Buxton, Sir Thomas Fowell 50
Buxus 130, *132*; *see also* box hedging

C

Caerhays, Cornwall 41, 70, 92
Calamagrostis 108
Callicarpa 110
Callistemon 147

BORDE HILL GARDEN
201

Cambridge, University of 29, 49, 57
Cambridge University Botanic Garden
    14, 42, 55
Camellia 36, 40, 61, 105, 108, 115, 117, 157,
    164
  C. cuspidata 33
  C. forrestii 153
  C. japonica 'Donckelaeri' 154, *154*
  C.j. 'Imbricata' 153
  C.j. 'Mathotiana Alba' 153
  C.j. 'Mathotiana Rosea' 153
  C. 'Leonard Messel' 134–35
  C. saluenensis 100, 164, 191
  C. 'Salutation' 42, 45, 98–101, *100*, 164,
    186, *186*, 190
  C. × *williamsii* 'Donation' 4, *41*, *44*, 45, 52,
    92, 154, *162*, 164, *168*, 171, 187, *187*,
    190
  C. × *w.* 'Francis Hanger' 108, 164, *168*, 171
Campanula 120, 123
Campbell, William Macdonald 42
Cardiocrinum 164, *164*
Carya glabra 52, 190
  C. ovata 166, 182
Catalogue of the Trees and Shrubs at Borde Hill, Sussex
    (1935) 29, 30, 32, 33, 38, 39, 43, 178
Catalpa 105, 108, 110
Catt, George 59, 61
Celastrus 147
Cephalotaxus 95
Cercis 114
Cestrum 147
Cetrelia 172
Ceylon (Sri Lanka) 23
chaenomeles 144–45, 147, *147*
Chamaecyparis 178
Chambers, Anne and Johnny 65–66
champion trees 65, 74, 89, 130, *133*, 157,
    160–61, 166, 192–93
Chatsworth, Derbyshire 13, 31
Chelsea Flower Show 14, *40*, 68, 84
Chenault's Nursery, France 81
cherry trees 129, *130*
Chile 39
Chimonanthus 164
China 13, 31, 33, 35, 37, 43, 157
Chittenden, Frederick 35, 38
Clarke *see also* Stephenson Clarke
Clarke, Agnes Maria (née Bridger) 23–25,
    24–25, 29
Clarke, Charles Bridger Orme 30
Clarke, Constance Gwendoline (Gwennie,
    née Bellamy) 46–47, *47*, 49
Clarke, Desmond 59, 162
Clarke, Dorothy (née Vanholt) 21, *21*

Clarke, Edith Gertrude (née Godman)
    25, 30, *31*, 33, *34*, 46, 49
Clarke, Goland 35
Clarke, John (*fl. c.* 1530) 21
Clarke, John (1753–1792) 21–22, *22*
Clarke, Louis Colville Gray 29, *30*, 43, 57
Clarke, Ralph 21, 22
Clarke, Robert (1715–1786) 21, *21*
Clarke, Robert (1781–1849) 22–23
Clarke, Stephenson 22, 23–25, *24*, 29
Clarke, Colonel Stephenson Robert (Stephie)
    19–20, *20*, 29, 46
  Azalea Ring 166–67, 170–71
  buys Borde Hill 20, 25, 30, *30*
  Catalogue 178
  children 30, 33–34, *34*, 46
  death 47
  develops garden 32–33
  early life 29–30
  extends house 33
  Garden of Allah 157, 162
  honours and awards 44–45, *45*
  military career 34, *35*
  Old Rhododendron Garden 76–81
  plant hunting and collecting 9, 13–14, 32,
    34–35, 37–45, 68
  second marriage 46–47, *47*
  South Lawn 105
  Stephanie's Glade 178
  Warren Wood 178–82
  West Bank 115
  West Garden 154
Clarke and Burgess 22–23
Clarke family tree 196
Clematis 98, *101*
Clothworkers' Company 22, 25, 30, *51*, 55
Coal Factors' Society 21, 22, 30
Colesbourne, Gloucestershire 33
Comber, Harold 40, 45
Comber, James 40
conifers 170
Conner, Angela, *Aquapoise* 68, *131*, 135
Conservative Party 51
Cornus 32, 81, 117, 153, 154, 164, 171–73, *172*
Correggio 29
Corylopsis 164
corylus 110
Cotinus 83, 108, *108*, 110
Cotoneaster 39, 152
Country Life 32, 33, *33*, 67–68, 84, 162
Cox, Euan 60
Cox, Kenneth 181
Cox, Peter 60
Crataegus 110, 115
Crinodendron 98

Crocosmia 109, 110, 152
crocuses 101
Croydon Lodge 22, 30
Crûg Farm Plants, North Wales 70, 143
Cryptomeria 117
Crystal Palace, London 13
Cupressus 129
  C. guadalupensis 61, 191
Cyclamen 106, 117
Cytisus 45, 92

D

Dacrycarpus 147
daffodils 83, 106, *106–107*, 174
dahlias 104–105, 110
Darmera 142
Davidia 28, 31, 33, 83, 178, *179*
daylilies 108, 123
Decaisnea 38
Deep House 92, 95
Delavay, Père 182
Delphinium 89, 96–97
Denmark 23
Devonshire, Duke of 31
Dietes 134
Dillon, Helen 89
Discaria 130, *133*
Doe, Brian 53–54, *53*, 55
Douglas, David 31, 182

E

Echinacea 151
echinops 108
echiums 151
Edgeworthia 164
Edinburgh Botanical Garden 14, 37, 38, 39,
    41, 55, 68
Elaeagnus 129, 135, 152
Eley, Charles 41
Elizabeth II, Queen 40, *51*
Elliott, Clarence 39
Elwes, Edith 30
Elwes, Henry John 29, 30, 32, 33, 76, 178
Emmenopterys henryi 43, 170, 172, 187, *187*
Epilobium 124–25
epimediums 81
Erica 32
Erigeron 46, 125, *127*
Eriobotrya 92
Eriophyllum 124
Erskine, Charles 153
Erysimum 134
Eton Ramblers Cricket Club 59
eucalyptus 98, 129, 130, *133*
Eucomis 140–41

Euphorbia 117, *125*, 127, *127*, 135, 151
Eutrochium 118–19, 125
Evison, Raymond 98
Exbury Gardens, Hampshire 40, 60

F
Fagus 43, 182; *see also* beech trees
Farfugium 143
Farrer, Reginald 32, 35, 37, *37*, 60
Fatsia 138–43
ferns *10–11*, 117, 127, 143, 154, *164*
Fig House *94*, 95
Findlay, Thomas Hope 60
fir trees 170
First World War 35, 49
Fitzroya 42
　　F. cupressoides 61, *191*
Fitzwilliam Museum, Cambridge 29
Fleet Prison, London 19
Fleming, Walter 44–45, 49, 52, 53, 60, 92, 98
Forestry Commission 52
forget-me-nots 83, *83*
Forrest, George 31, 32, 35, 37–38, *38*, 41,
　　43, 44, 52, 61, 63, 157, 164, *170*, 172
Fortune, Robert 31, 76, 171
Fortunearia 44
Foster, Maurice 172
Fox, Alfred 50
France 13
Fraxinus 166; *see also* ash trees
Fritillaria 130, *131*, 134
Fuchsia 95, *100*, 101, 117, 147, 152

G
Galanthus see snowdrops
Garden of Allah *4*, 43, *48*, 68, *72–73*, 74,
　　156–65, 157–64, 171, 174
The Gardeners' Chronicle and Agricultural Gazette 31, 171
Gardener's Magazine 31
Gardiner, Jim 67, 68, *68*, 69, 89
Gardiner Grove 68
Gardner, Hatton 52
Garrya 110
Gatland, Walter 20
Gentiana 39, 42
Geranium 83, 101, 110, 117, 118–20, 122–25,
　　125, 127
Geum 109
Gillenia 125
Gladiolus 122, 127
Gleditsia 'Sunburst' 83
Glendoick Nursery, near Perth 60, 181
Glendurgan Garden, Cornwall 50
Godfrey, Robert 171
Godman, Alice 30

Godman, Edith Gertrude *see* Clarke, Edith
　　Gertrude
Godman, Frederick Du Cane 30
Godman, Joseph 30
Goldsworth Nursery, Surrey 44–45
Gore's Wood 43, 59, 60
grasses 108, *109*, 130, 151, 152
Gravetye Manor, West Sussex 32
Great Exhibition, London (1851) 13
greenhouses 13, 62, 67, 74, 92–95, *94–95*, 147
Gunnera 138, 142–43, 164

H
Hakonechloa 108, 152
Hakoneya Nurseries, Japan 42
Halesia 170, 172
Hamamelis 74, 164
Hampton Court Flower Show 68, 153
Hanger, Francis 52
Hardy, Alan 60
Harrow, R.L. 42
Harry's Lake 67
Harry's Playground 69
Hawaii 31
hazel trees 178
Hedera 154
hedychiums 135, 143
Helenium 104–105, 108–10, *109*
helichrysum 92
hellebores 74, 117, 154, 162, 164, *164*
Hemerocallis 123, 127; *see also* daylilies
Henry VIII, King 19
Henry, Augustine 33
Heritage Lottery Fund 95
Heuchera 110
Hidcote Manor, Gloucestershire 13, 43
High Beeches, West Sussex 65
Highbrook Church, West Sussex 25, 29, 47,
　　55, 57
Highbrook Enterprises 58, 59
Hillier, Edwin 42, *42*
Hillier, Sir Harold 29, 42, 52–53, 61, 182
Hillier, Jean 42
Hillier & Sons, Winchester, Hampshire
　　42–43, 45
Himalayas 31, 33, 76, 153
Hoathly Hill, West Sussex 58
Hoheria angustifolia 52, 154, 190
　　H. 'Borde Hill' 81, 188, *188*
　　H. 'Glory of Amlwch' 98, 101
holm oak trees 81, 152
'Holy Trinity' 157, *160–61*
Hooker, Joseph Dalton 31, 33, 76, 171
hostas 154, 164
Howick, Lord 153

Howick Hall, Alnwick, Northumberland 153
Humphris, John 52, 54, *54*, 55, 58, 60–61, 67
hurricane (1987) 43, 63, *63*, 65, 67, 92, 117,
　　152–53, 154, 166, 178
Hyacinthoides see bluebells
Hydrangea 42, 101, *101*, 108, 164, *164*
　　H. quercifolia 110, 190
Hylotelephium see sedums
hypericum 152

I
Ibis (journal) 29, 34
Ilex 33
Imperial War Museum, London 49
India 13, 31, 35
Indigofera 147
Infinity Box 153
Iraq 52
irises 101
Isle of Wight 22, 29, 66
Italian Garden 13, 68, *70*, 74, 115, 117, 120,
　　127, 128–35, *128–37*
Italy 13
ivy 154

J
Jack Vass Walk 76, *76–77*, 82
Jackson, Albert Bruce 43, 44, 45
James I, King 19
Japan 42
Jasminum 92
Jay Robin's Rose Garden *8*, *54*, 62, 65, 68, 71,
　　74, 83, 84–89, *84–91*, 98–99
Jekyll, Gertrude 32, *32*
Johnston, Lawrence 43
Johnstone, George 41, 52
Jones, Rosie 94
Josephine's Way 152
Journal of the Royal Horticultural Society 43, 81, 115,
　　152, 157, 170
Juniperus 181–82

K
Kenya 35
Kew Gardens, London 13, 14, 31, 42, 55, 70,
　　153, 162
Kiftsgate Court Gardens, Gloucestershire 13,
　　65–66
Kingdon Ward, Frank 32, 35, 38, 39, *39*, 41,
　　44, 89, 110, 157, 164
Kingsbury, Noel 152
Kirengeshoma 164
Kirstenbosch, South Africa 53
Kleinwort family 61
Knap Hill Nursery, Woking, Surrey 170–71

INDEX
203

Knepp Castle, West Sussex 20
Kniphofia 122, *124–25*, 127

L
Lacey, Stephen 69
Lagerstroemia 127, *146*, *147*, *149*
Lanarth, Cornwall 41
Lancaster, Roy 61
landscape gardens 13
László, Philip de 25, *25*, 30, 34, *35*, 50, *50*
Laurus 147
Lavandula 87, *90–91*
Lear Associates 67
Leeds, University of 45
Leggett, Miss 40
Leonardo da Vinci 29
Leonardslee, West Sussex 40, 65, 70
Lepechinia 125
leucojums 117, 154
Libertia 152
lichens 151, 172
Ligularia 143
Ligustrum 98
Lilium 101, 134, *134*
Liquidambar 110, 164
Liriodendron chinense 43, *43*, 60, 62, 162, *164–65*, 191
Liriope 89
Lloyd's of London 57
Lobelia 89
Loder, Sir Edmund 40
Loder, Sir Giles 40
Loder, Robin 65, 70
Long Barn, Kent 43
Long Dell 43, 65, 67, 68, 151, 152–53, *152–53*
Lord, Dr Tony 68, 108
Loudon, John Claudius 31
Loyal Tooting Volunteers 22, *22*
Luculia 42
Lysimachia *138*, 143

M
Maackia 89
Macmillan, Harold 55
Magnolia 30, 37, 40, 41–42, 68, 74, 76–81, 154, 171–72
  M. Black Tulip 157, *157*
  M. campbellii 43, 166, 172, 181
  M.c. subsp. *mollicomata* 52, 154, 157, *159*
  M.c. subsp. *mollicomata* 'Borde Hill' *159*, *188*, 188
  M. dawsoniana *78–80*, 81
  M. delavayi 152, 182
  M. fraseri 157, *160*, 190

M. 'Gold Star' 154
M. grandiflora 'Goliath' 106
M.g. 'Kay Parris' 130, *134*
M. hypoleuca 40
M. 'Lois' 154
M. macrophylla 143
M.m. var. *ashei* 52
M. obovata 157, *161*
M. officinalis 40, 157, *160*
M. 'Premier Cru' 172
M. sargentiana var. *robusta* 52, *78–81*, 81, 135
M. sieboldii 81
M.s. subsp. *sinensis* 'Grandiflora' 81
M. × *soulangeana* 156, 157
M. × *s.* 'Brozzonii' *12*, *80*, 172
M. sprengeri 42
M.s. var. *diva* 76, *78*, 189, *189*
M. 'Susan', 81
M. tsarongensis 41, 42
M. × *veitchii* 154, 157, *158*
Mahonia 44, 154
Malus 87, 110, 166, 182
Margaret, Princess *51*
Mediterranean Garden 74, 92, *92–93*, 98
Melanoselinum *140–41*
Melianthus 92
Meliosma alba 70, 178, *182*, 189, *189*
Melon House 92, 95
Messel, Colonel Leonard 40, 45, *51*, 157, *160*
Messel family 52
Metasequoia 152, 182
Meynell, Ev, *Welcoming the New Year* 130, *133*
Mid-Summer Border 68, 74, *104–105*, 108–10, *108–109*
Millais, David 41, 55, 67, 69, *69*, 181
Millais, John Guille 41, 60
Millais, Ted 60
Miscanthus 108, 110, 152
Missouri Botanical Garden 42
Mitchell, Alan 67
Montpellier, University of 19
Moraea 147
Morocco 53
Munstead Wood, Surrey 32
Murless, Brendon, *Aphrodite* 87, *90–91*
Musa 138, *142*
Muscari 106, 124
Myosotis 83
Myrtus 130

N
Narcissus see daffodils
Natal 34
National Garden Scheme 45
National Trust 52, 55, 59, 70, 108

Natural England 71
Nature Conservancy Committee for England 52
Nepeta 39, 87, *87*, 95, 117
Nerine 14, 43, 49, 53–54, 95, 127
  N. 'Angela Limerick' 53, *54*, 190
Nerine Society 54
Nile, River 30
Nobbs, G. 42
North Park 43, 157, 164, 166
North Shields 21
Nunn, Maria Elizabeth 22
Nunn, William 22
Nymans, West Sussex 13, 40, 52, 55, 65, 70, 135
Nymphaea 134

O
oak trees 81, *102–103*, 105–106, *106–107*, 117, 120, 154, 164, 166, 178
Oemleria 154
Oenothera 100, *101*
Old Potting Sheds 13, 24, 63, 68, 117, 144–51, *147–51*
Old Rhododendron Garden 28, 76–83, *76–83*, 84, 178
Old Surrey & Burstow Hunt 55
Olearia chathamica 45, 190
Ophiopogon 117
Orange River Colony 34
orchids 43, 92
origanum 120
Osborne House, Isle of Wight 42
osmunda ferns 164
Ouse Valley 20, 105
Ouse Valley Viaduct *18*, 19, *19*, 43, 67, 105, 162, 166
Oxford University Press 29

P
Paeonia (peonies) 83, *83*, 89, 95, 101, 122, 147, 151
  P. lutea 'Jack Vass' 191
  see also tree peonies
palms 143, 153
Panicum 152
Paradise Walk 68, 74, 110, 117, *118–27*, *120–27*, 138
Parmigianino 29
Paulownia 152
Paxhill Park, West Sussex 20
Paxton, Joseph 13, 31
Peach House 92, 95, *95*
pelargoniums 92, *93*, 130, *132*, 134–35
Pennisetum 152

peonies *see Paeonia*; tree peonies
perovskias 92, 95, *124–25*, 127, 134
Persia (Iran) 13, 40, 129
Petrarch 19
Petworth, West Sussex 13
Philadelphus 153
Philip, Prince *40*
Phlomis 108, 151
phlox 101
phygelius 95, *109*, 110
Physocarpus 108
Picea 43, 138, 182
Picrasma 89
Pieris 164, *180–81*, 197
Pinetum 33, 43, 63, 65, 67, 166
Pinus (pine trees) 42, 117, 129, 138, 178, 181
    P. wallichiana 61, 191
Pittosporum 89, 92, 95, 98, 130, 138, 153
plant hunters 13–14, 31, 32, 33, 35, 37–40
Platanus orientalis var. *insularis* 49, 52, 178, *183*, 190
Podocarpus 110, 178
Populus 143, 166
Powell Duffryn 51
Primula 117, 154, *154*, 164
Prunus 84, 86, 87, 135, 164; *see also* cherry trees
Pulbrook & Gould 54
Punica 92
pyracantha 110

Q
Queen's Nursing Institute 45
Quercus 42, 81, 106, 164, 166; *see also* holm oak trees; oak trees
Quest-Ritson, Charles 95

R
Rabelais, François 19
Raffill, Charles 42
Ramalina 151
Ramblers Association 51, 52
Rhodesia/Zimbabwe 35
Rhododendron 14, *28*, 31, 33, *36*, 39, 42, 43, 44, 52, 59–63, 74, 76, 95, 105, 106–108, 110, 115, 152–53, 154, *155*, 164, *174*, 174–75, 178, 181, 208
    R. annae 163
    R. arboreum 76, *181*
    R.a. 'Barchard's Variety' *82*
    R. argyrophyllum subsp. *hypoglaucum* 153
    R. barbatum 31, 76
    R. 'Bonfire' 106
    R. 'Cynthia' *180–81*
    R. davidsonianum 61
    R. 'Delicatissimum' *168–69*
    R. falconeri 31
    R. fortunei 76, 178
    R. galactinum 63
    R. 'George Hardy' 108
    R. glanduliferum 153
    R. griffithianum 76, 153
    R. 'Hinode-giri' *76–77*, 111
    R. houlstonii 33
    R. 'Humboldt Picotee' *168*
    R. hunnewellianum *152*, 153
    R. iodes 61, 191
    R. 'J.G. Millais' *163*
    R. 'Loderi King George' *56*, 154
    R. 'Loderi Sir Edmund' 40
    R. 'Loderi Venus' 171
    R. luteum *168–69*, 171
    R. maddenii subsp. *crassum* 38
    R. metternichii 61, 191
    R. molle 170, 171
    R. 'Nicola Newman' 154
    R. oreodoxa var. *fargesii* 82
    R. 'Palestrina' *76–77*
    R. phaeochrysum 61, 191
    R. 'Pink Pearl' 106
    R. 'Romany Chai' 106
    R. rubiginosum *162–63*
    R. sinograde 152
    R. sutchuenense 'Seventh Heaven' 61, 191
    R. thomsonii 76
    R. 'Wilgen's Ruby' 106
Rhododendron Society 41, 60
Rhododendron Species Foundation 59
Rhodoleia championii 42
Ribes 53
Richea scoparia 45, 190
Robertsmere *26–27*, 67, *112–13*
Robinson, William 13, 31–32, *32*, 33, 115
Rock, Joseph 44
Rodgersia 143
The Rookery, Tooting 21, *23*
Rosa (roses) 92, 95, *104–105*, 108, *108*, *109*, 110, 127, 130
    Jay Robin's Rose Garden *8*, 54, 62, 65, 68, 71, 74, 83, *84–89*, 84–91, *98–99*
rosemary 92, 151
Rosse, 6th Earl of 45
Rothschild, Lionel de 40–41, *41*, 55, 67
Rothschild family 60
Round Dell 63, 68, 70, 74, 117, *138–43*, 138–43
Royal Agricultural Society of England 52
Royal Botanic Garden, Edinburgh 14, 37, 38, 39, 41, 55, 68
Royal Botanic Gardens, Kew 13, 14, 31, 42, 55, 70, 153, 162

Royal Geographical Society 30
Royal Horticultural Society (RHS) 14, 30, 31, 40, 44, 45, 52, 53, 54, 55, 57, 60–61, *60*, 68, 190–91
Royal Sussex Light Infantry Militia 29–30
Royal Sussex Regiment 34
Rubens, Peter Paul 29
Rudbeckia 110, *115*, 117, 151, *151*, 152

S
Sackville-West, Vita 43, 55
St John's College, Cambridge 21
Salvia 70, 89, 92, *96–97*, 110, *124–25*, 134, 138, 147–51, *149*
Sandling Park, Kent 60
sanguisorba 101
Santolina 134, 151
Savill Garden, Windsor Great Park 60
schefflera 143
sculpture exhibitions 68, *94*, 135
Scutellaria ovalifolia 45, 190
Second World War 40, 42, 46, 49, 57, 58
sedums *109*, 110
Senecio 92, *93*, *98–99*, 101
Sequoiadendron 166
Sezincote, Gloucestershire 61
Shady Garden 89
Sharp, Private 46
Sheffield Park, East Sussex 55, 61, 65, 70
Sissinghurst Castle, Kent 13, 43, 55
Six Hills Nursery, Stevenage, Hertfordshire 39
Slocock family 44–45
Smith, Sir William Wright 41–42
Snowdon, Earl of 45, *51*
snowdrops 33, 74
Society of Beaujolais 57
soils 13, 32, 33
Solanum *148–49*
Sophora 147
Sorbus 110, 164
South Africa 53
South America 13
South Lawn *10–11*, 20, 33, 74, *102–103*, 105–108, *106–107*, *110–111*, 115, 117, 171
South Lodge, Horsham, West Sussex 30
South Park *16–17*, *26–27*, 43, 49, 63, 65, 67, 74, 120
Speke, John Hanning 30
spruce trees 178
Spry, Constance 54
Stachyurus *152*, 153
Stephanie's Glade 2, 33, 43, 74, 174, 178, *178*, 182
Stephens, Harvey 70, 89, 147

INDEX
205

Stephenson, Jane 21, 22
Stephenson Clarke *see also* Clarke
Stephenson Clarke, Andrew 49
Stephenson Clarke, Andrew John 9, 14, 30, 34, 65–66, 69, 74
  at Borde Hill 65–71
  children 66, *69*, 71
  early life 58, *58*, 66
  Italian Garden 130
  Jay Robin's Rose Garden 84
  South Lawn 108
  Warren Wood 182
Stephenson Clarke, Anne 50, *51*
Stephenson Clarke, Edith Mary 34
Stephenson Clarke, Edmund (Eddie) 34, 35, 49
Stephenson Clarke, Eleni 9, 14, 50, 65–71, *65*, *69*, 74, 84, 108, 130, 154, 164, 172
Stephenson Clarke, Harry Ralph 66, *69*, 71, *71*
Stephenson Clarke, Jay Robin 66, *69*, 71, *71*, 84
Stephenson Clarke, John Philip 34, 46, 51
Stephenson Clarke, Juana Nidia Gereth (née Bickersteth-Wheeler) 57–59, *58*, 66
Stephenson Clarke, Maria (née Williams) 59, 61–62, 130
Stephenson Clarke, Marylynn 58, *58*
Stephenson Clarke, Sir Ralph 49–55, *49–51*, *54–55*
  awards 52
  at Borde Hill 14, 52–55
  and the *Catalogue* 43
  children 24, 45–46, 50, 51, 57
  death 55
  early life 25, 30, 34, 49
  family history 21
  as a farmer 55
  in First World War 35
  Garden of Allah 157
  makes Borde Hill a charitable trust 55
  marriage 49–50, *50*
  military career 49
  as MP 51–52
  plant collecting 52–53, 178, *183*
Stephenson Clarke, Rebekah Mary (Becky, née Buxton) 14, 46–47, 49–50, *50*, 52–55, *55*, 57, 59, *157*, 164
Stephenson Clarke, Robert (son of Stephie) 33, 34, 46
Stephenson Clarke, Robert Nunn 24, 38, 39, 57–62
  awards 60–61
  at Borde Hill 14, 44, 57–63, 67, 143
  Bride's Pool 115, 130

  children 58, *58*, 66
  death 14, 57, 63, 67
  early life 46, 50, *51*, 57–58
  interests 57
  South Lawn 106
  West Garden 154
Stephenson Clarke, Roland 58, *58*, 63, 65, 66, *66*
Stephenson Clarke, Simon 46, 50, *51*
Stephenson Clarke and Company 19, 21, 23, 51, 57, 66
Stern, Sir Frederick 54
Stevens, Andy 70, 89, 170
Stewartia pseudocamellia 172–73
  S. serrata 45, 190
Stipa 152
Stowe, Buckinghamshire 13
Strachan, Captain James 22
strelitzias 95

T

Tantardini, Antonio 24, *24*, *54*, 63, 130
Tasmania 40
Taxodium 115, 143
Taylor, Sir George 55, 59
Tetrapanax 140–42, 143
Teucrium 89
Thalictrum 89, 96–97
'Three Sisters' 157, 160–61
Tibet 33, 37, 38–39
Toona 152
Toxicodendron 110, 164
Trachelospermum 98
Trachycarpus 92, 135, 138, 152
Tree, Isabella 20
tree peonies 89, *100*, 151
Trewithen, Cornwall 41, 70
Tulipa (tulips) 106, *106–107*, 130
Turkey 33

U

Uganda 35
University College Dublin 42
Upson, Dr Tim 55, 69

V

Vanholt, Dorothy *see* Clarke, Dorothy
Vass, Jack *54*, 55, 59, 60, *60*, 61, *61*, 76, 110
Veitch, Harry 31, 33, 83
Veitch, John Gould 181
Veitch, Peter 154, *158*
Veitch Memorial Medal 41, 45, *45*
Veitch Nurseries 31, 43, 76, 154, 162, *165*
Veratrum 143
Verbena 95, 108, 110, 154

Vernonia 101
veronicastrums 101
Viburnum 83, 154, *155*
Victoria, Queen 22, 45
Victoria League for Commonwealth Friendship 50
Victorian greenhouses 13, 62, 67, 74, 92–95, *94–95*, 147
Vitis 92, *93*

W

Wada, K. 42
Wagg, Elsie 45
Walker, Sophie 68, 70, 138, 143
Warren Wood 33, 43, 49, 52, *52*, 68, 74, 174–82, *174–85*
water lilies 134
Waterer, Anthony 170–71
Waterer, John Sons & Crisp, Bagshot, Surrey 44, 171
West Bank 36, 63, 75, 114–17, *115–17*, 151
West Garden 56, 154, *154–55*
West Garden Lodge 147, 154
West India Dock Company 22
Whitbread 30
White, Henry 22
White Garden 74, 98–101, *98–101*
White House Farm, Kent 172
Whitgift School, Croydon 25
wild garlic 28, 83, *83*, 122, 164, 174
Williams, J.C. 41, *41*, 92
Williams, Maria *see* Stephenson Clarke, Maria
Williams, P.D. 41
Williams, Robin 68, 84–87, 89, *89*, 92, 130
Williams, Robin Templar 130
Wilson, Ernest Henry 'Chinese' 31, *31*, 32, 33, 35, 41, 43, *43*, 44, 76, 81, 83, 101, 157, 160, 162, 170, 178, 182, *182*
Winchester 19
Winchester College 29
Wisley 14, 35, 38, 42, 60
wisteria 154
Wood, Sir Kingsley 20
wood anemones 174
Wynn-Jones, Bleddyn and Sue 70, 143

Y

yew trees 84, 87, 130

Z

Zelkova 153
Zingiber 143
Zoffany, Johann 22, *22*

First published 2022 by Merrell Publishers,
London and New York

Merrell Publishers Limited
70 Cowcross Street
London EC1M 6EJ

merrellpublishers.com

Text copyright © 2022 the authors

Illustrations copyright © 2022 the copyright holders; see p. 199

Design and layout copyright © 2022 Merrell Publishers Limited

All rights reserved. No part of this publication may be reproduced, stored in a retrieval system or transmitted, in any form or by any means, electronic, mechanical, photocopying, recording or otherwise, without the prior written permission of the publisher.

British Library Cataloguing in Publication Data.
A catalogue record for this book is available from the British Library.

ISBN 978-1-8589-4690-0

Produced by Merrell Publishers Limited
Designed by Nicola Bailey
Project-managed by Claire Chandler
Additional picture research by Nick Wheldon
Proofread by Rosanna Fairhead
Indexed by Hilary Bird

Printed and bound in Singapore

Jacket, front: The view across Jay Robin's Rose Garden towards the east side of Borde Hill House.

Jacket, back, from top: *Magnolia dawsoniana* and *M. sargentiana* var. *robusta* in the Old Rhododendron Garden; Italian Garden; Paradise Walk.

Frontispiece: Shafts of sunlight through the trees of Stephanie's Glade illuminate drifts of bluebells in May.

Page 4: In March, Borde Hill's award-winning *Camellia* × *williamsii* 'Donation' flowers by steps leading from the Garden of Allah to the north front of the house.

Pages 10–11: Cool-green ferns and fiery acers provide rich interest beside the South Lawn in autumn.

Pages 16–17: Early-morning mist in the South Park.

Pages 72–73: Agapanthus line the wall above the Garden of Allah in August.

Page 197: The front of Borde Hill House. In the foreground are a purple rhododendron, a pink azalea and the young scarlet shoots of *Pieris formosa* var. *forrestii*, collected by George Forrest (No. 26518).

Overleaf: Rhododendron petals create a bright splash of colour in spring amid leaf litter and twigs among the roots of an old tree.

Note on text: Plant names have been checked against the Royal Horticultural Society's directory, available at rhs/org.uk/plants. In the 'History' section of the book, plant names are generally those that were in use at the time.

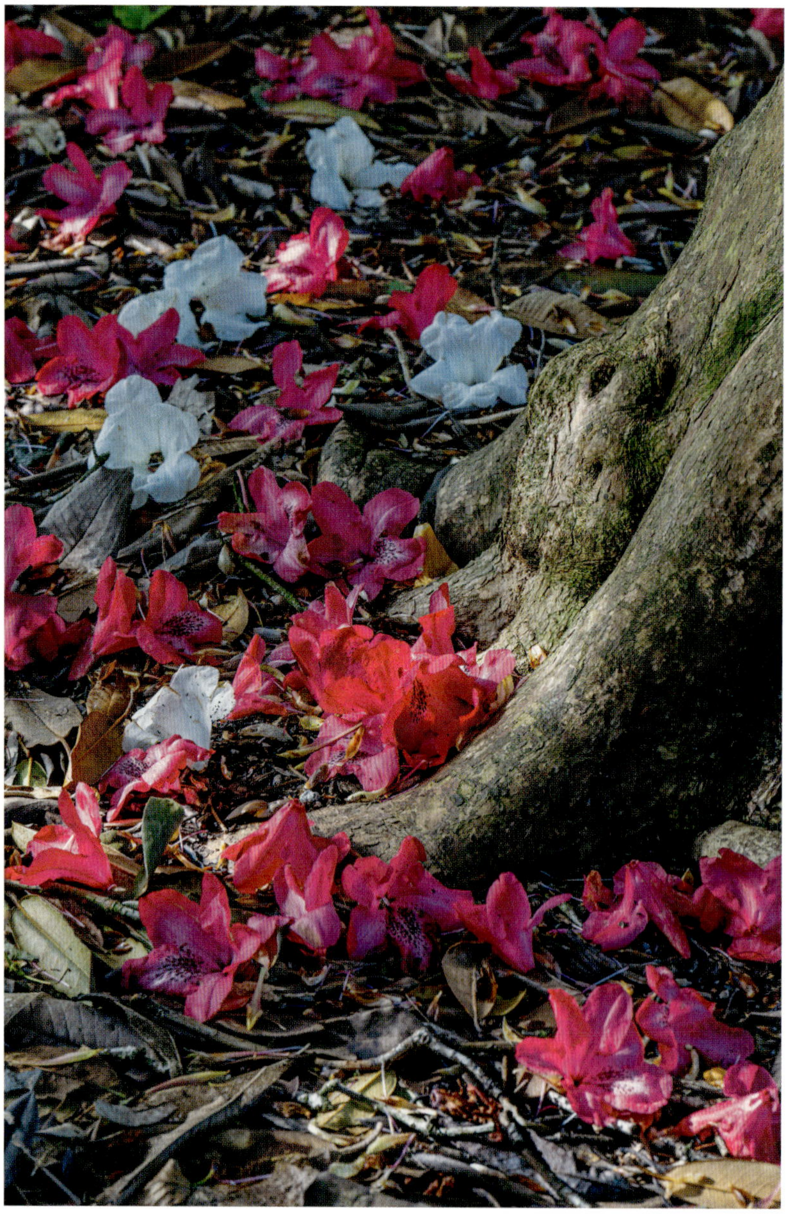